Welcome to

It has been a busy two years since our last
some major financial troubles around the wo
government cuts, austerity
Some of these problems
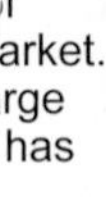
f
collectors, which in turn, w arket.
Yet it is not as gloomy a rge
number of dealers across Britain, it sounds as if the has
held up pretty well.

▲*Shipping special*

There have, of course, been changes in the market, with prices moving up and down in some subject areas.

One of the clear trends to emerge over the past two years is that common cards are struggling to sell. The internet has exposed just how common these cards are, with many of the same or similar cards up for sale. On the other hand, we have seen some staggering prices made at auction for rare cards... WW1 Silk badges, Railway Stations and Real photographic topography and social history among them.

As you would expect, we have made a large number of price revisions, both up and down, too numerous to mention specifically here. You will have to read the market reports for each section and check the categories you are interested in.

We hope this catalogue will be an invaluable guide to pricing old and modern picture postcards..now get out there and start buying and selling!

SPECIAL FEATURES

Page 12 Modern postcards A fresh look at the new wave by Brian Lund

Page 16 Auction News top prices realised on some super single lot cards

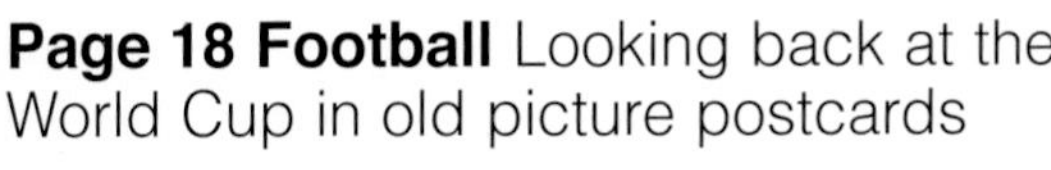

Page 18 Football Looking back at the World Cup in old picture postcards

Page 20 Military WW1 in postcards by Andrew Read

Page 176 Scotland Topographical An experts insight from Richard Stenlake

We have canvassed experts across the many subjects and fields of postcard dealing and collecting to adapt and bring up to date the valuations and reporting in this book..

Good hunting, ***Phil & Dave Smith...***

Special thanks goes to the following team of experts, without whom this catalogue would be impossible...

Nicky Hillman, Bill Kirkland, Brian Lund, Tony McKendrick, Andrew Read (Military), Tom Stanley (Shipping), Richard Stenlake (Scotland) plus Bill Pipe & Tim Pedley

Compiled by P & D Smith - www.postcardvalues.co.uk

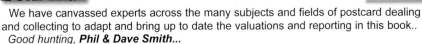

Published by: PPV Publications 173 Sunny Gardens Road, Hendon, London, NW4 1SG

Tel: 020 8203 2211 philsmith173@yahoo.co.uk

Reprographics and Production by DX IMAGING

Tel: 01923 227644 www.dx-imaging.co.uk

POSTCARD TRADERS
PTA
ASSOCIATION

AN INTRODUCTION TO POSTCARD COLLECTING

Here is a brief introduction to postcard collecting, a fascinating and rewarding hobby. We look at the historical background, and view the present state of the art.

The Early Beginnings

The first plain postcards appeared in Austria in 1869. One year later Britain followed, and shortly afterwards in the mid-1870s, the first picture postcards began to appear. The Paris Exhibition of 1889 gave a tremendous boost to this still novel form of sending a message, and from then on picture postcards were produced in ever increasing numbers by almost every country in the world. Britain joined the game in earnest in 1894 when the first picture cards were permitted and in 1902 was the first country to divide the back, thus allowing the message and address on one side and a complete picture on the other, a move which saw an explosion in picture postcard production as other countries quickly followed. This period is dealt with in more detail in the catalogue under 'Early Cards'.

The Golden Age

The period from 1902-1914 has been termed the 'Golden Age' of picture postcards, for it was in these years that the hobby reached a height of popularity that it has never exceeded. It was a time when nearly everybody sent postcards, because in a pre-telephone era they represented the cheapest and most reliable form of communication. And what cards they were ! Almost every conceivable subject could be found on picture postcards, as publishers competed with each other to produce the most attractive designs. As a result, postcard collecting became a national pastime where almost everybody young or old had their own albums into which went cards showing Father Christmas and fire engines, cards showing pigs, pretty ladies and political figures, and cards of just about any other subject you care to name! And the hobby was not confined to Britain, for by now every country in the world was producing postcards, resulting in uncountable millions being issued worldwide throughout this period.

The First World War

For reasons of quality and price, the majority of British postcards had been printed in Germany, and the guns of 1914 brought this quickly to an end. 2014 sees the 100th anniversary of the outbreak of war. With this we predict a surge in interest in the subject. For more detail on this please turn to page 20 for a feature by Andrew Read on this topic.

Between the Wars

From 1918 a number of things combined to bring about a virtual end to the hobby. A nation trying to come to terms with the tragedies of the Somme and of Flanders, was in no mood for the fripperies of the picture postcard. In addition, the doubling of the inland postage rate for postcards, the wider acceptance of the phone as a means of communication, not to mention the difficulties which many firms found themselves in after the war–all these factors combined to bring about the end. Perhaps quite simply, nobody, neither the postcard houses, nor the collectors, wanted to 'start again'. Of course, postcards were still being produced, but in much smaller quantities. The seaside comic market was still there, and some firms were producing local views, while others reflected the current Art Deco craze with some fine issues, but effectively the 'Golden Age' had passed.

▲*WW2 WAAFS £8*

The Second World War

The Second World War saw a minor revival in postcard production, with a number of military and aviation series being produced, as well as other cards dealing with issues of the time, but the hobby lay relatively dormant until the late 1950s.

The Postcard Revival

Throughout the post war years, a small band of enthusiasts had kept things going, until in 1959 two collectors, James Butland and Edward Westwood established a regular magazine.'*The Postcard Collectors' Guide & News*, full of articles about the hobby, and closing with a short sales list. 1961 saw the foundation by Drene Brennan of the 'Postcard Club of Great Britain', and at this time in the early 1960s, several collectors' shops could be found stocking old postcards. The hobby gathered momentum until in 1968 J.H.D. Smith, the former compiler of this catalogue established the monthly 'IPM' sales magazine. This was the first real attempt to establish classifications for postcards and to put the hobby on to a commercial basis, and this issue also carried the first auction of picture postcards. From then on things further progressed. Postcard Fairs were already being held under the aegis of the PCGB and these were complemented by the first big specialist events held by John Carter, and in the early 1970s by RF Postcards. The hobby received a massive boost with the Victoria & Albert Museum Centenary Exhibition of 1970, later to travel round the country, and supported by an ever increasing number of books, magazines and sales lists, culminated in 1975 with the appearance of the first IPM Catalogue. The following year, 1976, saw the formation of the Postcard Traders Association, the first sale held by "Specialised Postal Auctions', and the foundation of the annual British International Postcard Exhibition, while in 1977 came the first Postcard Fair at Bloomsbury Crest Hotel, now an institution among collectors. Our regular monthly journal 'Picture Postcard Monthly' first saw the light of day in 1978, and set the seal on what has become known as the postcard revival. For now we had the dealers, the collectors, the fairs and auctions, and the magazines, books and literature. Everything was there, ready to move postcard collecting into the national hobby it has now become, taking its place alongside Stamps and Coins as one of the top three collecting hobbies in the country.

The Present Day

The hobby today supports some 500 Dealers and many more smaller collector/dealers. The internet has changed postcard collecting, with thousands of postcards available, all categorised and easy to find with the search engines available. There are an estimated 20,000 serious collectors, many of whom belong to one of nearly 70 postcard clubs. We have over 20 auction houses specialising in picture postcards, and a national network of postcard fairs. There is the PPV Postcard Catalogue, a national magazine, and a substantial number of books on the subject. We can now look briefly at the operation of the hobby today.

The Collectors

Why do people collect picture postcards? Why do people collect anything! For pleasure, interest, and perhaps profit, are some of the reasons which may be advanced. Yet in this hobby, the collecting of postcards is now divided into two worlds. That of Art & Subject Cards, and that of Topographical, or Local History. The former are perhaps the 'real' postcard collectors, while the latter group are essentially more interested in representations of their own locality as it used to be, than in picture postcards as an art form.

The Dealers

The postcard trade operates in much the same way as the stamp or coin trade, in that we have a national network of dealers whose task it is to find and supply postcards to collectors. Many of them carry substantial stocks of up to 100,000 cards, all priced, and filed in boxes or albums under their respective subject or location headings, although others carry smaller stocks, perhaps specialising in several chosen themes or areas. Some dealers will conduct business through the post, sending approval selections of your choice, while many more can be found at postcard fairs throughout the country. A comprehensive list of dealers will be found in '*Picture Postcard Annual*', while dates of current Fairs are listed in '*Picture Postcard Monthly*. Most dealers now trade on the internet via sites such as *delcampe* or *ebay*.

Auctions

There are now 20 Auction Houses holding regular specialised sales of picture postcards. All produce catalogues obtainable on subscription, and all will accept postal bids for the Lots on offer. While the more common cards tend to be lotted in some quantity, there is now an increasing trend for the better cards to be offered as individual items in single lots, a reflection of the current strong demand for these cards. A word of advice, when buying at auction do try to ensure that cards are in the best possible condition, particularly if buying through a postal bid. This is made easy by certain leading Auction firms, whose descriptions always include a very clear statement of condition, but is less visible in the catalogues of some firms, where at times you will find nothing at all regarding condition.

Fairs

Led by the IPM Promotions Fair which has been held every month for 30 years at Bloomsbury, and has now moved to The Clerkenwell Centre, Lever Street, London EC14 there are now over 40 organisations holding regular Postcard Fairs throughout the country, dates of which may be checked with the diary published in '*Picture Postcard Monthly*'. The largest regular fair is the 'London Postcard Fair', which almost every month has up to 80 stands packed with picture postcards and related ephemera, Other large provincial events include the 2-day Fairs held at York, Shepton Mallet, Twickenham, Woking and with major one day events at Birmingham, Nottingham, Canterbury, Wickham and many other locations. While every weekend many smaller events are held regularly up and down the country. Here you will find the Postcard Trade at work, and will be able to meet the dealers in person. Ask them for what you want, and you will find them all very helpful, particularly in guiding the new collector.

What to Collect

This depends entirely upon the individual. Visit the fairs and look around at the enormous selection of cards you will find there. Perhaps after a few visits you may find yourself attracted to one particular artist or subject, or possibly you may wish to specialise in old views of your town or village. Whatever you choose, remember to look for cards in the finest possible condition. This is not perhaps so important in the topographical field where only a few copies of a particular card may remain, but it is important in art & subjects. Generally you will want to ensure that the higher the price asked, the better the condition of the card.

How to Collect

At the Fairs. and in Dealers' advertisements, you will find a good range of accessories offered. Many collectors store their cards in albums, while others prefer loose storage in cardboard boxes. You may also consider it advisable to protect your loose cards by keeping them in protective plastic envelopes now available. (*see pages 6&7 for suppliers details*) Some collectors prefer the old-fashioned Edwardian paper albums. rather than the modern Polypropolene/plastic types. It is entirely up to you.

Postcard Clubs

As your interest grows, you may wish to join one of the many Postcard Clubs, a list of which may be found in *Picture Postcard Annual.* Here you will meet other local collectors who share your interest in the subject and who will be able to broaden your horizons by showing you some of their own collecting themes.

Investment

This is not something to be attempted by the new collector, for while it is always pleasant to see your collection grow in value, to set out to buy postcards with the sole aim of making money is an exercise fraught with difficulties. Wait until you know a lot more about the hobby. Then it may be possible to put some spare cash into an area you feel is under-valued, but a study of past Catalogues and past prices will clearly reveal that while some cards have risen dramatically in price, others have remained on the same mark for years, while some cards have even fallen in value.

Selling your Cards

All collectors wish to sell at different times. Perhaps they are giving up, or maybe turning to another subject. Whatever the reason, you have five basic methods of disposing of unwanted cards. You can take a table at one of the Postcard Fairs, and with your stock properly marked up and laid out, you can become a 'Dealer' yourself! If you know of other collectors in your field, you could offer your cards to them for sale by private treaty. Alternatively you can offer your stock to a dealer, but his response will depend very largely upon what sort of cards they are, their condition, and at the end of the day, whether he wants them! All cards must have a Catalogue value, but it does not necessarily follow that anyone wants to buy them! Most dealers will only willingly buy those cards in the collectable categories which they have some chance of re-selling at a profit. You can, of course, sell your cards on an internet auction site, which is readily available to everyone. Finally you can offer your cards for sale by Public Auction, but remember that here you take a chance on the final price. You may of course put a reserve on your cards, and if they fail to meet this figure they will be returned to you. You may be pleasantly surprised at the price you obtain at Auction, or in some cases you could be disappointed. Certainly you may do better with particularly good single items if offered for sale by this method, but you have to meet the auctioneer's commission, which may be up to 20% of the price realised. If you have a valuable collection, you may wish to discuss various methods of sale with an established auctioneer or dealer.

Modern Cards

The past 20 years have seen a phenomenal growth in the production of modern postcards, and this can be seen as almost a separate industry, with cards on every conceivable subject now being issued by many leading companies. After some initial hesitation by the traditional postcard collecting world, Modern cards are now making considerable inroads into the hobby. Perhaps the great advantage of Modern Cards lies in their price, where for a nominal 50p, or so,one may buy superbly designed and printed cards on almost any subject you care to name.Also look out for free promotional cards given away by companies to promote thier products, particularly books, art, music and film. ***(Turn to page 12 for Brian Lund's guide to what makes a good modern postcard)***

Conclusions

In this brief survey we have tried to show how the hobby originated, and how it operates today. It is still growing, and we sincerely hope that all of you, particularly if you are a new collector finding out about postcards for the first time, will gain through this, and through the pages of this Catalogue, something of the nostalgia we collectors all feel for those long hot summer days at the turn of the century. It was a time of endless summer, when small boys looked for tiddlers under the bridge, oblivious to the voices calling them home across the fields, peacefully unaware of the later call of destiny which they would face in 1916 in the green fields of France.A time without television, video, or computer games, when young girls and boys spent their evenings carefully putting all their new cards into their postcard albums. It is these cards which are so highly prized today, and which form the subject of this Catalogue.

ACCESSORY SUPPLIERS

ROB ROY CARDS
Crosshall, Chelsfield Village, Orpington, Kent (See advert above) 01689-828052

VERA TRINDER LTD.
38 Bedford Street, London WC2 9EU (See advert inside front cover)
020-7836-2365

STANLEY GIBBONS PUBLICATIONS
7 Parkside, Christchurch Road, Ringwood, Hampshire BH24 3SH (see advert page 9)
0800 611 622

TAUNTON STAMP SHOP.
66 Bridge Street, Taunton, Somerset 01823-283327

MEMORIES, IPM PROMOTIONS, 130 BRENT STREET, LONDON,NW4 2DR
TEL 020 8203 1500 FAX 020 8203 7031 www.memoriespostcards.co.uk

The firms listed above are trade wholesalers and between them carry an extensive range of Accessories including: Postcard Catalogues - Books - Albums - Leaves - Plastic Envelopes - Film Front Bags - Postcard Wallets etc.

Vera Trinder and Stanley Gibbons also specialise in Philatelic and Numismatic albums and accessories, while **Rob Roy Cards** carry large stocks of Cigarette Card albums and leaves.

Most of the firms above will deal with individual customers, but a telephone call will confirm this, and determine whether the firms have the item you require currently in stock.
In addition many postcard dealers carry smaller stocks of Books, Albums and Accessories.

POSTCARD TERMS AND WHAT THEY MEAN

Applique
A term used to describe a postcard which has some form of cloth, metal, or other embellishment attached to it.

Art Deco
Artistic style of the 1920's & 30's recognisable by its symmetrical designs and straight lines.

Art Nouveau
Artistic style of the turn of the century, characterised by flowing lines and flowery symbols, yet often depicting impressionist more than representational art.

Bas Relief
Postcards with a heavily raised surface giving a papier-mache appearance.

Catch-phrases
Many pre-1914 Comic postcards are captioned by phrases such as "When Father says turn", often alluding to other spheres of contemporary life.

Chromo-Litho
The finest of all colour-printing methods, the colour being applied in solids as opposed to modern screen printing. There are no 'dots' in chromo-lithographic printing. Cards produced by this method have a rich and deep colour, where often the original shiny surface remains. Usually found in 'Gruss Aus' and other early undivided back cards.

Chromo-Litho Court card

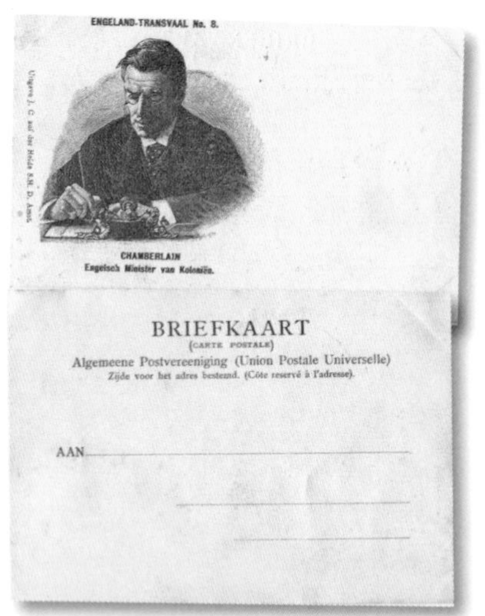

Early card with Undivided back

Composites
A number of cards which together form a large picture.

Court Cards
The official size for British picture postcards between 1894-1899, measuring 115mm x 89mm.

Divided Back
Postcards with the back divided into two sections, one for the message, the other for the address. Great Britain first divided the back in 1902.

Later card with divided back

Early
A term loosely used to describe any undivided back card.

Embossed
Postcards with a raised surface. Often found among Greetings and Heraldic types.

Fab Cards
Produced by W.N. Sharpe of Bradford. These cards contain a small printed silk square which could be removed and used for other purposes.

Giant Postcards
Novelty cards, some of which were as large as 305mm x 165mm.

GLOSSARY OF POSTCARD TERMS

'Oilette' postcard produced by Tuck

Glitter
Postcards sprinkled with tinsel.

Gruss Aus
German for "Greetings From". A generic term used to describe these highly pictorial early cards regardless of which country they originate from.

Hold to Light
Often referred to as "HTL". Postcards with small cut out windows, through which appear different colours when held to a strong light.

Intermediate Size
The link between Court Cards and Standard Size, these were cards of 130mm x 80mm.

Kaleidoscopes
Postcards where a rotating wheel reveals a myriad of colours when turned.

Midget Postcards
Novelty cards of size 90mm x 70mm.

'Pullout' card with xmas pictures hidden by the flap

Montage
A term usually employed to describe a picture formed by cutting up postage stamps.

Novelty
A postcard which deviates in any way from the norm. Cards which do something or have articles attached to them, or are printed in an unusual size or on strange materials, such as metal or even wood.

Official
Postcard printed by a Government or other established body to advertise their services. The Railway companies printed many 'Official' cards.

Oilette
A trade name used by the publishers Raphael Tuck to describe postcards reproduced from original paintings.

Panel Cards
These are postcards printed on heavy board.

Poster Advert card

Poster Advert
A reproduction of an advertising poster, or a postcard done specifically in that style. (as shown right) Also see more on pages 32-37

Pullouts
Postcards containing a strip view insert concealed under a flap.

Real Photographic
Often abbreviated to 'R/P'. Used to describe a card which has been produced by a photographic rather than a printing process.

Reward Cards
Given away to reward school-children for good work.

GLOSSARY OF POSTCARD TERMS

e back and the front of a typical Reward card

divided Back
tcards with a plain back where the whole of space would be used for the address. rm often used loosely to describe Early ds, although undivided backs were in com- use until 1907.

gnette postcard with an early military image

rite-Away
term used to describe a postcard bearing e opening line of a sentence, which the nder would then continue. Usually found early Comic postcards.

Standard Size
Introduced in GB in November 1899, this size of 140mm x 89mm corresponds to 5.5 x 3.5 in.

Topographical
A term used to describe post-cards showing street scenes and general views, where the view is more prominent than any other feature, e.g. if a Post Office or Public House were to form the dominant feature of a card, then it would be classified and priced under that heading.

Transparencies
Postcards which change colour or reveal a hidden object when held to a strong light.

Vignette
Usually found on undivided back post-cards, and consisting of a design which does not occupy the whole of the picture side. Vignettes may be anything from a small sketch in one corner of the card, to a design covering three-quarters of the card. The essential idea was that some space should be left for the message, as the reverse of the card could only be used for the address.

What's HOT in the world o

Defining what constitutes a modern postcard is not that simple. In the early days of the postcard revival in the 1960s it was pretty obvious –

everyone wanted pre-1914 cards – or at the latest pre-1939 ones. Now we're 50 years on from that era and the definition of 'modern' has had to be revised. Probably the best way is to call postcards published 1945-80 as 'semi-moderns', those from 1981-1999 as 'modern' and any from this century 'contemporary'. Another way of separating 'old' from 'modern' is by size, a rule that many collectors use. Anything 'Golden Age' size (140 x 89mm) is an 'old' postcard, those in a 150 x 100mm format (once called 'continental' size but now universal) or larger 'modern'. The problem with this second method is that some publishers from the 1980s – most notably J/V Postcards and Dalkeith Publishing – issued cards in 'Golden Age' size! Perhaps it would be simplest merely to define postcards by the decade in which they were

1 Aviation is a hot theme at the moment, with some postcards from the 1960s attracting seriously high prices (sometimes £100+!). This example, a Delta Airlines official postally used in 1991, might be nearer £1.

2 Football is a perenially popular theme, and this is one of the best series from the past 20 years. Published by The Homes of Football in Ambleside (now relocated to Manchester), this is card 6395 and shows an anti-racism demonstration at Highbury. Other cards show grounds of teams from non-league to Premiership. Pick them up while you still can at 50p each.

3 The postcards of John Hinde are becoming recognised as iconic examples of their era (1980s & 1990s). Their vibrant colours and marvellous composition make them well worth collecting. This card of Plymouth was from an Elmar Ludwig photo. It should be worth more than its current likely retail price of £1.

4 Part of the raison d'etre of postcard collecting is as a reminder of your life and the history you lived through. Postcards like this featuring websites should have an attraction for the generation that grew up as the internet evolved. A snip at 50p (originally it was free!).

5 Shipping moderns are extremely popular. This card of a Sealink ferry leaving Newhaven was published by Judges and would rate 50p, but older cards from the 1960-1990 period are fetching pounds.

MODERN POSTCARDS

Compiled by Brian Lund, editor of "Picture postcard monthly"

published. The bottom line, after all, is that postcards are postcards, and it might be thought perverse to exclude examples from your topographical or subject collection purely on the grounds of age or size.

It is a common perception that modern postcards are worth next to nothing, but street scenes from the 1950s can cost much more than their century-or-more-old Edwardian equivalents, and some artist-drawn Glamour cards are highly sought-after. A new edition of the catalogue Collect Modern Postcards, the latest edition of which was 1998, is badly needed to inform collectors just what modern cards are worth and to stimulate interest. Demand for collectable modern cards probably peaked in the 1980-95 period, and currently is a little depressed, partly because of the lack of regular new interesting material. Despite this, there is a wealth of postcards that have been produced over the past 50 or 60 years in most collecting categories, and much of it is still available -Some themes–transport, cricket and politics – are available on modern postcards in abundance.

6 In the public consciousness, saucy comics from the 1970s are synonymous with the word 'postcard'. For postcard connoisseurs, these cards are just a fraction of the output, but they obviously have the potential to attract a wider audience. Some named artists such as Pedro, responsible for this design on a postcard published in the 'Sunny Pedro series' would currently sell for £1.

Pedro
WHERE DID YOU LEARN THAT DOUBLE-TICKLE BERT?

7 Road transport. This postcard is 50 years old and 'Golden Age' size, but most collectors would instantly categorise it as 'modern'. It shows the first motorway service station on the M6, and a road almost devoid of traffic. Now that's nostalgia! The card was published by J. Arthur Dixon and would attract a price tag of £2.50.

8 Art. John Lennon is pictured here by the artist Philip Castle in the superb 'Illustrateurs' series published by Nugeron. The series includes many Fantasy designs and deserves a base price of £1.50. This one (H215) would make at least £5.

9 Railway postcards are among the most popular of all subjects, and collectors have an extensive range of Moderns to choose from. This is from the excellent series by Pete Shaw on the Settle-Carlisle line. Available at retail price of 40p.

10. **Map cards** used to be among the most popular of all, and still have plenty of potential. This 1960s card was published by Photo Precision Ltd and is worth 50p. but are less in vogue at the moment. £1.50

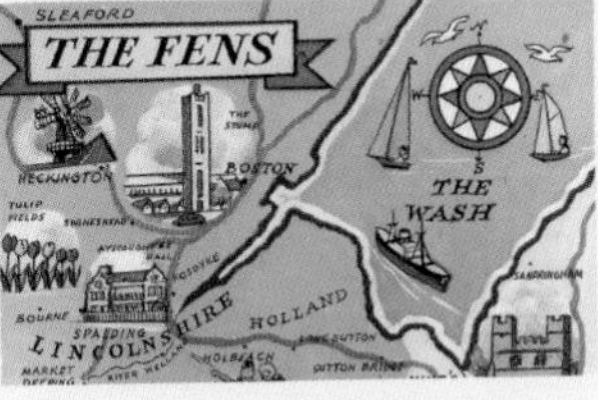

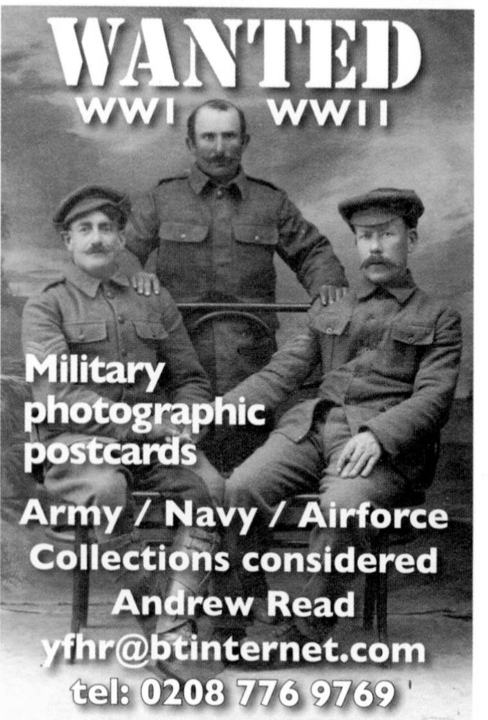

WANTED
WWI WWII
Military photographic postcards
Army / Navy / Airforce
Collections considered
Andrew Read
yfhr@btinternet.com
tel: 0208 776 9769

YORK INTERNATIONAL POSTCARD EXPO
80+
DEALERS
YORK RACECOURSE
April 4th & April 5th
FRI 11 - 7 pm
SAT 10 - 5 pm
DETAILS
01347 822722
01268 743222
2014

AUCTION NEWS

Together with our friends Warwick & Warwick Aucti[ons] here are some hammer pr[ices] from the last year, with so[me] super cards shown to giv[e an] idea of what to look out fo[r]

▲Social History, London Life. Rotary Photographic Co. no. 62 "G.P.O. Royal Mail Motor" RP £95

▲Sport, Football. Manchester City chromo-litho by Valentine, unused £85

▲Mucha, "Dawn (Aurore)" unused and in good condition. £75

◀Artists Rifles T 28 London, in good condition £290

▶Emboidered. S.I.H. (South Irish Horse), in good condition.£105

For info about Warwick & Warwick auctions see inside back page

▲Wilts. Pewsey Post Office, with postmaster and postmen, unused RP £65

▲Political, Suffragettes, 1 of 4 RPs of a 1910 London procession, (4 cards sold for £345)

▲Sport, Football. Tottenham Hotspur stadium entrance, p.u. 1928, £135

▲Surrey. Woking fire station, 1926 RP, with 3 motor appliances and crew. £38

Postcard from Rio

▲ Mexico 1970 Aral publish card of the great Pele, £10

Brazil 2014 is just months away... here's some collectible cards from World Cups gone by

Welcome to the world of World Cup cards...
Rio 2014 is likely to stimulate interest in this topic, so we've put together a selection of postcards from previous tournaments to whet your appetite.
If you are about to start your own collection then our valuation will help as a guide to what you would reasonably expect to pay.
Looking to the future, both Rio 2014 and Russia 2018 will result in new cards. Expect to pay from 50p to £1. there is a market for these modern cards and at that sort of price, these are a good buy.

▲ 1998 - Retro series published by Carlsberg, for the French world cup £2

▲1938 - This early advertising card was issue for the French World Cup £45

rance 1998 FPCC pub-
ed card for £1

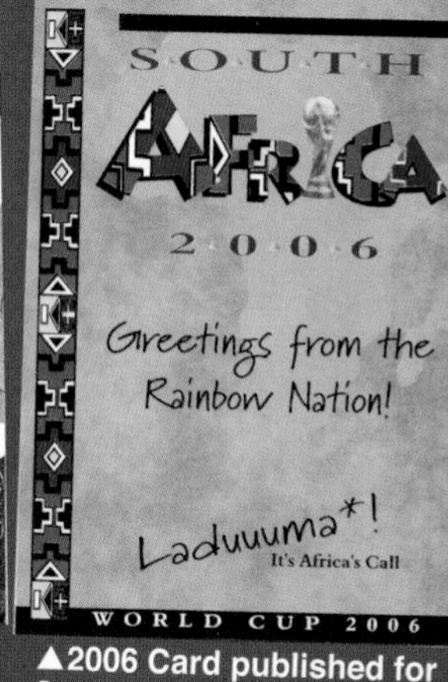

▲2006 Card published for South Africa £1

▲ 1970, Bobby Moore, Mexico , £10

USA 1994, by Jaque
rdie, £7.50

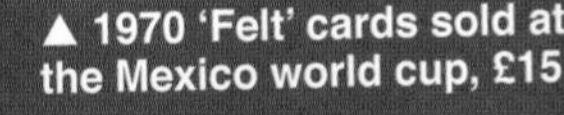

▲ 1970 'Felt' cards sold at the Mexico world cup, £15

VIGO 82
COPA DEL MUNDO DE FUTBOL ESPAÑA 82

◀1982 Spain This card is one of 15 official posters, £4

90 Bari stadium card for
World cup, £6

MasterCard
OFFICIAL CARD
EUROPEAN FOOTBALL CHAMPIONSHIP '92 – WORLD CUP '94

▲1994 USA Mastercard advert price £1.50

▲Mexico 1970, Aztec stadium and Jules Rimet trophy £15

THE FIRST WORLD

By ANDREW READ

When the First World War broke out in 1914, hundreds of thousands of men found themselves separated from friends and family – and they turned to the post-card to stay in touch.

For both photographers and postcard publishers this was a golden commercial opportunity and to satisfy demand they produced a huge number and range of cards which provide a fascinating snapshot of the times.

With 2014 being the centenary anniversary of the outbreak of war we can anticipate a surge in interest in this subject and values of all types of postcards published during the war years should see an uplift in popularity and consequently in value.

For gootness sake Halt !
der East Yorks
are koming

COMIC Anti German £6

SAY GOOD-NIGHT, DADDY, NOT
GOOD-BYE!
Dis-moi bonne nuit, papa, et pas adieu!

SENTIMENTAL £4

Commercially produced postcards in circulation during the period of the Great War tend to be of three main genres; Sentimental, Patriotic and Comic. In the first two years of conflict they were predominantly patriotic in tone. Many were jingoistic; harnessing popular opinion in support of the Allied cause. Some might contain a poem or verse playing on the theme of self-sacrifice and heroism; whilst others played on the notion of martial power: the dominance of Britain's Navy or the size of her Empire. Many cards supported the idea of a "just war" rallying to the aid of "defenceless little Belgium" against an aggressive and ruthless Germany. This found further expression, as war progressed, in the growing number of cards produced in response to high profile public outrages, such as the Zeppelin and Gotha Raids on London and Kent ; the shooting of Captain Fryatt ; the Bombardment of Scarborough and the execution of Nurse Edith Cavell. As emotions ran high, anti-German sentiment also manifested itself in postcards of a more comic nature. These presented Germany and their Allies as an inferior power and poked fun at such objects of ridicule as Dachshunds, German Waiters, and more pointedly, the Kaiser himself.

As those who joined Kitchener's " New Army " in the early weeks of the war, moved away from home to established military camps for basic training, so the need and desire to correspond with loved ones increased. Some posted sentimental cards with a focus on parting and separation. Others chose postcards which expressed their new sense of regimental pride and patriotic duty, illustrated by regimental badges and crests, coupled with patriotic flags or a verse. Others preferred the anti-Kaiser theme which depicted comic caricatures of the Kaiser or panicking German soldiers, hiding in barrels or running from "the 10th Worcesters" or the "Wimbledon Boys".

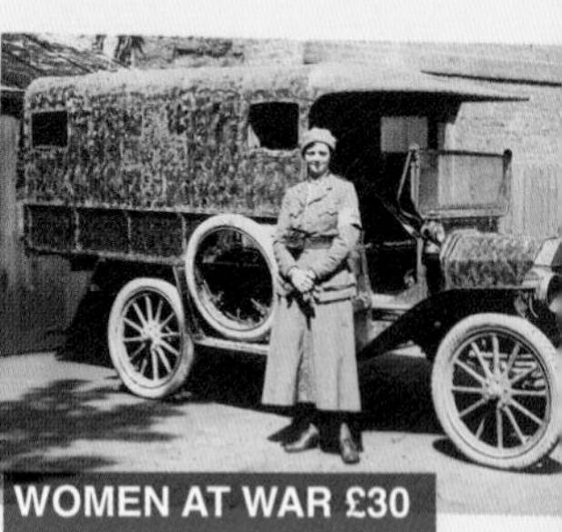

WOMEN AT WAR £30

ANTI KAISER cartoon £8

WAR *in Postcards*

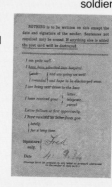

Responding to these new recruits and their preoccupation with the rigours of camp life and basic training, postcard publishers also produced a large and varied selection of mainly comic postcards. These portrayed the lot of the ordinary soldier in a light-hearted manner; Illustrated by self-mocking "Poem" and "Song" cards and comic depictions showing the various stages of military training. As soldiers neared the end of their training and prepared for service overseas; their " Loved ones " responded with postcards of a predominantly romantic or sentimental nature, expressing a sweetheart's last goodbye or a family's desire for the safe return of a father, son or brother. For those men already "on Active Service" the choices were more limited. Many communicated with home using official Field Postcards which baldly stated "I am quite well", or "I have been admitted to hospital. Wounded". However, these could be supplemented by postcards of French manufacture, made available to troops at rest or on leave, from shops and cafés in the larger towns behind the "lines", such as Arras, Le Havre and Amiens. Most were sentimental, romantic or patriotic in their content, with "Silk" cards being a particular favourite; offering more individually tailored designs. In addition, soldiers could buy books of postcards which showed printed photographic scenes of military activity behind the "Front"; or stark images of devastated French and Belgian towns and villages. Alternatively, postcards could be purchased, when out of the "line ", at the many Army Canteens and Recreational huts run by voluntary organisations, such as the YMCA. These retailed their own letter cards and stationery but also stocked some of the more popular postcards available at "home ".

NOTHING is to be written on this except the date and signature of the sender. Sentences not required may be erased. If anything else is added the post card will be destroyed.

I am quite well.
I have been admitted into hospital.
{ sick } { and am going on well.
{ wounded } { and hope to be discharged soon.
I am being sent down to the base.
I have received your { letter. / telegram. / parcel
Letter follows at first opportunity.
I have received no letter from you
{ lately.
{ for a long time.

Signature only: Fred
Date: 4 · 9 · 16

(Postage must be prepaid on any letter or postcard addressed to the sender of this card.)

▲**MUNITIONS superb photographic postcard inside a gas mask factory £45**

Continued ▶▶▶

THE FIRST WORLD WAR.. *in Postcards*

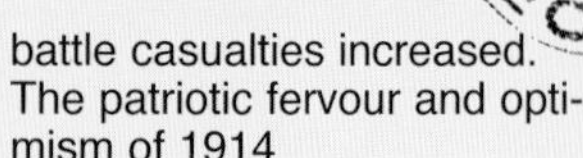

Cont'd ▶

As the country gradually transformed itself into a "wartime" economy; with the realization that the war would not be "over by Christmas", so the postcard began to reflect the popular issues and concerns of the day. These ranged from the shell shortage, to conscientious objectors and food rationing, to name but a few. In addition, postcards also found new forms of expression associated with the war effort, ranging from support for initiatives such as the raising of subscriptions for Comforts and Tobacco funds for those at "the Front", to the promotion of national Campaigns and Appeals, such as those for Government War Bonds and YMCA Hut Funds.

WOMAN working the land £6

By 1916, due to the large numbers of men on active service, those remaining on the "home front" comprised mainly of women, children, the elderly and those too infirm or medically unfit to fight, including increasing numbers of servicemen disabled due to wounds and sickness. In consequence, many of the postcards published after 1916 reflect this changing social landscape, depicting women at work and wounded soldiers convalescing in hospital. Some of the cards have a serious message, supporting the war effort, whilst others are of a more comic nature; sometimes self-effacing or positively ribald in content. Parallel to this is a change in mood. Any notion of a quick victory had receded by 1916, as the number of battle casualties increased. The patriotic fervour and optimism of 1914 and 1915 was replaced by a more stoical desire to see it through to the bitter end. A mood reflected in the content and style of the many "trench humour" postcards so memorably portrayed by Bruce Bairnsfather and his numerous imitators. One of whom, F. Mackain, produced a number of comic series depicting the soldier in training, at the base, up the line and at rest. These cards had a certain resonance and appeal to the British "Tommy"

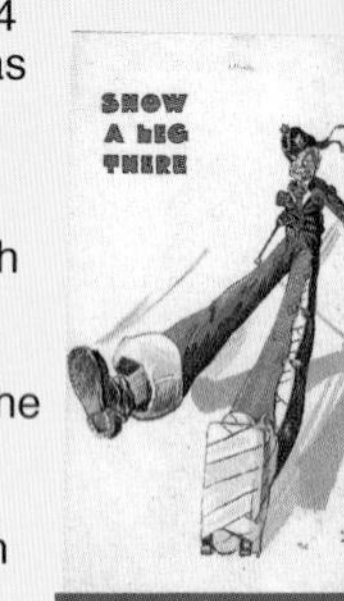

COMIC casualt

MILITARY HOSPITAL, and inset a postcard showing the staff sisters. These were sent from a wounded British soldier to his wife telling her he was 'going on alright'.

whose mood, tinged with an ever present sense of death and wounding, became more fatalistic and dark in tone as the war progressed. In parallel to this, there was also a desire by those "at home" to empathise more fully with those serving abroad; whether a father, husband, brother or son. This desire was reflected in the publication of an increasing number of "active service" postcards, produced by The Daily Mail and others, from Official War photographs and those of a less unofficial nature that documented the various allied Campaigns and offensives – such as the Dardanelles, the Somme and Palestine.

TRENCHES by Reg Maurice £4

In parallel, to the commercially produced postcards that spanned the First World War, photographic postcards also increased greatly, with many local photographers reaping the benefits from the huge demand from soldiers for a portrait of themselves in uniform, to send home or give to a new friend or acquaintance. The rather transient lifestyle of a soldier in training - making numerous friends and acquaintances - whilst always being on the move, made the postcard an ideal and cheap way of providing a keepsake or contact details for a new friend. A habit that continued even after a soldier proceeded on "active service", with many soldiers sending home postcards of themselves behind the lines or, in some cases, in the trenches themselves. For those taken prisoner, it was perhaps the best way of confirming to friends and family that they were safe and well, after being posted missing; in many cases, arriving before any official confirmation was received concerning their plight. These photographic images of individuals and their friends provide a lasting memory of an individual's life, a moment in time, which (sometimes rather tragically) could also have been their last.

On another level, these images can provide much historical detail. How soldiers were clothed and equipped. Many of the photos can illustrate the process of training from basic drill and route marches, through to manoeuvres and final firing. They provide photographic evidence of billeting or accommodation in a particular location, where the physical evidence has long since gone. As the first industrial war, these images can also help document the growing reliance on technology and the means of prosecuting "modern war" - whether it is a soldier armed with a Maxim Gun; a dispatch rider astride his motorcycle or a crew seated in the cockpit of their aeroplane. Individual and group photographs can also illustrate and document the cost of war: a group of dishevelled soldiers, newly-captured, dispirited and cowed together with their German guards; a wounded soldier in hospital blues recovering from wounds or the Grave Marker of an individual killed in action.

ACTION studio photo of an Australian soldier with his Maxim Gun £15

Whatever the motivation for collecting postcards connected with the First World War, the diversity of subject matter coupled with the photographic images themselves and the ephemeral details (the messages written or the addresses and censor marks provided) gives a rich source of original evidence - whether you are interested from a family history perspective, as a local historian, or a military researcher.

PROUD soldiers wanted a photographic memento to send home

■ Turn to page 104 for more Military postcards and their values

WHAT THE PRICES MEAN

With a few exceptions, all cards in this Catalogue have been given a single price, representing a broad average figure for the majority of cards in their respective classification. For example:

ART and SUBJECT CARDS

The stated price may be taken as a broad average figure for all Art and Subject cards. You will find C.E. Flower listed at £2. There are many common cards by this artist which are worth no more than £1, while his rare cards would certainly be worth £3. The great bulk of his output therefore would be expected to sell at the broad average figure of £2.

TOPOGRAPHICAL and SOCIAL HISTORY

With any relevant entry, e.g. Motor Bus .Tram . Street Market . Windmill etc. the stated price, or broad average figure, is for a card, *either RP or Printed, fully identified and showing a 'Close-up at a named location',* with real photographic cards being the most desirable. (Logically it will be appreciated that to qualify for listing at all, a Bus or Tram etc. has to be a *"Close-up"* in the first place and as such would represent the *majority of cards in that classification*). Generally speaking, anything less would be classified as a street scene at a lower price. If you think of a Bus or Tram in the middle distance, that is a street scene, while a Windmill in the middle-distance would similarly be priced at a lower figure.

With this in mind, it is then necessary to apply certain other criteria before formulating a final price, as with all Topographical and Social History cards, it is neither realistic nor practical to subdivide each entry into considerations of: Real Photographic . Printed . Close-up . Far Distance . Located . Unlocated . Identified . Unidentified . Common . Scarce . Publisher . Condition etc., not to mention whether the card is in a saleable area or even if it forms part of a remaindered stock! (You will begin to appreciate the problems in pricing these cards!). Put simply, the card has to be a Close-up to qualify for the price given. Consideration of all these other factors will then enable you to arrive at a final valuation.

A real photographic Motor Bus is catalogued at £35. A distant view of a Bus trundling along a country road may fetch £5, while a common, mass produced card of Buses in Trafalgar Square would only be worth 50p. On the other hand, a spectacular real photograph of a bus in a provincial town, taken by a local photographer, where the image fills the whole of the card, may fetch £50. Real Photographic cards are generally worth more than Printed cards, but a middle distance RP would be worth less than a superb Printed close-up. Admittedly, this is not easy for collectors new to the hobby, but as you gain more knowledge you will quickly see how it all works! Pricing is not an exact science, nor would we ever wish it to be!

It is further pointed out that in all relevant classifications, 'Accidents' would carry a price toward the higher end of the scale.

FURTHER INFORMATION

It must always be borne in mind that an exceptional card or complete set in any classification may fetch a price well in excess of Catalogue valuation. There are many reasons for this. In the dealer's stock any particularly rare or desirable item may be felt to be worth a premium, given the number of potential buyers, while at auction the same card, or complete set, would be offered to a totally different world-wide clientele, with a resulting number of high bids being received. It does not therefore follow that any auction realisation can be taken as representing current market value as perceived by the majority of dealers throughout the country.

In many Subject classifications, for example, Animals, Children, Greetings etc. one finds many cards printed by the early chromo-litho method. The superior quality of these cards would put them at the higher end of the price range.

It is not possible to be more specific given the huge numbers and types of postcards produced, neither is it realistic to have an entry for 'Chromo-Litho' under hundreds of Subject listings!

A single figure has been for all classifications where the majority of cards are of similar content, e.g. Bamforth Song Cards. One would expect to find such cards in any dealer's stock, priced at around the stated price.

The Price Range has been retained for classifications where one finds a wide divergence of content in available cards, e.g. 'Advert Cards/Poster Type'. Here only knowledge and experience can be your guide, though it is quite practical to take a middle average price for any particular card. This will enable you to form a realistic assessment of the value of your collection.

Unless otherwise stated, all cards in this catalogue are priced as being commercially published. Private and family photographs have no value other than what they may be worth to a particular collector. There are certain exceptions e.g. 'Contemporary Fashion, Weddings' and similar collectable cards.

Unless clearly stated in the text, all prices are for single cards.

In all cases, prices are for cards in fine condition, with no marks or bent corners etc. This is particularly so with Art and Subject cards, whereas in the Topographical and Social History fields, the image may be felt to outweigh considerations of condition.

The cards listed in this Catalogue are with very few exceptions pre-1939 and all standard size 5.5 x 3.5 in. This date may be extended to 1945 for the issues of World War 2, and as far as 1990 for GB Topographical Views, Civil Aviation, Cinema and one or two other subjects as indicated in the listings.

Certain issues in the larger 6 x 4 size did occur during this period, and are listed as appropriate, but with the odd exception
All prices in this Catalogue, many of them covering thousands of cards with one figure, must be taken as a broad average of that particular classification. Please do not say "PPV gives £3 for this". PPV does not give £3 for this. PPV suggests £3 as a mean average figure for the majority of cards of that type. Some cards may be worth £1, while others may be worth £5. Please bear this in mind when buying or selling.

N.B. It must be pointed out to non-collectors wishing to sell cards, that perhaps 75% of all postcards are virtually worthless! Postcards are like Stamps or Coins, in that huge quantities of common, or low-denomination material exists in today's market. I refer to Greetings cards - Landscapes - Seasides - Tourist Areas - Churches - Cathedrals - common Foreign views etc. All these cards are catalogued, and all must have a price, but it does not follow that anyone wants to buy them! Such cards may be picked up from auctions or trade sources in bulk at nominal cost. Effectively, what dealers want to buy are the better cards catalogued at £1.50 and upwards, which they can sell again. Please bear this in mind when offering cards for sale.

MODERN CARDS

As a brief guide it can be assumed that while certain subject themes may have a value of up to several pounds each, the vast majority of subject cards can be purchased new for 50p or less and secondhand or used for a few pence each.
Please see page 12 for Brian Lund's 2014 modern review.

As for topographical views, the same price structure applies, although it is pointed out to prospective vendors that views of foreign holiday areas are worth very little.

ARTISTS / COLLECTIONS

The years at the turn of the century saw the production of a number of selected postcard series now justly celebrated as representing the high-water mark of postcard art and design. In this respect France was very much to the fore, and I give below a list of these series, together with details of other leading European collections. This is almost entirely the province of the European collector, for although these cards do come along from time to time in our Auctions, the interest in Britain is limited to a few people.

Market Report
A highly specialised area which has seen steady interest, prices tend to be determined at auction, generally outside the scope of the UK market.
Present price ranges are considered adequate.

AUSTRIA

WIENER WERKSTATTE 1908-1913

Recognised by the title design on the reverse, these cards were produced perhaps as a reaction to the swirling lines of Art Nouveau, being typified by a spare and severe style which gave way to Cubism and Art Deco. Artists include: Mela Koehler and Oskar Kokoschka.
Price Range: £60/£2500

FRANCE

COCORICO

Probably the most celebrated of all French series. There are 12 designs only. Artists include: De Feure and Steinlen.
Price Range: £150/£750

COLLECTION DES CENT. 1901

A series of 100 cards by leading Artists of the day. Cards have this title printed at the edge. Artists include: Alphonse Mucha, Caran d'Ache, Jules Cheret and A. Steinlen.
Price Range: £50/£500

COLLECTION JOB 1895-1914

There were three series together totalling 78 cards. Reprints of calendars and posters from the period above. Artists include: Angelo Asti, Jules Cheret and Alphonse Mucha.
Price Range: £50/£300

CONCOURS DE BYRHH 1906

A competition held to select advertisements for this aperitif. 113 designs were published as postcards. Artists include: Maurice Denis, Raphael Kirchner and G. Meunier.
Price Range: £50/£300

EDITIONS CINOS 1898

A series of 35 cards by famous artists of the day. Artists include: Alphonse Mucha, Jules Cheret and Toulouse-Lautrec.
Price Range: £100/750

GERMANY

JUGEND 1899

Three series totalling 75 cards, in the Art Nouveau style. Artists include: Hans Christiansen.
Price Range: £50/£300

BAUHAUS 1923.

This series consisted of 20 designs, with reputedly only about 25 copies of each design printed Artists include: Paul Klee and Kurt Schmidt.
Price Range: £250/£50,000

CHROMO-LITHO

Generally acknowledged as the finest of all colour printing methods. Briefly, the design was etched onto a limestone block and printed in solid colours, as opposed to modern screen printing, where the dots can be seen through a strong glass. Chromo-Litho printing was used extensively for postcards from 1890-1910, particularly in the `Gruss Aus' and `Early Vignette' classifications. The reader is directed to the specialist books in this field which will list many of the hundreds of publishers engaged in this form of printing.The price of any Chromo-Litho card may be found by reference to its subject or artist, but there exist a great many unsigned Chromo-Litho cards of general landscape type.

Chromo-litho Italian military, lovely printing, but this type of card can be found for just £5

TOPOGRAPHICAL ART

In recent years the collection of chromo-litho topographical art has become popular in its own right. Prominent names in this field include Manuel Wielandt, Michael Zeno Diemer, Raoul Frank, Paul Kley, K. Mutter and A. Prosnocimi. These and others are listed in the main Artist index.

Many cards in this genre however are unsigned, and a guide to the price of these is given below:

French Views	£3
German Views	£4
Italian Views	£4
Swiss Views	£3
Other countries	£3+

ART REPRODUCTIONS

Friezes/Red Border types	£2
Miscellaneous reproductions	£1

Chromo-Litho/Heavy Board

Misch & Stock/Sborgi/Stengel	£2-£5

Gallery Reproduction Series

Photochrom Co.	.75

Misch & Stock Art reproduction of Rafael's 'The Madonna of Foligno' Vatican, Rome £2

ART TYPES

Colouring Cards/Pairs

Tuck R. & Sons	£2
Miscellaneous Types	£1

Oilfacism

Tuck R. & Sons	£1.50
Miscellaneous Oil Facsimiles	£1

Hand Painted

Professional Work	£5
Amateur Work	£2
Mass produced	£1

SCULPTURE

Art Sculpture on black card	£1
Gallery/Museum types	.75

Montage scenes

Mastroianni D.	£2

A winter sporting theme by Artelius, a fine art deco artist from Sweden, £15*

ART DECO

This subject remains an important postcard classification, reflecting as it does the work of many leading artists of the twentieth century. Art Deco began in the early years after 1900, as a reaction to the swirling and complex designs of Art Nouveau. The style was characterised by a more severe and economical line, and was later to be inspired by cubism. It reached its height in 1925 with the Paris Exposition des Arts Decoratifs et Modernes, but died out in the 1930s. At its peak, the Ar Deco style reached into many other branches of the arts. **Market Report** "Collectors have been looking for quality items by the more important artists. Brunelleschi, Montedoro, Mela Koehler, and the 'hand-painted' versions by Meschini have all been in demand. Glamour related Chiostri has also sold well, although not so much those featuring children. Scandinavian artists have continued to have a loyal following, with Rylander and Nerman amongst the more notable names. Certain themes have also featured, with sports and advertising related subjects being strong categories. Less popular have been unsigned examples, silhouettes and the more common artists such as Corbella and Nanni".

A beautiful 'hand-painted' and signed card by Giovanni Meschini. Examples like this fetch up to £40

A popular artist, with pierrots appearing on several series by Sofia Chiostri. This type card is worth between £25 and £30

ART NOUVEAU

This is a highly specialised field which, like Art Deco, reaches into the Fine Art World, with the consequent high price structure of many of its Artists. Typified by a swirling, flowing style, Art Nouveau reached its apogee at the turn of the century in the work of Mucha, Kirchner and Basch, among others, but died out about ten years later.

Market Report

Many of the classic Art Nouveau artists such as Alphonse Mucha and Eva Daniel are getting more and more difficult to find at fairs nowadays with only a few UK based dealers carrying the top names. Visiting continental dealers often have a better selection. Early examples by Kirchner are still in demand, as are cards by Arpad Basch Carl Jozsa and Henri Meunier. Certain Russian artists have begun to fetch high prices, driven by the surge of interest from collectors and dealers in that country. However, there are many beautiful unsigned examples of this period to be found, often at very reasonable prices, so a discerning collector can still build up a very fine collection over time.

.bove: An unusual example of Art Nouveau landscape by the Russian artist Ivan Bilibin £65.
'op: Alphonse Mucha, 'months of the year' £150

RAPHAEL KIRCHNER

Kirchner was born in Vienna in 1875 and died in America at the height of his fame in 1917. His work dates from 1897 to 1916 and during this time he produced nearly 800 postcard designs, grouped together in over 120 sets and other issues, published by some 77 separate firms. Kirchner was one of the leading figures in the Art Nouveau movement, although some of his later work lay more in the field of straight Glamour. His cards have been catalogued by Antonio and Pia Dell'Aquila in,"Raphael Kirchner and his Postcards" published in 1996. This magisterial work illustrates every known card and gives a full listing of all known publishers. Readers who wish to look further into the life and work of this great artist can have no better guide. All one can do within the confines of a general catalogue such as this, is give a brief guide to those cards which by reason of publisher or other factors, are most often found on the British market, together with an indication of price. This in itself can only be a very broad assessment, as many of these series were reprinted by other publishers, often in different formats, with added greetings or other variations. It is further noted that certain rare cards not listed here, can be worth anything up to £500+ each. One problem remains with Kirchner in that some of his cards are unsigned. There is not much we can do about this other than refer the reader to Dell'Aquila where every card is identified. What follows is merely a general guide which I hope will be of some help to collectors.

All prices below are for single cards. A complete set may attract a premium over this figure. It must be noted that prices apply to cards in flawless condition, with no marks or damage of any kind. With highly rated cards such as these, condition is everything and those in less than perfect state would be worth considerably less.

'Raphael Kirchner and his Postcards' may be purchased from: Reflections of a Bygone Age, 15 Debdale Lane, Keyworth, Notts. NG12 5HT at the price of £29.95 including postage.

Early Kirchner with cycling subject, £60

A Quatre Feuilles	Set 6	£65
Girls' heads in clover leaf		
Enfants de la Mer	Set 10	£65
Girls at the Seaside		
Fruits Douces	Set 6	£65
Girls with fruit between green borders		
Geisha	Set 10	£45
Scenes of Japanese life		
Greek Virgins	Set 12	£65
Girls in beige & gold design		
Les Cigarrettes du Monde	Set 6	£65
Girls smoking cigarettes		
Maid of Athens	Set 6+	
Studies of young girls		
Coloured		£40
Bw series		£25
See also Tuck listing		
Mikado	Set 6	£50
Japanese Girls		
Santoy	Set 6	£60
Scenes of Japanese Life		
Demi Vierge	Set 6	£65
Girls on gold background between green borders		
Femmes Soleil	Set 6	£65
Girls' faces on background of sunrays		
Same designs on pale blue without sunrays		

Erika Set 6 £65
Girls' heads on floral background

Marionettes Set 6 £55
Girls with puppets

Bijoux Set 6 £65
Girls in goblet/heart shaped panels

Les Peches Capitaux Set 7 £35
Girl with inset pierrot head

Kirchner Girls Set 24 £25
Bruton Galleries
Delta Fine Art Co. EC2

Kirchner Girls Set 12 £25
Bruton Galleries
Alphalsa Publishing Co. EC2

Les Amours de Pierrot Set 10 £35
Girl with inset pierrot head on titled card
Reinthal & Newman/New York

Librairie de l'Estampe/Paris £35
Glamour/WW1 period. 32 cards
Numbered and titled on back

Cards published in Britain by Raphael Tuck & Sons.

Connoisseur 2555 Salome Girls' large faces with scenic background
Coloured Set 6 £60
Black & White Set 6 £30

Connoisseur 2642
Les Ephemeres Set 6 £100
Three girls in flowing dresses

Oilette Connoisseur 2709
Flashing Motorists Set 6 £60

Continental 3002 Set 6 £85
Continental 3003 Set 6 £85
Girls' faces in circle with mauve background

Continental 3004 Set 10 £85
Continental 3005 Set 10 £85
Girls standing in Flowers

Continental 4002

Continental 4003
Maid of Athens
Coloured Set 6 £40
Black & White Set 6 £25
Continental 4008 Set 6 £85

Continental 4009 Set 6 £85
Girls in panels with pink borders

Continental 4016 Set 6 £85

Continental 4017 Set 6 £85
Girls in panels with olive borders

Continental 4024 Set 6 £65

Continental 4025 Set 6 £65
Greek Virgins
Diaphne 3501 Set 5 £200
Diaphne 8902 Set 5 £200
Vitraux d'Art
Girls in stained glass windows

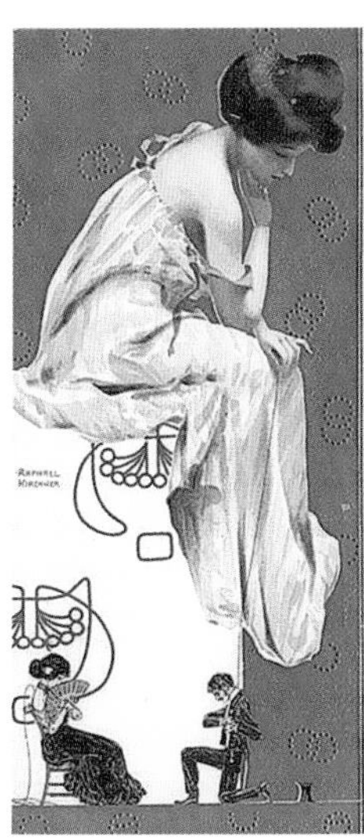

Marionettes £55

The postcards of Raphael Kirchner can be divided into three main periods:

The Early Beginnings: 1897 - 1899

The Golden Age: 1900 - 1907

The Glamour Age: 1910 - 1917

Bruton Galleries £25

ADVERTISING

A popular and widely collected of postcard themes. Many different types of Advertising cards were produced during the early years of this century, both by the companies whose products they advertised, and by the independent publishers. They range from the very attractive 'Poster Types', designed in the form of an advertising poster, or sometimes reproducing an established poster such as Fry's classic 'Five Boys' design, to the many plainer types known as 'Giveaways'. These were published by the company for promotional purposes, and were often given away with the product, although many more do show themes such as the gathering, processing, or manufacture of the product. Companies across the whole spectrum of industry produced Advertising cards of one sort or another, and we have cards from the Food and Drink industry, Animal Feed Manufacturers, Newspapers and Magazines, the Tobacco Industry, and many more. In addition, many of the Railway and Shipping companies, as well as other more specialised issues are listed under those respective sections. We also include 'Reward Cards' under the main entry, as these were given away to school-children for good attendance.

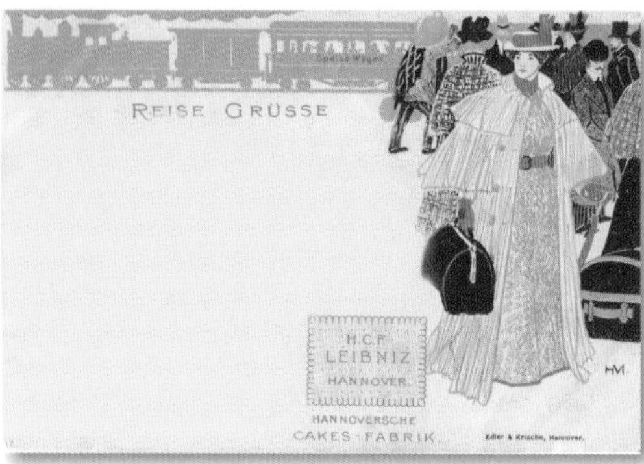

Market Report

The internet has affected this category disproportionately because of the difficulty in distinguishing reproductions from the genuine article. Rare cards still command good prices but many classic poster types are worth half of what they were a few years ago.

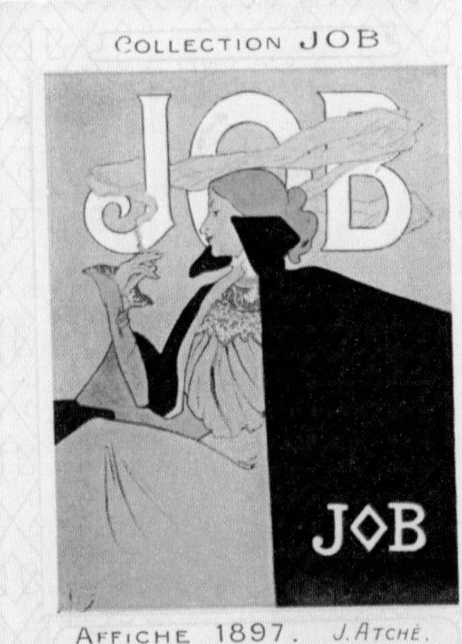

Collection Job, Tobacco advert, £50

POSTER TYPE

Beecham's Pills	
Tom Browne designs	£30
Beer & Baccy	
Victoria State 1896	£30
Berry's Boot Polish	£20
Bird's Custard	£20
British Army	
Recruiting Poster	£30
Bryant & May	£35
John Bull Tyres	£35
Cadbury's	£40
Camp Coffee	
Harry Payne designs	£60
Other designs	£30
Campbell's Soups	
G. Weidersheim designs	£25
Capern's Bird Foods	£15
Cerebos Salt	£25
Champion Vinegar	£12
Claymore Whiskey	
Defenders of the Empire	£10
Continental Tyres	£25
C.W.S	
Pelaw Metal Polish	£18
Other Products	£18
Epps Milk Chocolate	£20
Fletcher's Sauce	£25
GP Government Tea	£15
Gossage's Soap	£20
Heinz H.J. & Co.	£18
H.P. Sauce	£30
Horniman's Tea	£25
Hudson's Soap	£25
James Keiller	£15
John Knight Soap	£25
Mustad Horse Nails	£25
Nestle's Milk	£30
North British Rubber Co.	£30
Ovaltine	£15
Palmer Tyres	£25
Peek Frean	
Tom Browne designs	£25
Raleigh Cycles	£35
Schweppes	£12
Skipper Sardines	£10
Wood Milne Rubber Heels	£15
Miscellaneous Products	£10/£30
Suchard Chocolate/Cocoa	

One of the earliest companies to employ the medium of the picture postcard for advertising purposes, Suchard were producing cards from c.1890 onwards.

Early Vignette/Gruss Aus type	£20

Wood Milne poster advert £15

TUCK R. & SONS
Celebrated Posters

There exists a considerable variance in price for these cards, even for the same card, if sold at auction or by a dealer. Basically the lower numbered series are the more common, and would range from about £15-£30 depending upon the artist, design, product, condition etc. But even here we find particular cards occurring more frequently than the others. Indeed some are positively commonplace!
The higher series from 1504 onwards are less often found, with the contrary position that certain cards seem almost non-existent! Here the price range would be from £30-£75, although prices as high as £150 for particular cards have been noted in the stocks of certain dealers!
For a more comprehensive study of this subject we recommend 'The Picture Postcards of Raphael Tuck & sons'. by J.H.D.Smith. (Currently out of print)

SETS & SERIES

C.W.S. Packet Teas

Dickens sketches/Trade back £8
Time Around the World/Trade back £10

Epps Cocoa

Nature series £8

Famous Posters in Miniature

H.M.& Co. £30

GP Government Tea

Set 6/KEVII at Windsor
Price per set £130

Lemco

Coronation series £15
Types of Lemco Cattle £10

Quaker Oats

Smiles/Set 10 £12

Shell Oil

Original series... see listing below £25-£75
Later series 50s & 60s £6-£10
Reproductions 1.50

The following are early postcards issued by Shell (1900 – 1914). *By Alan Roman.*
The SQ numbers are assigned to each card to ease identification. These numbers appear in my book "The Shell Picture Postcard Book" and on my web site www.arpostcards.co.uk

SQ1 (22) aviator/ car driver holding Shell can £45
SQ2 (23) Avoid inferior spirit as you would a trap£45
SQ3 (24) Illustrates petrol can with one word 'Shell' on each £40
SQ4 (25) The Keystone to Motoring £40
SQ5 (32) Kindred Spirit £45
SQ6 (33) Votes for Women £60
SQ7 (34) They all want Shell £45
SQ8 (35) Speeding the Parting Guest £50
SQ9 (38) See that you always have Shell £45
SQ10 (37) Best for Cars. Best for Boats £40
SQ11 (38) For all times and all Climbs £50
SQ12 (39) More records on Shell than any other £50
SQ13 (40) CAUTION! See that every can...... impression of a Shell £50
SQ14 (41) The Spirit of Great Strength £50
SQ17 (66) When you think of Speed think of Shell £50
SQ18 (66) As Above but overprinted Four-Inch Race September 24 1908 £55
SQ20 (71) Of amazing Power £35
SQ21 (72) Best on Earth. Best in the Air £45
SQ22 (73) Invincible. Illustrates Bulldog £25
SQ23 (74) Shell is the Password to Successful Motoring £40
SQ24 (75) Helping Father £40
SQ25 (76) Always ahead of Time £40
SQ26 (77) King Petrolemy Sendeth....Precious Spirit £30
SQ27(78) 1st Unsuccessful Motorist £30
SQ28 (79) The Best Mascot £35
SQ29 (83) Scottish Reliability Trials £40
SQ32 (134) Souvenir of Blackpool Aviation week £40
SQ33 (135) Must have Shell at all costs! £35
SQ34 (136) Illustrates planes and balloon above a tower £40
SQ35 (143) General Election 1910 £70
SQ36 (145) The Key to successful Motoring £30
SQ37 (146) waiter offering a can of Shell £25
SQ38 (147) Holds more honours than any other £25
SQ39 (148) The Spirit of many Triumphs £25
SQ40 (149) Safeguard your interests by using Shell £25
SQ41 (159) What makes them go so far £25
SQ42 (155) Triumphs of the Air. Mr Pulham £40
SQ50 (180) Best for Hill Climbing £25
SQ51 (181) Scottish Trials. boy with Bagpipes £20
SQ52 (182) With Captain Scott R.N. in the Antarctic En route to the South Pole £50
SQ53 (183) The Spirit of the Coming Age £40
SQ54 (184) Old King Cole was a merry old soul.. £20
SQ55 (185) girl sitting in a sea shell £25
SQ56 (200) Waiter (presenting wine list): What brand sir?... £30
SQ57 (201) The Favourite with every engine £40
SQ58 (202) What a find for the Shell collector £45
SQ59 (203) Give a Camel food and water and it wil go on "Fast" for 8 days £30
SQ64 (227) Witch flying on a can of Shell £50
SQ65 (228) More miles on Shell than any other! Illustrates dog pulling a can of Shell £35
SQ66 (229) Illustrates school master in classroom with three boys £45
SQ67 (230) For uniform excellence £40
SQ69 (246) On the Track of a good thing £45
SQ70 (247) angel flying and holding a can £35
SQ71 (248) A Friend in Need £35
SQ72 (249) Stone Age car £30
SQ76 (267) a man hoisting a Shell Motor Spirit Flag £50
SQ77 (270) two Heralds £45
SQ78 (272) a car, boat, and a motor cycle £45
SQ79 (273) As 272, just the car and boat £45
SQ81 (286) Mr Hamel on a Bleriot.. £50
SQ83 (289) Where's that Shell? £45
SQ84 (290) small car by the side of a large car £45
SQ85 (291) He sell the "Shell" on the sea shore £40
SQ86 (292) Highest in public esteem £45
SQ87 (293) Buoyed up by the "BEST OF SPIRITS" £40
SQ102 (-) Best on Land and Sea £45
SQ103 (-) As above Tourist Trophy Race 1906 £50
SQ104 (-) C.S. RollsTourist Trophy Race £50
SQ105 (-) driver pouring from Shell can £45
SQ106 (-) For Power and Economy £60
SQ107 (-) Always turns up Trumps £45
SQ108 (-) I thought so! It's everywhere £45
SQ114 (-) Shell carried unanimously £50
SQ118 (-) drivers on Rocket to the Moon £60

Above: Drivers on Rocket £60

Walker, Harrison & Garthwaite

Phoenix Poultry Foods	£10
Viscan Pet Foods	£12
VC Winners	£15

CHROMO-LITHO

Standard-size cards, mainly of French origin, and printed Chromo-Litho, usually in early vignette style. They carry the brand name of a product on an often quite unrelated design.

Arlatte Chicory
Tuck R. & Sons/Flowers £10

Belle Jardiniere
Art sketches £20

Chocolat Lindt
Children/Art sketches £20

Chocolat Lombart
Children/Art sketches £20

Lipton
Language of Flowers £18

Scott's Emulsion
French Departments/Set 92 £8

COURT SIZE

These are among the earliest examples of Advertising cards. Smaller than standard postcard size, and usually printed chromo-litho in vignette style.

Hutchinson Novels
Literary adverts £25

Johnston's Corn Flour
Some Methods of Travelling/Set 24 £35

Nestle's Swiss Milk
Military vignettes £40

St. Ivel Cheese £20

FRIENDLY SOCIETIES

Not exactly Poster Type, although some very attractive designs may be found on these cards.

Grand United Order of Oddfellows £6

Hearts of Oak Benefit Society £6

Independent Order of Rechabites £6

Order of the Sons of Temperance

Heraldic Designs	£6
Bridges/Castles/Churches	£10

Twentieth Century Equitable Friendly Society £6

POSTER TYPE/SERIES

FRY J.S. & SONS

Prices... As with Tuck Celebrated Posters, a wide divergence exists in the current market value of these cards. Some are very common, others remarkably scarce.

Tom Browne designs	£30/£45
With Capt Scott at the South Pole	£70
Other designs	£20/£40

Caption	**Artist**
Showcard Replica Series	
What's good for the bee	
His heart's desire	
A perfect dream	
The tired traveller	
On the top	
A perfect food	
Sweeter than honey	
Vivian Mansell &Co.	
Unapproachable	
This is my brother Billy	
A source of delight	
Is the best	
Keeps out the cold	
Various Publishers	
John Bull says support home industries	R.C. Carter
Cow being milked	R.C. Carter
The prize winner	Chas. Pears
If you feel cold	Chas. Pears
My eye! Ain't Fry's Chocolate nice	Chas. Pears
Far too good to share	Chas. Pears
The diver's lucky find	
Cocoa Sah!	Edgar Filby
Good old mater	
Fry's Milk Chocolate (White Cow)	
Fry's Milk Chocolate (Pyjama boy)	
With Capt. Scott at the South Pole	
Keeps out the cold	
No better food after a good bath	Maud Fabian
The five senses	
Five girls want	
Always merry and bright	Ernest Noble
Great Scott! What a find.	John Hassall
Avec les compliments	
Disgraced but not defeated	Edgar Filby
I fully endorse	
I am ... etc.	
Yes, it's Fry's	
It's worth the risk	
Unrivalled ... etc.	
A double first	
The bloom of health	
A perfect breakfast table	

Caption	Artist
No better food	
Design as above/C.W. Faulkner	
The little connoisseur	
Over the top and the best of luck	
Fry's for good	
So near and yet so far	Tom Browne
Highway robbery	Tom Browne
See their eyes as she buys	
Fry's	Tom Browne
One touch of nature	Tom Browne
Right up to date	Tom Browne
Fry's Cocoa (rich girl)	Tom Browne
Hello Daddy	
Whom God preserve	
Compliments of J.S. Fry & Sons Ltd.	
Fry's Coca (Boy with train)	
Fry's Chocolate for endurance	
Well, if you know of a better cocoa!	
Going by leaps and bounds	
Jolly good for the money	
Sustaining and invigorating	
Fry's, it's good	
The best is good enough for me	
Fry's Pure Cocoa/	
Design as above/J.S. Fry & Sons Ltd.	
Tuck CP 1500	Gordon Browne
Fry's Milk Chocolate/Tuck CP 1502	

TOBACCO

A special classification for these cards reflects a shared interest with the cigarette card world.

Adkins Tobacco
Tom Browne posters £150+

Cavander's Army Mixture
Poster type £25

Dimitrino Cigarettes
Chromo-Litho £15

Gallaher's Park Drive Cigarettes
Poster type £15

Gitanes Cigarettes
Poster type/Art Deco £30

Godfrey Phillips

Set 30/Beauty Spots of the Homeland	£8
Set 24/Coronation Series	£8
Set 26/Famous Paintings	£8
Set 24/Film Stars	£60
Set 48/Film Stars	£60
Set 30/Garden Studies	£6
Set 12/Jubilee Series	£6
Set 30/Our Dogs	£90
Set 30/Our Glorious Empire	£12
Set 30/Our Puppies	£40

Grapevine Cigarettes
Southend Lifeboat 1906 £15

Wills Capstan Gold Flake, (courtesy of Warwick & Warwick, see inside back cover page) £80

Gray's Cigarettes
Views £3

Job Cigarette Papers
Vercasson/Poster type:
Chromo-Litho £50
Early vignettes £25

Lea R. & J./Chairman Cigarettes
O.E. Pottery and Porcelain/Set 24 £6
With supplier's imprint £8

Mitchell's Prize Crop
Glasgow Exhibition 1901 £50

Murad Turkish Cigarettes £30

Nicholas Sarony
Film Stars £3

Ogden's
Poster type £90

Players
Poster type £75
Other types £30

Sandorides Lucana Cigarettes
Poster type £20

U.K. Tobacco Co./The Greys
Beautiful Britain £2

Wills W.D. & H.O.
Poster type: Capstan/Gold Flake/
Three Castles/Westward Ho! £80+

Miscellaneous Companies
Poster type £15/£40
Views etc. £2+

GIVEAWAY/ INSERT CARDS

This section covers those cards given away or distributed by commercial firms, news-papers and magazines, etc., for promotional purposes. Subjects depicted are varied, and often have no relation to the product advertised. Here again the total number of firms who produced these cards is incalculable. We list below the more common and collectable cards.

Amami Shampoo
Prichard & Constance £2

Answers £4

Bazaar, Exchange & Mart
Comic sketches £8

Beecham's Pills
GB views £1.50

Bees Ltd. £1

Bensdorp Cocoa
Pierrots £15
Dutch Scenes £6
London views £6
Isle of Marken £1.50

Books/Magazines/Newspapers
Military/Mail/Front Page £3
French Newspapers/Front Page £3
Other publications £3

Boon's Cocoa
European views .75

Bovril
Art Reproductions £1

Brett's Publications
GB views £1.50

British Dominions Insurance
Art studies/Set 24 £1.50

Bromo Cocoa
Plantation sketches £2

Brooke Bond
Silhouettes of Manchester £12

Butywave Shampoo
Film Stars £3

Cadbury Bros.
Bournville village £1.50

Canadian Dept. of Emigration
Canadian views £1.50

Canary and Cage Bird Life
Cage Bird Studies/32 cards
/pc back £5
/trade back £3

Capern's Bird Foods
Cage bird studies/pc back £4
/trade back £3

Captain Magazine
Tom Browne sketches £8

Carter Paterson
Removal trucks £10
Art sketches £2

Carter's Seeds £2

Chelsea Flower Show £3

Chick's Own £5

0Chivers & Sons
Studies of English Fruits £2
Aerial views of Histon £4

Christian Novels
GB views £1.50

Colman's Starch
Postmen of the Empire £12
GB sketches £3

Connoisseur
Art Reproductions .50

Cook E./Lightning Series
Aviation studies £8

Formosa Oolong tea, Japanese print £5

Feathered World
Poultry studies £5

Field J.C./Toilet Soaps
Childhood sketches £4

Field The
Military sketches £4

Fine Arts Publishing Co.
Burlington Proofs .75

F-M-N Complete Novels
Theatrical portraits £1.50

Formosa Oolong Tea
Sketches on Rice Paper £10
Japanese prints £5

Fry J.S. & Sons
Non-poster types £8
Views of Somerdale Works £2

Garden City Association
Letchworth Garden City/
Set 12/Frank Dean £4
Set 6/W.W. Ratcliffe £4

Gentlewoman
Royal Artist Post Card Series £4

Girl's Own Paper
Art sketches/4 designs £10

Glaxo
Various subjects £3

Goss W.H.
Oates S. & Co. £8

Guinness A.
Cartoons/6x4 size/
Three sets of 6 cards (per card) £10

3 sets of six cards produced on heavy card and larger size 6" x 4" with an envelope.
Set A. features Alice in Wonderland.
Alice Studies Natural History
Mushroom Growth
Why was the Hatter Mad
Bottle & Jug
My Mother Said....
Bottle Royal.
Set B. features Animal Posters.
Lion & Keeper
Pelican
Kangaroo & Keeper
Sea Lion & Keeper
Polar Bear
Toucan.
Set C. features "Guiness for Strength"
Posters.
Girder
Pillar
Car

Tree Chopping
Wheelbarrow
Horse & Cart
Brewery scenes £8
Brewery scenes/6x4 size £4

Harland & Wolf
Valentine & Sons £6

Hartley W.P.
Jam production scenes £2

Haydock Coals
Art Reproduction/GB views £1

Health and Strength
Physical Culture studies £8
Hoffman's Starch £1.50

Home Words
Various subjects £1.50

Horner's Penny Stories
Various subjects £3

Horniman's Tea
Invisible Picture £8
GB views £2

Hotels/Restaurants
GB/Artist sketches £3
GB Photographic/Printed £5
Foreign/Gruss Aus type £4
Foreign/Later issues £1

Ideas Weekly
The Imps £8

Idle Moments
Various subjects £1.50

Imperial Fine Art Corporation
Art Reproductions .75

International Horse Show £8

Jacob W. & R.
Biscuit production scenes £3

King Insurance Co.
GB Royalty sketches £6

Lever Bros.
Port Sunlight village £1.50

Liberty's £8

Liebig Fray-Bentos
Oxo Shackleton Expedition £25
Meat processing scenes £4

Lipton
Tea Estate sketches £2

Liverpool, China & India Tea Co. Ltd.
Atlantic Liners £15

Lord Mayor Treloar Home
Institution scenes £1.50

Maggi
European views .75

Manchester Dock & Harbour Board
Topographical sketches £6

Mazawattee Tea & Chocolate
Louis Wain Cats/Postcard £85
/Trade Back £50

Mellin's Food
Costume & Flags/Set 12 £6
Various subjects £6

Melox
Animal Foods £6

Menier Chocolate
Paris sketches £1

Miniature Novels
Various subjects £1.50

Mirror Novels
Theatrical/Bookmark type £3

Molassin Meal/Dog Cakes
Various subjects £8

My Pocket Novel
Various subjects £1.50

My Queen & Romance
Various subjects £1.50

Nestle's
Animals & Birds/Set 12 £6

New Zealand Govt. Department
Topographical sketches £1.50

New Zealand Lamb
Dairy Farming scenes .75

North British Rubber Co.
Golfing sketches £45

Norwich Union
Motor Fire Engine £12

Ocean Accident & Guarantee Corp.
Insurance Post Card Series £5

Odol Dentifrice
Posters £8
Actresses £4

Oetzmann's Cottages
Exhibition cards £1.50

Old Calabar
Animal Foods £10

Oliver Typewriters
Writing through the Ages £6

Overprints
Advertising copy overprinted on to otherwise standard commercial postcard. Value as latter plus nominal premium.

Schweppes, Poster advert £30

Oxo
Oxo Cattle Studies £15
Oxo Novelty (plain back) £10
Oxo Football teams £45

Peark's Butter/Tea
Various subjects £2

Pears A. & F.
Various subjects £2
Bubbles £1

Peek Frean
Invisible Picture £10
GB views £2

Pickfords
Transport sketches £8
Reproductions .50

Pitman Health Food Co.
Ideal food series £5

Poole Pottery
Phototype showing pottery techniques £6

Postcard Connoisseur
Dore's London/1904 Facsimile £50

Pratts motor oil £20

Price's Candles
Military sketches £8
Nursery Riddles £8

Princess Novels
Various subjects £1.50

Red Letter/Red Star Weekly
Greetings/Coloured £3

Regina Shaving
Cartoon £6

Remington Typewriters
Poster type £20

Ridgway's
Tea Estate scenes £3

Rowntree
Louis Wain Cats £75
Rowntree's Postcard Series £2

Rudge motor cycles
Poster adverts £35

St. Bartholomew's Hospital
Reconstuction Appeal £1

St.Ivel
GB views/Set 12 £1.50

St. Paul's Hospital/Set 12
£1,000 Competition £1

Sainsbury's Margarine
Crelos/Early Days of Sport £15
/Fairy Tales £15

Schweppes
Poster type £30
factory views £20

Selfridge Co. £3

Shippam's
Food production scenes £5
Shops/Stores
Artist sketches £8-£15
Photographic/Printed £15+
Shurey's Publications
Twopenny Tube/Set 12 £6
Various subjects £1.50
Singer Sewing Machines
Sewing Machines Worldwide £8
Aviation studies £6
Battleships £3
Sketchy Bits
Various subjects £1.50
Smart Novels
Dance Band Leaders/Set 10 £6
Greetings/Coloured £1.50
Various subjects £1.50
Spillers £12
Sportex Cloth
Dog studies £8
Spratt's Dog Foods
Dog studies £8
Standard Cars
Poster art cartoons £30
Sutton & Sons
Flowers/Vegetables £1.50
Swan Fountain Pens
Comic sketches £6
Symond's London Stores
Comic sketches £8
T.A.T.
The `Months' Series £4
Other subjects £1.50
Thomson D.C.
Various subjects £1.50
Thorley
Cattle photographs £6
Time Magazine
Subscription cards .75
Tiny Tots
Greetings/Coloured £8
Tit-Bits
Poster type £6
Tower Tea
Proverb Series £10
Trent Pottery
Trent Bridge Publishing Co. £6
Tussauds Madame
Tableaux/Set 12/Tuck R. & Sons £3
Two Steeples Hosiery
Hunting sketches £3

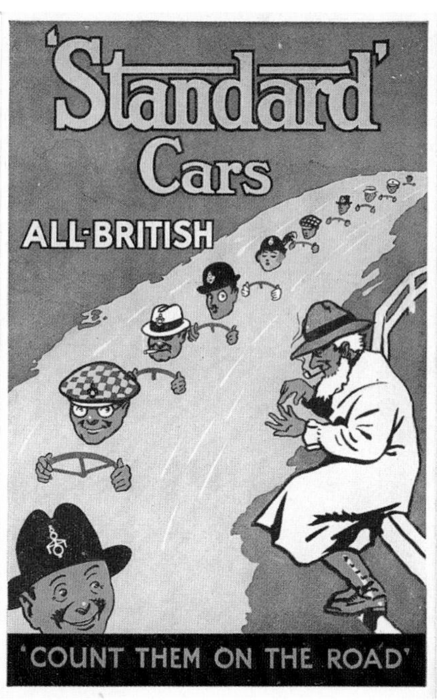

Standard Cars, Poster advert £30

Rudge motor cycles, poster advert £35

Waterman pens £20

Typhoo Tea

Various subjects/Oilette	£3

Underwood Typewriters

Poster type	£20

Van Houten's Cocoa

MGM Film Stars	£5
Colouring Cards of Birds/ Set of 6 in Folder/Price per card	£4
Dutch scenes	£2
Art Sketches/Uncaptioned	£1.50

Virol

Children of all Nations	£6

Vitality

Physical Culture studies	£6

Ward Lock

Naval photographs	£3

Weekly Tale-Teller

Various subjects	£1.50

Weekly Telegraph

Tom Browne sketches	£8

Weldon's Bazaar

KE VII Coronation Souvenir	£10

White Horse Whisky

Maggs Coaching studies	£2

Wolesley Motor Cars

Full view of vehicles	£25

Wolesley motor cars £25

Watson's cleanser £20

Wood-Milne Rubber Heel
Glamour studies/Sager £25
GB views £1.50
Wrench
Insurance cards £8
Yes or No
Various subjects £1.50

REWARD CARDS

Given away for good school work and attendance etc.

COMPANIES

Cadbury Bros.
Birds/Set 25 £6
Birds and their Eggs/Set 12 £6
Butterflies/Set 32 £8
Map Cards £8
Ficolax
Fruit sketches £4
Milkmaid Condensed Milk
Royalty sketches £8
Nectar Tea
Bird sketches £6
Tea Estate sketches £4
Reckitt
Naval History £6
Scott's Emulsion £5

EDUCATION AUTHORITIES

Barking Education Committee
Homeland Series/Court Size £6
County Borough of West Ham
Court Size £8
Erith Education Committee
Tuck R. & Sons/Castles etc. £3
Hampshire County Council
GB views £1.50
Huddersfield Education Committee
GB views £3
Isle of Ely Education Committee
Nature Notes £3
Leyton School Board/Pre-1902
Various sizes and series £5
London County Council
Battleships/6 x 4 size/ S. Cribb £5
Various Subjects £1.50
Oxfordshire Education Committee
British Wild Flowers £3
Reading EducationCommittee
Animals/Historical £3
School Board for London
Various subjects/Pre-1895 £5
Various subjects/1895-1902 £3
Surrey Education Committee
GB views £2
Walthamstow Education Committee
Paintings/Views £3
Wanstead School Board
Flowers £4

Younger Ales £15

ANIMALS

If postcard collecting was originally the province of the young girls of the Edwardian age, then it is to them, and their interest in this subject, that we owe the great legacy of Animal cards bequeathed us. Always an attractive collecting area, then as now. Animal cards were produced in considerable quantity, with almost every type of bird or beast depicted somewhere.

Market Report

Artist drawn anthropormorpic cards, especially cats, frogs and wild animals, are currently the most popular categories. Demand for Louis Wain has eased recently but there is still strong demand for artists such as Maurice Boulanger, Arthur Thiele and G H Thompson. Poultry breeds (again art type) also have a keen following, as do real photographic cards of animals in a social history context. Not so much interest in general run-of-the-mill art cards of cats, dogs and horses."

ANTHROPORMORPHIC

(Animals in human dress)

Chromo-Litho	£10
Photographic/Printed	£3

BIRDS

NVP Sluis Birdfood	£1.50
Racing Pigeons	£5
Scilly Isles/C.J. King	£1
Art Studies	£2-£4
Photographic Studies	£1
Tuck R. & Sons	
British Birds & their Eggs/ Aquarette Series 9218/9399/9519	£5

BUTTERFLIES

Art Studies	£3
Photographic Studies	£1
Tuck R. & Sons	
Butterflies	£6
British Butterflies and Moths	£6
Butterflies on the Wing	£6
Educational Series No. 8/Set 6	£8

CATTLE

Miscellaneous Studies	£1.50

A Happy Birthday
A Birthday Greeting let us send,
To-day to you, our dearest friend,
May all you wish be on the way,
To bring you joy this happy day.

Cat unsigned art study, on a patriotic birthday greeting £6

CATS

Chromo-Litho	£12
Mainzer, Alfred/Post-war	£2
Art Studies	£3-£6
Photographic Studies	£1.50
Inter Art	£6

Also see Artists section p.46 and Louis Wain p.23

DOGS

Military Dogs/WW1	£6
Spratt's Dog Foods	£8
Art Studies	£3-£10
Photographic Studies	£2

Also see Artists section p.46 and Louis Wain p.23

Dog Carts

Belgian/Netherlands	£4
French Milk Carts	£50+
French other Carts	£60+
Swiss	£5
Other European types	£6

Within these prices, named breeds would be worth more than un-named.

Nice artwork of a strong saleable breed £5

DONKEYS

Donkey Carts/RP	£8+
Seaside	£3
Domestic	£3

FISH

Art Studies	£3
Photographic Studies	£1.50

HORSES

Horses and Carts	£6
Ponies and Traps	£4
Working Horses	£3
Art Studies	£4
Photographic Studies	£2

COACHING

Vanderbilt Coach	£12
Holiday types	£3
State/Ceremonial Coaches	£1.50
Old Coaching Inns of England/ Set 16/J.C. Maggs	£1

PIGS

Early/Chromo-Litho	£10
Farmyard scenes	£3
Art Studies	£5
Photographic Studies	£3

POULTRY

Easter Chicks	£1.50
Art Studies	£4
Photographic Studies	£1.50

Tuck R. & Sons

Prize Poultry/Oilette	£6

TAXIDERMY

Booth Museum/Brighton	£3
Bramber Museum	£1.50
Stuffed Animals/Fish	£3

WILD ANIMALS

Frogs	£5
Rabbits	£3
Art studies	£3
Photographic Studies	£1

Tuck R. & Sons

Wild Animals/Oilette	£3

Donkeys, Artist drawn seaside greeting £3

ZOO ANIMALS

Art Studies	£3
Photographic Studies	£3

Official Issues

London Zoo/Whipsnade	£2-£5

Series

Zoological Society of London/ H.A.J. Schultz & Co.	£5
Hartmann	£4
L.L. series	£6

SERIES

Tuck R. & Sons

Educational Series	£9

WELFARE SOCIETIES

Abattoir scenes/U.S.A.	£10
Anti-Bloodsports	£18+
Anti-Vivisection	£18
Cat Protection Organisations	£10
National Canine Defence League	£12
Our Dumb Friends League	£15
R.S.P.C.A./R.S.P.B.	£12+
Vegetarian Society	£10
Veterinary Services	£15

ARTISTS

This is a select index of better known artists who designed for the picture postcard in both Subject and Topographical fields. It is not comprehensive, as many thousands of artists world-wide have contributed to the medium during the past century. The price stated may be taken as a guide to the most typical and representative work of the artist concerned, although in the Subject field, this price may be qualified by the theme depicted. With all artists so much depends upon the individual card, the design, the period, the publisher and of course the condition. I have done nothing more than indicate the general price area into which the artist falls,but certain rare cards by particular artists may dramatically exceed this figure. The great majority of artists listed below are either British, or have produced cards which are collected in this country. There are some excellent catalogues available which list the artists of France, Italy, Russia, USA etc. but I do not consider it practical to copy out several thousand names which would have little relevance to the British market. We have intoduced more new artists to the section and illustrations, which we hope will help.

Market Report
A R Quinton continues to forge ahead. Most other artists are price sensitive and it is a buyers market generally. There are plenty of opportunities for collectors at the moment. Condition is crucial to the sales of the more expensive artists, prices must reflect this.

M.A.	Comic	£1
S.A.	Comic	£1.50
T.A.	Comic	£1.50
Abeille, Jack	Art Nouveau	£60
	Glamour	£50
Acker, Flori Von	General	£1
Ackroyd, W.M.	Animals	£3
Adms, C.J.	General	£1
Adams, Frank	General	£3
Adams, J.T.	General	£1.50
Adams, M	General	£1
Adams, Will	Comic	£1.50
Addison, W.G.	General	£1.50
Ainsley, Anne	Animals	£3
Albertini	Glamour	£6
Aldin, Cecil	Animals	£6
Allan, A	General	£1
Alanen, Joseph	Patriotic	£10.00
Allen, S.J.	General	£1
Allen, W.	General	£1.50
Alys, M	Children	£1.50
Ambler, C	Animals	£3
Anders, O	Animals	£6
	Comic	£3
Anderson, Alan	Railway	£3
Anderson, Anne	Children	£6
Anderson, Carl	Comic	£5
Anderson, V.C.	Children	£4
Andrews, E	General	£1.50
Andrews, ET	Early	£10
Anichini, Ezio	Art Deco	£15
Anttila, Eva	Children	£6
Aranda, Pilar	Art Deco	£8
Ardizonne, E	General	£3
Aris, Ernest	Comic	£3
	General	£1.50
Armitage, A.F.	General	£1.50
Asti, Angelo	Glamour	£6
Attwell, Mabel Lucie	Children/	
	Pre-1918	£10
	1918-1939	£5
	1940 on	£3
	Modern Repros	.50
Atche	Glamour	£30
Austen, Alex	General	£1
Austerlitz, E	Comic	£3
Austin E.H.S. Barnes	Animals	£12
Austin, Winifred	Animals	£4
Aveline,F	Glamour	£6
Aveling, S.	General	£1.50
Azzoni, N.	Children	£4

Mabel Lucie Attwell, 1918-1939 period £5

H.S.B.	Comic	£1.50
J.O.B.	Comic	£2
Baertson	Military	£4
Bady, Carlos	Glamour	£5
Bailey G.O.	Glamour	£4
Bairnsfather, Bruce	Comic	£4
	Theatre	£30
Baker, G.	Military	£4
Baker, H Granville	Military	£6
Bakst, Leon	Art Deco	£50
Balestrieri, L	Glamour	£8
	General	£4
Ball, Wilfred	General	£2
Bamber, George A	Comic	£2
Baness	General £1	
Bannister, A.F.D.	Aviation	£4
	Shipping	£4
Bantock	Art Deco	£8
Barbara, S	Art Nouveau	£20
Barber, Court	Glamour	£6
Barber, C.W.	Children	£3
	Glamour	£3
Barde	Flowers	£1.50
Barham, S	Children	£8
Barker, Cecily M	Children	£12
Barnes,A.E.	Animals	£20
Barnes, G.L.	Animals	£15
	Comic	£8
Barraud, A	General	£1.50
Barraud, N	Animals	£5

Carl Anderson Comic, £5

"Traffic chaos—Red, Yellow and Green, Stop-and-Go signals, all at Oncesh!"

Ricardo Brook, Comic £4

Barrett, A	Military	£3
Barribal, W	Children	£12
	Glamour	£12
	Theatre	£25
Barthel, Paul	General	£1.50
Bartoli, Guiseppi	General	£5
Basch, Arpad	Art Nouveau	£110
Bask, W	General	£1
Bateman, H.M.	Comic	£8
Bates, Leo	Glamour	£5
Bates, Marjorie C.	Literary	£5
	General	£3
Baumgarten, Fritz	Children	£6
Bayer, R.W.	Flowers	£1.50
Beale, Sophia	General	£2
Beards, Harold	Comic	£1.50
Bebb, Rosa	Animals	£6
	General	£1.50
Becker, C.	Military	£8
	Sport	£8
Bee	Comic	£1
Beecroft, Herbert	General	£4
Beer, Andrew	General	£1.50
Beerts, Albert	Military	£5
Belcher, George	Comic	£4
Belet, A	Pierrotts	£8
Bell, Steve	Political	£2
Bem, B	Children	£12
Benois, Alexander	Various	£25
Beraud, N	Animals	£4
	Military	£5
Berkeley, Edith	General	£1

Bertiglia, Children £6

Berkeley, Stanley	Animals	£3
Berthon, Paul	Art Nouveau	£80
Bertiglia, A	Children	£6
	Political	£8-£15
	Sports	£15
Bianchi	Glamour	£4
Bianco.T.	Glamour	£4
	Political	£12
Biggar, J.L.	Comic	£2
	Tennis	£12
Bilibin, Ivan	Art Nouveau	£65
	Misc	£15-£55
Billing, M	General	£1.50
Billinge, Ophelia	Animals	£5
Birch, Nora-Annie	Children	£4
Bird, H	Sport	£5
Birger	Art Deco	£16-£20
	Winter sport	£12
Birtles, H.	General	£1.50
Bizuth	WW2 Comic	£4
Bjorklind, Hans	Art Deco	£12
Bjornstrom, Theodor	Fantasy	£8
Black, Algernon	Shipping	£8
Black, Montague B.	Shipping	£8
Black, W. Milne	Comic	£4
Blair, Andrew	General	£1.50
Blair, John	General	£1.50
Bob	Comic	£2
	General	£1.50
Boccasile, Gino	Art Deco	£45
Boecker, A.G.	Flowers	£1.50
Bohrdt, Hans	Shipping	£20
Boileau, Philip	Glamour	£10
Bolton, F.N.	General	£1
Bompard, S	Glamour	£6
Boriss, Margret	Children	£6
Borrow, W.H.	General	£2
Bothams, W	General	£1
Bottaro, E	Glamour	£10
Bottomley, Edwin	Animals	£3
Bottomley, George	Glamour	£3
Boulanger, Maurice	Animals	£10
	Comic	£10
Bouret, Germaine	Children	£6
Bourillon	Military	£5
Boutet, Henri	Art Nouveau	£35
Bowden, Doris	Children	£6
Bowers, Albert	General	£2
Bowers, Stephen	General	£2
Bowley, A.L.	Children	£12
Bowley M.	Animals	£6
Boyne, T	General	£1
Bradshaw, Percy V	Comic	£6
	Political/Sport	£8
Braun, W	Glamour	£6
Breanski, Arthur de	General	£2
Brett, Molly	Children	£3
Bridgeman, Arthur W	General	£2
Briggs, Barbara	Animals	£4
Brisley, Nina	Children	£5
Broadrick, Jack	Comic	£2
Brook, Ricardo	Comic	£4
Brown, Maynard	Glamour	£4
Browne, Stewart	Theatre	£15
Browne, Tom	Adv/Inserts	£10
	Adv/Literary	£10

Barbara Briggs, Comic Dogs £4

	Posters	£15/£75
	Cathedrals	£6
	Comic	£4
	Theatre	£20
Brundage, Frances	Children/ Chromo-Litho	£15
	Others	£6
	General	£4
Brunelleschi, U	Art Deco	£110
Buchanan, Fred	Comic	£3
Buchel, Charles	Theatre	£18
Budge	Comic	£1
Bull, Rene	Comic	£4
Burger, R	General	£1
Burgess, Arthur	Shipping	£8
Burnard, Victor W.	General	£1.50
Burton, F.W.	General	£1.50
Bushby, Thomas	General	£3
Busi, Adolfo	Art Deco	£12
	Glamour	£6
Bussiere, G	Art Nouveau	£30
Butchur, Arthur	Children	£4
	Glamour	£4
Butler, G.	Animals	£2
Buxton, Dudley	Comic	£2
A.S.C.	Comic	£1.50
C.C.	Comic	£1.50
Caffieri, V	General	£2
Caldecott, Randolph	Children	£1.50
Calderara, C	Art Deco	£8
Calland, H.J.	Animals	£5
Cameron, Archie	Comic	£1.50
Cane, Ella Du	Flowers	£1.50
Capiello Leonetto	Art Nouveau	£75
Caport	Comic	£1
Carey, John	Comic	£2
Carline, George	General	£1
Carnell, Albert	Comic	£3
Carr, Paddy	Children	£2
Carrere, F.O.	Glamour	£8
Carruthers, W	General	£1.50
Carson, T.	Art Nouveau	£20
Carter, R.C.	Comic	£2
Carter, Reg	Comic	£1.50
	Southwold Rly.	£4
Carter, Sydney	Comic	£2
	General	£2

F.J.S. Chatterton, Animals £5

Cascella Basilio	General	£10
Cassiers, H	General	£6
	Royalty	£10
	Shipping	£18
Castelli, V	Children	£6
Cattley, P.R.	Comic	£2
Cauvy, Leon	Art Nouveau	£50
Cenni, Eldi	Glamour	£4
Chalker	Comic	£1.50
Chandler, E	Comic	£2
Chapalet, Roger	Shipping	£5
Chaperon,Eugene	Military	£8
Charlet, J.A.	Glamour	£10
Chatterton, F.J.S.	Animals	£5
Cheret, Jules	Art Nouveau	£75
Cherubini, M	Glamour	£6
Chidley, Arthur	Military	£12
Chilton, G.	Art Deco	£20
Chiostri	Art Deco	£25
Christiansen, Hans	Art Nouveau	£100
Christie, G. Fyffe	Comic	£4
Christy, F. Earl	Glamour	£6
Church, Bernard, W	Shipping	£6

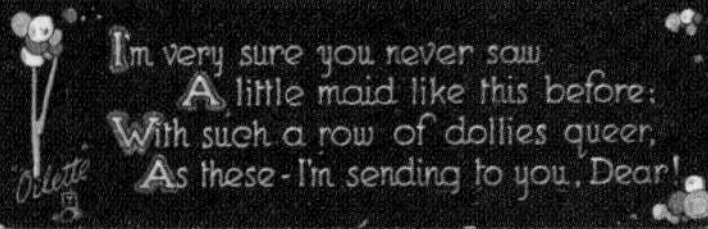

Phyllis Cooper, Children £12

Clapsaddle, Ellen H.	Children	£8
	General	£4
Clarkson G.T	Aviation	£6
Clarkson, R	General	£1
Cloke, Rene	Children	£8
Coates, A	General	£1
Cobbe, B	Animals	£4
Cock, Stanley	Comic	£3
Cock, Stanley	Comic	£3
Cockcroft, E.M.	UK Glamour	£6
Colbourn, Lawrence	Comic	£2
Cole, Edwin	General	£1
Coleman, W.S.	Children	£8
	General	£6
Coley, Hilda M.	Flowers	£1
Colls, H.	General	£1.50
Colombo, E.	Children	£6
	Glamour	£8
Combaz, Gisbert	Art Nouveau	£100
Comicus	Comic	£1.50
Conrad, George	Art Nouveau	£100
Cook, C.K.	Comic	£4
Cooper, A. Heaton	General	£1
Cooper, Phyllis	Children	£12
	Later Issues	£2
Copping, Harold	Glamour	£4
	Literary	£4
	Military	£4
Coppola, A	General	£2
Corbella, Tito	Art Deco	£18
	Glamour	£8
	Political	£8
Cordingley, G.R.	General	£1.50
Corke, C. Essenhigh	General	£2
Cottom, C.M.	Children	£5
Cowderoy, K.E.	Children	£8
	Art Deco	£18
Cowham, Hilda	Children	£8
	Comic	£6
Crackerjack	Comic	£4
Craftanara	General	£2
Craig, Janie	Flowers	£2
Cramer, Rie	Art Deco	£20
	Children	£18
Crane, Walter	Political	£18
Cremieux, Suzanne	Glamour	£8
	Military	£8
Croft, Anne	General	£1
Crombie, C.M.	Comic	£4
	Golf	£25
Cross, Roy	Comic	£4
Crow	General	£3
Croxford, W.E.	General	£1.50
Cubley, H. Hadfield	General	£1.50
Cuneo, Cyrus	Military	£8
Cynicus	CourtCards	£15
	Und. back	£5
	Landscapes	£2
	Later Comic	£2/5
	Place Names	£3
	Political	£6
	Shakespeare	£8
J.C.D.	Comic	£1.50
J.W.D.	Comic	£1.50
Daniell, Eva	Art Nouveau	£110
Dauber	Comic	£2
Davey, George	Comic	£2
Davidson, Nora	Children	£3
Davies, Roland	Aviation	£3
Davo	Comic	£1
Daws, F.T.	Animals	£6
Dawson, Muriel	Children	£8
Dean, Frank	Sport	£4

	General	£4
Dedina, Jean	Glamour	£7
Dexter, Marjorie M.	Children	£5
Diefenbach, K.W.	Art Deco	£8
Diemer, Michael Zeno	Early ships	£12
	General	£4
Dinah	Children	£4
Dink	Sport	£8
Dirks, Gus	Comic	£6
Dixon, Charles	Shipping	£10
Dobson, H.J.	General	£1.50
Docker, E. Jnr.	Art Nouveau	£60
	Animals	£5
Dodd, Francis	Military	£3
Donaldini, Jnr.	Animals	£6
Doruzhinsky, Mstislav	General	£25
Douglas, J	General	£1.50
Downey, Thos. P.	Comic	£2
Doy, H.	Comic	£1
Drallek, Yaran	Comic	£1
Drayton, Grace	See under Wiederseim	
Driscoll	Comic	£1
Drog	Glamour	£3

George Conrad, Art Nouveau £100

W.R.Ellam, Comic cats £10

Drucker	Children	£3
Drummond, Eileen	Animals	£5
Drummond, Norah	Animals	£6
Ducane, E & F	General	£1
Duddle, Josephine	Children	£8
Dudley, Tom	General	£1
Dufresne, Paul	Glamour	£5
Duncan, Hamish	Comic	£2
Duncan, J. Ellen	Children	£2
Dunk	Military	£10
Drog	Glamour	£3
Dupuis, Emile	Military	£4
Dwig	Comic	£6
Dyer, Ellen	Flowers	£1
Dyer, W.H.	General	£1
Dymond, R.J.	General	£1
E	Comic	£2
A.E.	Comic	£2
Eaman, J	General	£2
Earbalestier, C.	General	£1.50
Earnshaw, Harold	Comic	£3
Ebner, Pauli	Children	£8
Eckenbrecker, T von	Shipping	£10
Edgerton, Linda	Children	£8
Edler, Edouard	Shipping	£12
Edmunds, Kay	Military	£1.50
Edwards, Edwin	General	£1
Edwards, Lionel	Comic	£4
Eliott, Harry	Comic	£8
Elks	Comic	£1
Ellam, W.R.		
Breakfast in Bed	Comic	£10
Other Series	Comic	£10
	Sport	£12
Elliot, K.E.	Flowers	£1
Elym	Political	£5-£8

Emanuel, Frank, L.	General	£2
Endacott, S.	General	£3
Esmond,	Comic	£5
Ettwell, Elliot	General	£2
Evans, Percy	Comic	£2
A.E.F.	Children	£1
Fabian, Maud	Advertising	£15
Fabiano, F.	Glamour	£15
Fay, John H	Shipping	£4
Federley, Aleksander	Patriotic	£10
Feiertag,	Children	£3
Felix, P.E.	Art Deco	£8
Fernel, Fernand	Comic	£8
Fernoel	Art Nouveau	£8
Feure de	Art Nouveau	£160
Fidler, Alice Luella	Glamour	£8
Fidler, Elsie Catherine	Glamour	£8
Fidus, H.A. von	Art Nouveau	£60
Filby, Edgar	Advertising	£25
Finnemore, J	General	£1.50
Fisher, Harrison	Glamour	£10
Fitzgerald, A	General	£2
Fitzpatrick	Comic	£1.50
Fleury, H.	Comic	£2
	Railway	£2
Flower, Charles E.	General	£2.50
Folkard, Charles	Children	£15
	Literary	£15
Fontan, Leo	Glamour	£12
Forestier, A	Advertising	£35
Forres, Kit	Children	£2
Forrest, A.S.	Shipping	£3
Forsberg, J.	General	£1.50
Foster, Gilbert	General	£1.50
Foster, R.A.	General	£1.50
Fowell, G.M.	General	£1
Fradkin, E.	Children	£1.50
Francis,	General	£1
Frank, Raoul	Shipping	£18
Fraser	Comic	£3
Fredillo	Art Nouveau	£20
Freer, H.B.	Shipping	£8
French, Annie	Art Nouveau	£100
Fry, John H.	Shipping	£10

Leo Font
Glamour
£12

Fuller, Edmund	Comic	£6
	Postal	£6
Fulleylove, Joan	General	£1.50
Fullwood, A.H.	General	£5
Furniss, Harry	Political	£5
Fych, C.D.	Glamour	£6
Gabard, E	Sport	£5
Gabb	Comic	£1.50
Gabriel, E	Shipping	£12
Gallon, R.	General	£1
Ganz	Comic	£3
Gardener, E.C.	General	£1.50
Garland, A.	General	£1.50
Gassaway, Katherine	Children	£6
Gay, Cherry	Children	£1.50
Gayac	Glamour	£15
Gear, M.	Animals	£5
Gerald, Brian	General	£1.50
Gerbault, H	Glamour	£6
Gervese, H.	Comic	£3
Gibbs, May	Comic	£25
Gibson Charles Dana	Glamour	£2
Giglio	Glamour	£5
Gilbert, Allan	Glamour	£4
Giles,	Comic	£6
Gill, Arthur	Comic	£3

T.Gilson £3

Gilmour	Comic	£2.50
Gilson, T.	Comic Military	£2-4 £3
Gioja, G	General	£5
Giris	Aviation	£15
Gladwin, May	Comic	£5
Glanville	Comic	£1.50
Gobbi. D	Art Deco	£20
Goethen E. van	Children	£10
Golay, Mary	General	£3
Goodman, Maud		
/Tuck Early	Children	£18
/TuckEarly	General	£18
/Hildesheimer	Children	£4
Gotch, Phyllis, M	Comic	£2.50
Gould	Comic	£1.50
Govey, Lilian	Children	£8
Gozzard, J.W.	General	£1.50
Graeff	Comic	£2
Graf, Marte	Art Deco	£10
Grant, Carleton	General	£1
Grasset, Eugene	Art Nouveau	£75
Green, Alec E.	Children	£3
Green, Roland	Animals	£3
Greenall, Jack	Comic	£2
Greenaway, Kate	Children/ 1903 printing	£65
	later printing	£15
Greenbank, A.	Glamour	£8
Greiner, M	Children	£10
Gresley, A.	Flowers	£1.50
Gretty, G	General	£1.50
Grey, Mollie	Children	£2
Gribble, Bernard F.	General	£2
Grimes	Comic	£3
Grin, C.U.	Comic	£1.50
Grosze, Manni	Art Deco	£10
Grunewald	Art Deco	£12
Guerzoni, C	Glamour	£8
Guggenberger, T	General	£4
Guillaume A.	Art Nouveau Comic	£75 £5
Gunar, Clement	Easter Witches.	£10
Gunn, A.	Glamour	£5
Gunn Gwennet	Comic	£2
Gurnsey, C.	Comic	£1.50
Guy, T.	General	£1
E.A.H.	Comic	£1.50
F.W.H.	Comic	£3
S.H.	Comic	£1
Hager, Nini	Art Nouveau	£80
Hailey, Edward	General	£1
Haller, A.	Flowers	£2

Lilian Govey, Children £8

Halliday	Comic	£3
Hamilton, E	Shipping	£8
Hamilton, J.M.	Sport	£15
Hamish	Comic	£3
Hammick, J.W.	Glamour	£3
Hammond, J.	Flowers	£1.50
Hampel, Walter	Art Nouveau	£85
Hanbury, F. Schmidt	General	£1.50
Hannaford	General	£1.50
Hansi	Children	£15
	Political	£15
Harbour, Jennie	Art Deco	£15
Hardy, Dudley	Comic	£6
	Glamour	£9
	Political	£12
	Shipping	£20
	Theatre	£20
Hardy, Florence	Children	£6
Hardy, F.	Art Deco	£10
Hardy, F.C.	Military	£4
Harriet	Comic	£1
Harrison, E. Florence	Glamour	£6
Hart, Josef	Art Nouveau	£25
Hartridge, Norman	Children	£10
Harvey, F.	Comic	£1.50
Haslehust, E.W.	General	£1.50
Hassall, John	Comic	£5
	Court Size	£15
	Theatre	£30
	General	£4
Hauby, S.	Art Nouveau	£12
Haviland, Frank	Glamour	£5
Hayes, F.W.	General	£1.50
Hayes, Sydney	Animals	£1.50
Hebblethwaite, S.H.	Comic	£3
Heinirch	General	£6
Henckel, Carl	Military	£6
Henley	Comic	£1.50
Henley, W.E.	General	£1.50
Henry, Thomas	Children	£6
	Comic	£6
Herouard	Glamour	£15
Herrfurth, Oskar	Children	£10
Heusser, Harry	Shipping	£8
Hey, Paul	General	£4
Heyermanns,S.	General	£1.50

Gunn Gwennet, Comic £2

Heyermans, John A	General	£1.50
Hickling, P.B.	General	£1.50
Hier, Prof. van	General	£1.50
Higham, Sydney	General	£1.50
Hiles, Bartram	General	£2
Hill, L. Raven	Political	£5
Hilton, Alf	Comic	£2
Hines, B.	General	£1..50
Hodgson, W. Scott	General	£1
Hofer, Andre	Glamour	£7
Hoffman, H.W.	General	£1
Hoffman, J.	Art Nouveau	£90
Hoffmann, Anton	Military	£8
Hohenstein, A	Art Nouveau	£35
Hohlwein, Ludwig	Advertising	£25
	Military	£10
Holloway, Edgar A.	Military	£12
Hollyer, Eva	Children	£8
Home, Gordon	General	£1.50
Hood, Eileen	Animals	£4
Hopcroft, G.E.	General	£1.50
Hopking, Noel	Animals	£1.50
Horder, Margaret	Children	£2
Horrell, Charles	Glamour	£4
Horsfall, Mary	Children	£6
	Glamour	£4

Horwitz, Helena	Glamour	£4
Howard, C.T.	General	£2
Howard, Jim	Comic	£1.50
Howell, E.	Comic	£1.50
Hudson, Gerald	Military	£4
Hughes, Alun	Comic	£1.50
Hughes, Lloyd	Comic	£1.50
Hughes, R.	General	£1
Hummel	Children	£4
Hunt, Edgar	Animals	£2
Hunt, Muriel	Animals	£4
Hunter, Mildred C	Animals	£4
Hurst, Hal	Comic	£3
Hutchinson, F.	General	£1
Hyde, Graham	Comic	£6
Ibbetson, Ernest	Comic	£8
	Military	£12
Icart, Louis	Glamour	£12
Innes, John	General	£2
Inskip, J. Henry	General	£1.50
Iranez, J	Children	£4
Ironico	Comic	£1.50
Irwin	Comic	£1
J.R.J.	Comic	£1.50
Jackson, Helen	Children	£18
Jackson, Ian	Glamour	£5
Jacobs, Helen	Children	£8
Jafuri, R.	General	£3
James, Frank	Animals	£1.50
James, Ivy Millicent	Children	£10
Jank, Angelo	Art Nouveau	£35
Jarach, A	Glamour	£12
Jaderholm-Snellman	Art Deco	£15
Jay, Cecil	Glamour	£5
Jenkins, G.H.	General	£1.50
Jester	Comic	£1.50
Jo	Comic	£1
Johnson, M.	General	£1.50
Johnson, S.	General	£1.50
Jossot	Art Nouveau	£160
Josza, Carl	Art Nouveau	£60
Jotter	Comic Types	£3
	Greetings	£2
	Hotels	£3/10
	Derbys/Cornwall	£1

Kyd, Comic £8

	Sheffield/Ireland	£4
	Views -Other	£2
Jung, Maurice	Art Nouveau	£500
A.H.K.	General	£1
C.K.	Comic	£1.50
E.M.T.K.	Comic	£1.50
Kaby	Glamour	£4
Kainradl, L	Art Nouveau	£100
Kammerer, Rob	General	£1.50
Karaktus	Comic	£1.50
Kaskeline, Fred	Children	£6
Katinka	Art Deco	£12
Kaufmann, J.C.	Animals	£2
Keene, Elmer	General	£1.50
Keene, Frank	Comic	£1.50
Keene, Minnie	Animals	£2
Keesey, Walter M.	General	£1
Kempe	Children	£6
Kennedy, A.E.	Animals	£6
	Comic	£6
	Theatre	£12
Kerr, Tom	Children	£1
Kid	Comic	£1.50
Kidd, Will	Children	£6
Kieszkow	Art Nouveau	£30

Kimball, Alonzo	Glamour	£5
King A. Price	General	£1.50
King, Edward	General	£3
King, Gunning	General	£3
King, Jessie M.	Art Nouveau	£85
King, W.B.	Comic	£1.50
King, Yeend	General	£1.50
Kinnear, J.	General	£2
Kinsella, E.P.	Children	£6
	Comic	£6
	Theatre	£20
Kircher, A.	Naval	£4
Kirchner, Raphael	/Early Art Nouveau	£50 - £100
/WW1 period	Glamour	£30
/Bruton Galleries	Glamour	£25
Kirk, A.H.	General	£1.50
Kirkbach	Children	£3
Kirkpatrick	General	£1
Kirmse, Persis	Animals	£5
Klein, Christina	General/ Chromo-Litho	£6
	Later Issues	£3
Kley, Paul	Chromo-Litho	£6
	Other printings	£2
Klodic	Shipping	£6
Knox, W	General	£1.50
Koch, Ludwig	Sport	£6
Koehler, Mela	Art Deco	£70
	Art Nouveau	£120
Koehler Mela Broman	Art Deco	£25
Kokoschka	Art Nouveau	£600
Konopa	Art Nouveau	£35
Kosa	Art Nouveau	£100
Koy	Comic	£1.50
Kulas, J.V.	Art Nouveau	£35

A.E.Kennedy, £6

Kupka	Art Nouveau	£75
Kyd	Comic	£8
	Literary	£12
	London Life	£10
Lacy, Chas J.de	Shipping	£12
Lajoux, Edmond	Military	£5
Lamb, Eric	General	£1
Lambert, H.G.C. Marsh	Children	£5
Lancere, Yergenyi	General	£15
Lang, W.	Art Nouveau	£35
Larcombe, Ethel	Art Nouveau	£35
Lasalle, Jean	Glamour	£2
	General	£2
Laskoff F	Art Nouveau	£50
Lauder, C.J.	General	£1.50
Lautrec, H. de Toulouse	Art Nouveau	£600
Lawes, H.	General	£1
Laz	Comic	£1.50
Leete, Alfred	Comic	£4
Leggatt, C.P.	Comic	£2
Lehmann, Felix	Sport	£6
Lehmann, Phil	Comic	£2
Leigh, Conrad	Military	£4
Lelee Leopold	Art Nouveau	£60
LeMunyon, Pearl Fidler	Glamour	£6
Leng, Max	Art Nouveau	£30
Leodud Di	Art Deco	£6
Leonnec, G.	Glamour	£15
Leroux Pierre Albert	Military	£5
Leroy	Military	£5
Lesker, H.	Art Deco	£8
Lessieux, E. Louis	Art Nouveau	£40
	Shipping	£25
Lester, Adrienne	Animals	£3
Lester, Ralph	Glamour	£3
Lewin, F.G.	Children	£6
	Comic	£4
Lilien, E.M.	Art Nouveau	£40
	General	£8
Lime, H.	Comic	£1
Lindsay, J.	General	£1
Lindsell, L.	Glamour	£3
Livemont, Privat	Art Nouveau	£100
Lloyd, T. Ivester	Glamour	£4
	Military	£5

Loffler Berthold	Art Nouveau	£100
Loffler, Lovat	Art Nouveau	£30
Loir Luigi	General	£6
Long, L.M.	General	£1.50
Longley, Chilton	Art Deco	£30
Longmire, R.O.	Political	£10
Longstaffe, Ernest	General	£1.50
Loreley	Art Deco	£15
Lorenz, Fabius	Glamour	£10
Love, H. Montagu	Military	£6
	General	£2
Lovering, I.	General	£1.50
Lowe, Meta	Children	£2
Luckcott G.Y.	Comic	£1.50
Ludgate	Comic	£2
Ludlow, Hal	Comic	£2
Ludovici, A.	Children	£5
	Comic	£3
	Political	£3
Luke W.	Comic	£2
Lumley, Savile	Military	£4
Lynen, Amedee	General	£4
C.M.	Comic	£1
M.S.M.	Glamour	£15
P.C.M.	Comic	£1.50
Mac/National Series	Comic	£2
Mac	Animals	£5
	Comic	£3
MacBean L.C.	Comic	£2
McGill, Donald	Comic/	
	Early Dated	£8
	Pre-1914	£5
	1914-1939	£3-6
	`New'	£1
McIntyre, J.	General	£1.50
McIntyre, R.F.	General	£1.50
McNeill, J.	Military	£12
Macdonald, A.K.	Art Nouveau	£35
Mackain, F.	Comic	£3
Macleod, F.	Comic	£2
Macpherson, John	General	£1
MacWhirter, J.	General	£1.50
Maggs, J.C.	Coaching	£2
Maguire, Bertha	General	£1.50
Maguire, Helena	Animals	£8
	General	£3

Mailick, A.	Glamour	£4
	General	£3
Mainzer, Alfred	Animals	£3
Mair, H. Willebeek le	Children	£6
Mallet, Beatrice	Children	£5
	Advertising	£12
Mallet, Dennis	Comic	£1.50
Manavian, V.	Comic	£3
Mann, James S	Shipping	£12
Marchant, Leslie P.	Comic	£1.50
Marco, M.	Glamour	£3
Marechaux, C.	Glamour	£4
Margetson, Hester	Children	£5
Marisch, G.	Art Nouveau	£75
Maroc	Comic	£1
Marshall, Alice	Children	£12
Mart	Comic	£1.50
Martin, E	Children	£8
Martin, L.B.	Comic	£3
	Children	£5
Martin, Phil	Comic	£2
Martineau, Alice	Glamour	£8
	General	£3
	Children	£8
Martini, A.	Adverts	£35
	Political	£25
Martino R. de	General	£1
Marty, Andre	Art Deco	£15
Mason, Finch	Comic/Sport	£4
Mason, Frank H.	Shipping	£5
Mason, George W	Comic	£4

You should learn to keep your mouths closed in war-time!

F.E.Morgan, Comic £3

Mastroianni, D.	General	£2
Mataloni, G.	Art Nouveau	£30
Matthison, W.	General	£1.50
Maurice, Reg	Comic	£2
Mauzan, A.	Children	£6
	Glamour	£10
	Political	£8
	Art Deco	£15
	General	£3
May, F.S.	Comic	£2
May, J.A.	Comic	£2
May, Phil	Comic/ Write-away	£8
	Oilette	£4
Maybank, Thomas	Children	£12
Mayer, Lou	Glamour	£8
Meadows, Chas	Comic	£2
Menpes, Mortimer	Children	£3
Meras, Rene	Glamour	£7
Mercer, Joyce	Art Deco	£25
	Children	£25
Meredith, Jack	Comic	£2
Merte, O.	Animals	£5
Meschini, G. Art Deco	Hand painted	£35
	Printed	£20
Metlicovitz, L.	Art Nouveau	£35
Meunier, Henri	Art Nouveau	£100
Meunier, Suzanne	Glamour	£20
Mich	Comic	£1.50
Midge	Comic	£5
Mignot, Victor	Art Nouveau	£35
Mike	Comic	£1
Miller, Hilda T.	Children/ Liberty	£15
	Other Pubs.	£8

Henri Meunier, Art Nouveau, £100

Alphonse Mucha, Months of the year £150

Miller, Laurence.	Humour	£4-£6
	Tennis	£15
Milliere, Maurice	Glamour	£15
Millor	Flowers	£1
Millot	Greetings	£1
Mills, Ernest, H.	Animals	£4
Monestier, C.	Glamour	£8
Monier, Maggy	Glamour	£10
Moore, A. Winter	General	£1.50
Moore, F.	Railway	£3
Montague, Love, H	Military	£8
Montague, R.	Shipping	£6
	General	£1.50
Montedoro, M	Art Deco	£60
Moreland, Arthur	Comic	£3-£5
	Political	£6
Morgan, F.E.	Comic	£3
Morris, M.	General	£1.50
Morrow, Albert	Theatre	£12
Moser, Koloman	Art Nouveau	£120
Mostyn, Dorothy	Glamour	£4
Mostyn, Marjorie	Glamour	£4
Mouton, G.	Glamour	£10
Mucha, Alphonse	Art Nouveau	£100+
	Exhibition	£100
	Slav Period	£50
Muggiai	Glamour	£15
Mulholland, S.A.	General	£1
Muller, A.	Animals	£4
Muller, Valery	General	£8
Muraton, E.	Flowers	£2
MurhaghanKathleen, I.	Children	£4
Musta, Ville	Ethnic	£3- £6
Mutter, K.	General	£4
Naillod, C.S.	Glamour	£6
Nam, Jacques	Glamour	£10

Nanni,G.	Glamour	£6
	Art Deco	£12
	Erotic/nudes	£15
	Sports	£15-£18
Nap	Comic	£2
Nash, A.A.	Children	£4
Nerman	Art Deco	£18
	Theatre	£25
Neumont, M	Glamour	£5
Neville-Cumming, R	Shipping	£8
Newton, G.E.	General	£1.50
Ney	Glamour	£10
Nicholson, J	Shipping	£5
Nielsen, Harry B.	Comic	£2
Nielsen, Vivienne	Animals	£3
Nixon, K.	Children	£10
Noble, Ernest	Comic	£3
Norfield, Edgar	Comic	£1.50
Norman, Parsons	General	£1.50
Norman, Val	General	£1.50
Norwood, A.Harding	General	£1.50
Noury, Gaston	Art Nouveau	£80
Nystrom, Jenny	Children	£8
	Glamour	£12
O'Beirne, F.	Military	£12
O'Kay	Comic	£1
O'Neill, Rose	Children	£8
Operti, A.	General	£5
Opper, F.	Comic	£1.50
Orens, Denizard	Political	£18
Ost. A.	Art Nouveau	£30
Ostrumova-Lebeva,A	General	£25
Outcault, R.F.	Children	£8
	Comic	£5
Outhwaite, Ida R.	Children	£25
Overell, J.	Children	£4
Overnell	Children	£5
Owen, Will	Comic	£4
	Theatre	£12
Oyston, George	General	£1.50
Paget, Wal	General	£1.50
Palmer, Phyllis, M.	Children	£5
Palmer, Sutton	General	£1.50
Pannett, R.	Glamour	£8
	Theatre	£18
Parker, N.	Animals	£4

Arthur Moreland, Political cartoon £6

Parkinson, Ethel	Children	£5
Parlett, Harry	Comic	£1.50
Parlett, T.	Comic	£2
Parr, B.F.C.	General	£1
Parr, Doreen	Children	£4
Partridge, Bernard	Political	£4
Parsons, F.J.	Railway	£3
Patek, August	Art Nouveau	£12
Patella, B.	Art Nouveau	£35
Paterson, Vera	Children	£3

Harry Payne, Military in London £5

Popini, Glamour £15

Paulus	Military	£3
Payne, Arthur C	General	£2
Payne, G.M.	Comic	£3
	Glamour	£3
Payne, Harry		
/Tuck Early	Horses	£40
/Tuck Early	Military	£40
/Metropolitan Police	General	£40
/Wild West	General	£30
/Coaching	Animals	£30
/Gale & Polden	Military	£15
/Stewart & Woolf	Military	£15
/Badges & Wearers	Military	£12+
/Oilettes	Horses	£6
/Oilettes	Military	£6+
/Military in London	Military	£6
/Rural Life	General	£5
/Other	General	£10+
Pears, Chas	Advertising	£15
Pearse, Susan B	Children	£12
Peddie, Tom	Glamour	£3
Pellegrini, E.	Glamour	£20
Peltier, L.	Glamour	£8
Penley, Edwin A.	General	£1.50
Pennington, Oswald	Shipping	£7
Penny, Theo	Comic	£1.50
Penot, A.	Glamour	£12
Pepin, Maurice	Glamour	£12
Peras	Glamour	£8
Percival, E.D.	General	£1.50
Perlberg, F.	Animals	£4
	General	£1.50
Perly	Comic	£1.50
Person, Alice Fidler	Glamour	£6
Petal	Comic	£1
Peterson, Hannes	General	£2
Pfaff, C.	General	£6
Philippi, Robert	Art Nouveau	£15
Phillimore, R.P.	General	£4
Phipson, E.A.	General	£1.50
Phiz	Dickens	£5
Pike, Sidney	General	£1.50
Pillard,	Glamour	£6
	Military	£6
Pinder, Douglas	General	£1
Pingers	Political	£6
Pinhey, Edith	General	£1
Pinkawa, Anton	Art Nouveau	£30
Piper, George	Children	£3
Pirkis	Comic	£3
Pitcher, Henrie	General	£3
Pizer, Herbert	Glamour	£8
Plumstead, Joyce	Children	£8
Pohola, Jouko	Helsinki Olympics	£12
Polzin, G.	General	£4
Pope, Dorothy T.	Animals	£8
Popini	Art Nouveau	£30
	Glamour	£15
Poulbot, Francisque	Children	£4
Poy	Comic	£1.50
Praga, Alfred	Shipping	£12
Presland, A.L.	Flowers	£1.50
Preston, Chloe	Children	£8
Prosnocimi, A.	General	£1.50
Purser, Phyllis	Children	£4
Pyp	Comic	£2
Quatremain, W.W.	General	£1.50
Quinnell, Cecil W.	Glamour	£4
	Literary	£4
Quinton, A.R.		
/Salmon J. & Co.	South Africa	£12+
	Ostende	£15+

	General	£3 +
	1960/70 Period	.75
	Reprints/7 digit computer nos.	.25
/Tuck R. & Sons	General	£4+
Quinton, F.E.	General	£1.50
Quinton, Harry	Comic	£2
Quips	Comic	£1.50
A.F.R.	Comic	£1.50
F.A.R.	General	£1.50
J.S.R.	Comic	£1.50
Rackham, Arthur	Children	£25
Raemaekers, Louis	Political	£3
Ralph, Lester	Glamour	£6
Raimondi, R.	General	£3
Rambler	General	£1
Ramsey, George S.	General	£1
Rankin, George	Animals	£3
Rappini	Glamour	£5
	General	£4
Ratcliffe, W.W.	General	£4
Rauh, Ludwig	Glamour	£15
Raven, Phil.	Comic	£1.50
Read, F.W.	Glamour	£3
	General	£1
Read, T. Buchanan	General	£1
Reckling, L.G.	General	£1
Reichert, C.	Animals	£4
Reiss, Fritz	General	£5
Remington Frederick	General	£8
Renaud, M.	Flowers	£1
Renault, A.	Flowers	£1
Rennie, M.	General	£1.50
Rex	Comic	£1
Reynolds, Frank	Comic	£4
	Literary	£5
Ribas	Glamour	£10
Richardson, Agnes	Children	£5
Richardson, Charles	Comic	£1.50
Richardson, R.V.	Comic	£2
Richardson, R.W.E.	General	£1.50
Richmond, Leonard	Railways	£10
Rickard, J.	Children	£8
Right	Comic	£2
Riley,W.E.	Military	£3

IS SOMEONE NEVER COMING ANY MORE?

Chloe Preston, Children £8

Ritchie, Alick P.F.	Comic	£3
Ritter, Paul	General	£4
Robert, Lucien	Glamour	£15
Roberts, Howard L.	Comic	£2
Roberts, Violet M	Animals	£20
Rob, G.	Comic/Patriotic	£5
Robida, A.	General	£5
Robinson, W. Heath	Comic	£6
Rodella, G.	Glamour	£5
Rog	Comic	£1.50
Romney, George	Railways	£3
Rooke, H.K.	Shipping	£10
Rose, Freda Mabel	Children	£3
Rosenvinge, Odin	Shipping	£12
Rossi, J.C.	Art Nouveau	£65
Rostro	Political	£15
Rousse, Frank	General	£2
Rowland, Ralph	Comic	£2
Rowlandson, G.	Military	£5
	Sport	£8
	Comic	£3
	General	£1.50

Rowntree, Harry	Animals	£12
	Comic	£12
Rubino, Antonio	Advertising	£30
	Children	£4
	Patriotic	£8
	Misc.	£5
Rust, A.	Comic	£1.50
Ryan, F.	Comic	£1.50
Ryland, Henry	Glamour	£8
Rylander	Art Deco	£20
S. (Capital)	Comic	£1.50
S. (Script)	Comic	£1.50
J.M.S.	Comic	£1.50
K.S.	Comic	£1.50
M.S.	Children	£1.50
S.E.S.	Comic	£1.50
Sachetti, E.	Political	£8
Sager, Xavier	Glamour	£15
	Golf /Tennis	£25
Salaman, Edith	General	£5
Salmony, G.	Glamour	£5
Samokiche, N	Military	£15
Sancha, F.	Political	£8
Sand, Adina	Glamour	£8
	Children	£5
Sanders, A.E.	General	£1.50
Sanderson, Amy	Children	£3
Sandford, H.Dix	Children	£6
	Black Humour	£8
Sandy-Hook	Shipping	£12
Santino. F	Glamour	£8-£12
Sarg, Tony	Comic	£2
Sartoi, E.	General	£1
Sauber	General	£6
	Social History	£6
Saville Rena	Children	£1.50
Sayer, Henry	Comic	£5

G.Vernon Stokes, Mastiff, £4

Schiele, Egon	Art Nouveau	£100+
Schiesl, R.	General	£3
Schmidt-Hamburg	Shipping	£10
	General	£1.50
Schonflug, Fritz	Comic	£4
Schonian	Animals	£4
Schubert, H.	Glamour	£5
Schweiger, L.	General	£4
Scottie	Glamour	£6
Scribbler	Comic	£1.50
Scrivener, Maude	Animals	£3
Severn, Walter	General	£1.50
Sgrilli	Children	£5
Shand, C.E.	Art Deco	£15
Shaw, H.G.	Animals	£6
Shaw, W. Stocker	Comic	£2
Shelton, S.	General	£1.50
Shepheard, G.E.	Comic	£5
Sherrin, A.	General	£1.50
Sherwin, D.	General	£1
Shmerling, Oscar	General	£7
Shoesmith, Kenneth	Shipping	£12
Short, E.A.	Flowers	£1.50
Sikes, F.H.	General	£1.50
Simkin, R.	Military	£15
Simonetti, A.M.	Glamour	£5
Sinty, Juan	Comic	£1.50
Skip	Comic	£1
Smale, B.H.	Comic	£8
	Military	£8
Small, D.	General	£2
Smith D. Carlton	Children	£5
Smith, Edna	Children	£2
Smith, Jessie Wilcox	Art Nouveau	£35
	Children	£30
Smith, May	Children	£8
Smith, Rob H	'The Lifeboat at work'	£5
Smith, Syd	Comic	£2
Smith, W.	General	£1.50
Smyth	Comic	£1
Sokolov, Yevgeni	General	£10
Solomko, Serge de	Glamour	£20
Somerville, Howard	Glamour	£4
	Comic	£2
Sonrel, Elizabeth	Art Nouveau	£50/60

Sowerby, Millicent	Children/	
	Chromo-Litho	£20
	Other types	£8
Spatz	Comic	£2
Sperlich, T.	Animals	£6
Spindler, Erwin	General	£6
Spurgin, Fred	Comic	£3
	Glamour	£5
	Military	£5
Spurrier, W.B.	Comic	£2
Spy	Political	£15
Stanlaw, S. Penrhyn	Glamour	£4
Stanlaws, Penly	Glamour	£6
Stannard, H. Sylvester	General	£2
Stannard, Lilian	General	£2
Stassen, F	Music	£15
Stead, A.	General	£1
Steele, L.	Children	£4
Steinlen, Alexandre	Art Nouveau	£90
Stenberg, Aina	Art Deco	£12
Sternberg, V.W.	Children	£2
Stewart, J.A.	Animals	£5
	Military	£5
Stoddart, R.W.	Comic	£2
Stokes G. Vernon	Animals	£2-£5
Stone, Frederick	Comic	£1.50
Stone, F.	Comic	£2
Stower, Willi	Shipping/	
	Early	£20
	Later	£8
	General	£6
Stretton, Philip	Animals	£5
Strong, G.W.	Comic	£1.50
Studdy, G.E.	Comic/	
	Bonzo	£8
	Others	£6
Sullivan, Pat	Comic	£5
Syd	Comic	£2
Syllikuss	Comic	£2
Symonds, Constance	Children	£8
Szyk, Arthur	Political	£6/£15
T.	Comic	£1
C.T.	Comic	£1.50
J.T.	General	£1.50
L.B.T.	Comic	£1.50
W.E.T.	Comic	£1.50
Tait	Comic	£1

Lance Thackeray, Tuck Oilette Comic £6

Talboys, A.	Animals	£3
Tam, Jean	Glamour	£12
Tanquerey, L.	Art Deco	£4
Tarrant, Margaret W.	Children/6	
	Pre-1945	£6
	1945 on	£2
Taylor, A.	Children	£1.50
	Comic	£1.50
Taylor, E.S.	Comic	£1.50
Tempest, Douglas	Children	£1.50
	Comic	£1.50
Tempest, Margaret	Children	£3
Terzi, A.	Glamour	£8

Stocker Shaw, Comic £2

Thackeray, Lance	Comic/Cricket	£15
	Write-away	£10
	Oilettes	£6
Theo	Aviation	£20
Thiede, Adolf	General	£1.50
Thiele, Arthur	Animals	£15+
	Comic	£15+
	Political	£25
Thomas, Bert	Comic	£5
Thomas, Paul	Animals	£5
Thomas, Victor	Children	£6
Thomas, Walter	Shipping	£10
Thompson, E.H.	General	£1.50
Thorne, Diana	Animals	£1.50
Titicus	Comic	£1.50
Toussaint, M.	Military	£6
Travis, Stuart	General	£1.50
Trick, E.W.	General	£1.50
Tringham, H.	General	£1.50
Trow	Comic	£1
True, W.	Theatre	£12
Truman, Herbert	General	£1
Tuhka, Augusti	Art Deco	£12
Turner, C.E.	Shipping	£8
Turrian, E.D.	Art Nouveau	£30
Twelvetrees, C.H.	Children	£6
Uden, E.	General	£1
Ullman, Max	Shipping	£15
Underwood,Clarence F	Glamour	£5
Upton, Florence K.	Children	£35
Usabal, Luis	Glamour	£10/15
Utrillo, A.	General	£6
Valles, F.	Comic	£1.50
Vallet, L.	Glamour	£10
	Military	£4

Louis Wain, £30

Clarence F Underwood, Glamour £5

Valter, Eugenie M.	Animals	£4
Valter, Florence E.	Animals	£4
Vaughan, E.H.	General	£1.50
Veal, O.	Comic	£2
Vera	Children	£2
Vernon, E.	Glamour	£6
Vernon, R.W.	General	£1.50
Villon Jacques	Art Nouveau	£300
Voellmy, F.	General	£8
Vouga, E.	Flowers	£1
F.W.	Comic	£1.50
J.S.W.	Comic	£2
Maurice Wagemans	*Military*	*£3*
Wain, Louis	Animals/Early	£50+
	Later	£30+
	Oilettes	£30+
	Advertising	£75+

(***For a more comprehensive listing of Louis Wain cards, please refer to page 66***

Wal.	Comic	£1.50
Walbourn, Ernest	General	£1.50
Walker, F.S.	General	£1.50
Walker, Hilda	Animals	£4

Brian White WW2 Comic £4

Wanke, Alice	Art Nouveau Children	£20 £10
Ward, Dudley	Comic	£3
Ward, Herbert	Military	£5
Ward, Vernon	General	£1.50
Wardle, Arthur	Animals	£8
Warrington, Ellen	General	£1.50
Watson, C.M. West	Animals	£5
Wealthy, R.J.	Animals	£3
Weaver, E.	Comic	£1.50
Webb, A.D.	General	£1
Weierter, Louis	Advertising	£25
Welzi, A.	Art Nouveau	£30
Wennerberg, Brynolf	Art Nouveau Glamour	£20 £15
West, A.L.	Animals	£2
West, Reginald	General	£1.50
Weston, Rita F.	Children	£1
Whatley, H	General	£2
Wheeler, Dorothy	Children	£4
Whishaw, A.Y.	General	£1.50
White, Brian	Children Comic WW2	£2 £4
White, D.	Comic	£2
White, Flora	Children	£5
White, H. Percy	Comic	£2
Whitehead, Fred	General	£1.50
Wichera, R.R.	Children Glamour	£6 £8
Wiederseim, G.G.	Children	£6
Wielandt, Manuel	General	£5
Wilcock, A.M.	Children	£4
Wilkin, Bob	Comic	£1
Wilkinson, Gilbert	Comic	£5
Wilkinson, Norman	Shipping	£10
Williams, Madge	Children	£3
Williams, Warren	General	£1.50
Willis, George	Comic	£1.50
Wilson, David	Political	£6
Wimble, Arthur	Glamour	£2
Wimbush, Henry B.	General	£2
Wimbush, Winifred	General Glamour	£3 £6
Wishaw, M.C.	General	£3
Wood, Lawson	Comic Gran'pop Theatre	£6 £5 £18
Wood, Starr	Comic	£5
Woodville, R. Caton	Military	£6
Woollett, Cress	Glamour	£3
Woude Sikko van de	General	£2
Wright, Gilbert	General	£4
Wright, Seppings,	General	£2
Wuyts, A	Children Glamour	£6 £6
Wyllie, W.L.	Shipping	£8
Xerxes	Comic	£1.50
H.Y.	Comic	£1.50
Young, A.	General	£1.50
Young Gwen Hayward	General	£3
Young, Hayward	General	£3
Zandrino, Adelina	Glamour	£10
Zirka, C.	Glamour	£6

Gibert Wilkinson WW2 Comic £5

LOUIS WAIN

Beagles
Coloured & Photographic £30

Boots
Famous Picture Series of 12 £35

Davidson Bros.
Various Cards £35

Dutton/N.Y.
Various Cards £35

Ettlinger & Co.
Series 5226. Father Christmas Cats £70
Series 5376. Father Christmas Cats £70

Faulkner C.W.
Series 182 • 183 • 189 • 190 • 374
453 • 454 • 484 • 485 • 503 • 515
541 • 1596 • plus many others. £30/£50

Gale & Polden
At least 1 design £45

Hartmann
Series 3068. Fluffikins Family £45
Series 3069. Manx Cats £60

Mack W.E.
The Cat's Academy (Not all by Wain) £25

Nister E.
Series 353 • 355 etc. £35
Valentine series £6

Philco series 2093 £30

Salmon series various cards £30

Theo Stroefer
Usually unsigned designs £20

Tuck R. & Sons
Series 130. Black/White und. back £18

Theatre Series 3885 • 3895 B/W £40

Write-Away Series
539 • 956 • 957 • 1003 • 1004 £40

Chromo-Litho Series
1260 • 1261 • 1262 • 1735 • 1748
1749 • 1782 • 5802 • 5892 £30

Chromo-Litho Nursery Rhymes/ Christmas/Pantomime
Series 297 • 298 • 8126 • 8127 £100

Diabolo Series 9563 £40

Valentine series, this is one of a set of six Un-numbered cards, all seaside themes £40 per card

Dressing Dolls Fairy Tales

Oilette 3385	£100+

Oilette and similar Series

1412 • 3266 • 6075 • 6084 • 6401 6444 • 8515 • 8612 • 8613 • 8614 8615 • 8816 • 8817 • 8826 • 8850 8864 • 9396 • 9540 • 9541	£30
Others/Odd cards/ Part Sets inc. C132/133	£30

Valentine

Coloured Series/Un-numbered	£40
Charlie Chaplin cards	£90

Wrench

Pantomime/Black Cat Series	£50

Anon

Jackson's Hats & Boots/Poster Type	£75
WW1 Set including a cat `Kaiser'	£75

Many other cards exist, sometimes pirate copies, often with Wain's signature removed. There are also a number of unsigned cards by other artists done in the Wain style.
All prices shown here are for single cards. A complete set may attract a premium over this figure.
It must be noted that prices apply to cards in flawless condition, with no marks or damage.

Louis Wain.
BUT
"THINGS LIKE THIS YOU KNOW MUST BE
AFTER A FAMOUS VICTORY."

Published by Mack W.E. The Cat's Academy (Not all by Wain) This card No 051 is not signed by Wain, but looks in the style of Wain, hence a price of £20

FLIGHT TO VICTORY

Now nearly 100 years since these postcards relating to The Royal Flying Corps were published, they give us a feel for the mood of the time.

During the early part of the war, the RFC supported the British Army, by artillery co-operation and photographic reconnaissance. This gradually led RFC pilots into aerial battles with German pilots and later in the war included the strafing of enemy infantry and emplacements, the bombing of German military airfields and later the strategic bombing of German industrial and transportation facilities.

At the start of World War I in 1914 the RFC had 2,073 personnel by the start of 1919 after merging with RNAS, the newly formed RAF had 4,000 combat aircraft and 114,000 personnel.

Shooting down the baby killer £6

Airco 9A de Havilland bi-plane photographed at Hendon £

The Spider drawn by Ellam £20

Glamour girl in RFC uniform £15

G.E. Shepherd comic £5

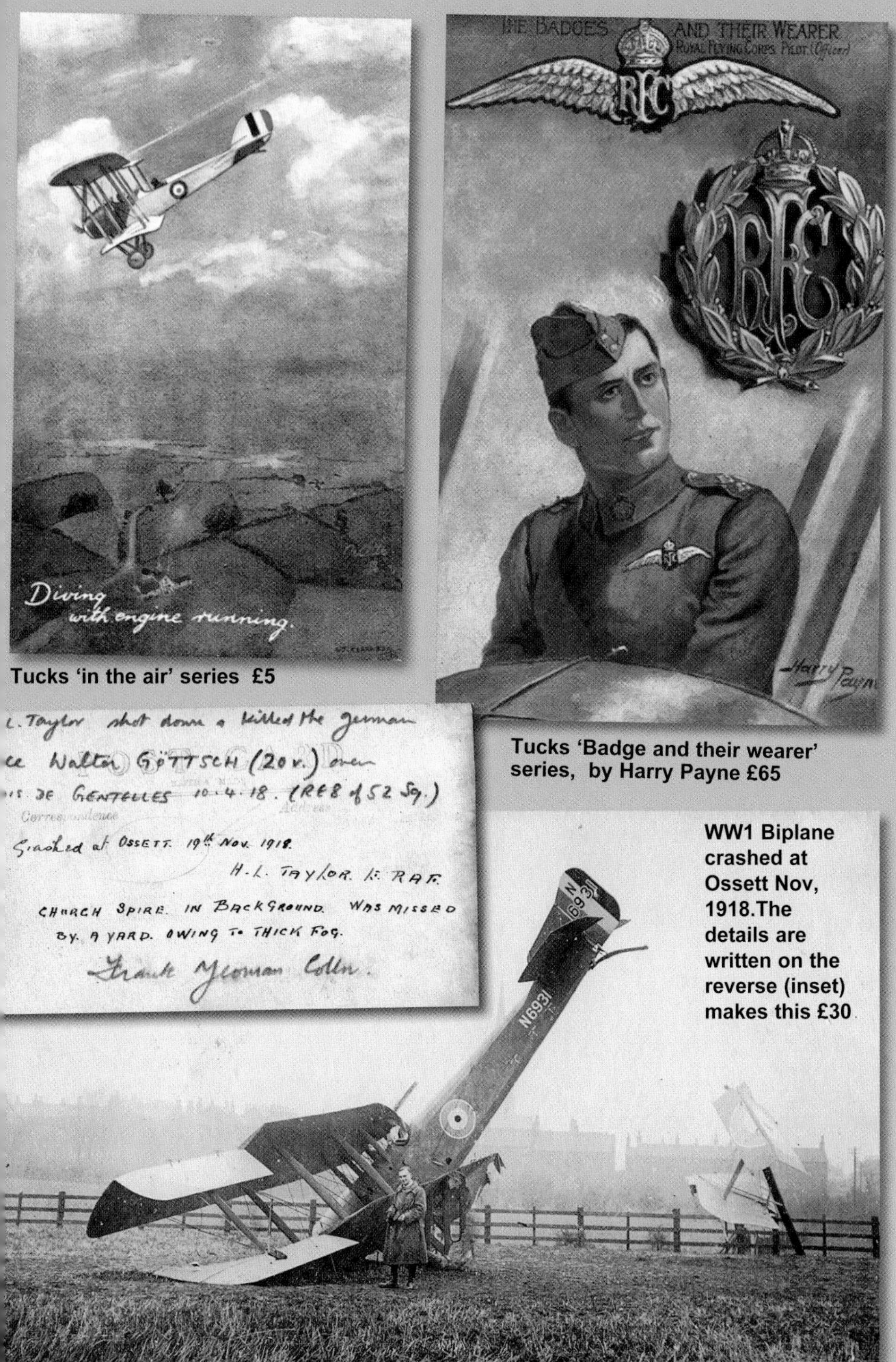

Tucks 'in the air' series £5

Tucks 'Badge and their wearer' series, by Harry Payne £65

L. Taylor shot down & killed the german
ace Walter GÖTTSCH (20 v.) over
Bois de GENTELLES 10.4.18. (RE8 of 52 Sq.)

Crashed at OSSETT. 19th Nov. 1918.

H. L. TAYLOR. F. RAF.

CHURCH SPIRE IN BACKGROUND. WAS MISSED
BY A YARD. OWING TO THICK FOG.

Frank Yeoman Colln.

WW1 Biplane crashed at Ossett Nov, 1918.The details are written on the reverse (inset) makes this £30

AVIATION

The early days of flying presented a challenge which postcard publishers were not slow to take up, with the resulting legacy of a great many fine studies both photographic and artistic on this theme. Postcards cover the whole spectrum of civil and military aviation from the early beginnings, through World War I to the nineteen-thirties and up to the present day. Generally speaking photographic cards are worth more than artistic studies, the former often having some related local history interest. It must be further emphasised that in all cases prices given are for unused cards. If postally used a much higher figure may be expected, depending upon type of postmark, date of flight, clarity of strike etc.

Market Report:
Most of the demand is in modern civil aviation and airline issue cards. Early aviation cards are sure to take off again at some point. Also interest in WW1 Royal Flying Corps is sure to increase with the centenary in 2014.

AIRCRAFT

AIRCRAFT Pre-1918

Flying at Hendon Series	£15-£25
Brooklands Aviation	£15-£30
Daily Mail Tour 1912	£10
At named locations	£30
French Aviation	£10
Civil aircraft	£10
Military aircraft	£8
Accidents	
Identified	£25
Unidentified	£5
Series	
Lefebvre Utile	£35
Lombart	£25
Educational Series	
Tuck R. & Sons	£20
The Lightning Series	
E. Cook	£15
Famous Aeroplane Series	
Tuck R. & Sons	£5
In the Air Series	
Tuck R. & Sons	£6
Artist/Derek Bannister	
Salmon J. Ltd	£5

AIRCRAFT 1918-1939

Schneider Trophy	£20+
Civil Aircraft	£10-15
Military Aircraft	£5-10
Joy Flights	£6-8
Accidents	
Identified	£25
Unidentified	£5
Amy Johnson	
England-Australia Flight/Set 6/ Tuck R. & Sons/3867B	£15
Portraits	£15
Imperial Airways	
Croydon Airport	£20
Official	£18
Pilots	£20

AIRCRAFT 1939 - 1960

Civil Aircraft	£8-15
Real Photograph Series	
Valentine	£3

PILOTS

Pre-1914	
With aircraft	£15-£20
Portraits	£15
1918-1939	
With aircraft	£15
Portraits	£12

Flying at Brooklands, Weybridge £15

Flying at Hendon series £20

French aviation £10

Aviator Harold Gatty and aircraft £18

Female aviator Mrs Stokes £15

Bournemouth advertising £30

Hendon Aviation meeting £20

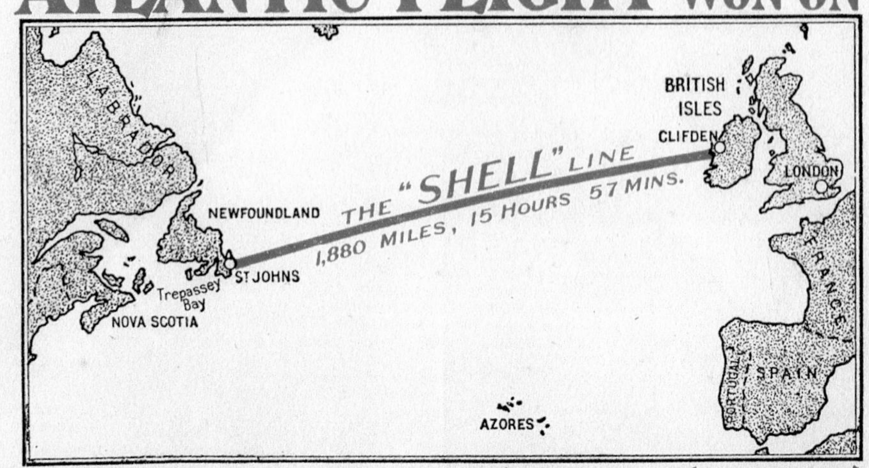

Shell advertising poster £60

London to Windsor flown card £30

AVIATION MEETINGS

Blackpool 1909/10	£20-£30
Doncaster 1909	£30-£35
Bournemouth 1910	£25-£30
Burton on Trent 1910	£30-£45
Lanark 1910	£30-£45
Wolverhampton 1910	£45
Poster Adverts	
Coloured	£60
Black & White	£30
Early Airline Poster Adverts	£85

FLOWN CARDS

Beckenham Coronation Balloon/9.8.02	
Flown	
Unflown	
Lifeboat Saturday/20.9.02	
Flown	£1,500
Unflown	£200
Lifeboat Saturday/29.8.03	
Flown	£1,000
Unflown	£200
Daily Graphic Expedition 1907	
Flown	£150
Unflown	£50
First U.K. Aerial Post 1911	
London-Windsor - Flown	£20/£40
Windsor-London - Flown	£30/£75
Unflown cards	£18

N.B. The value of flown U.K. Aerial Post Cards depends upon which colour type has been used, date of flight, clarity of strike etc. These factors are also relevant to any flown cards.

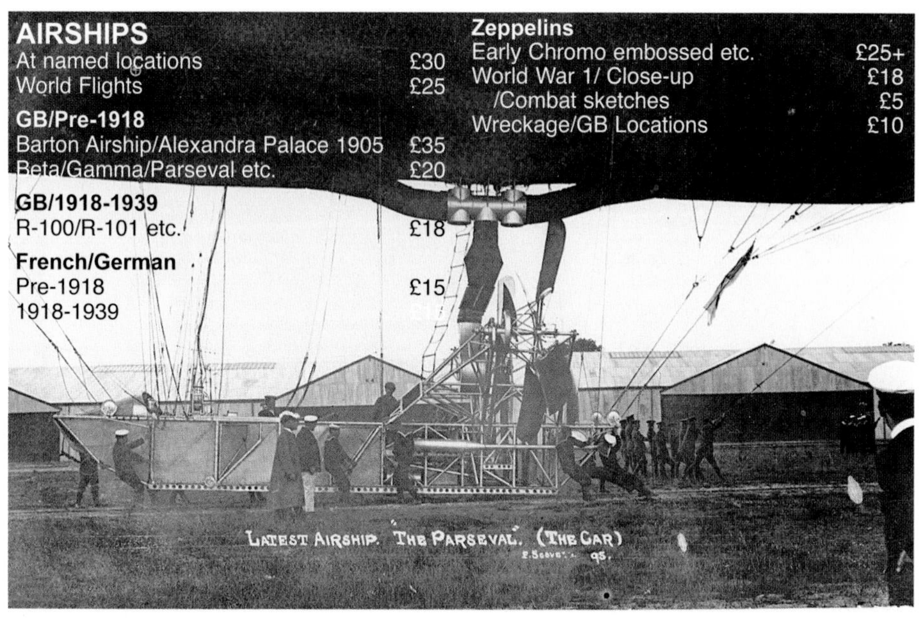

AIRSHIPS

At named locations	£30
World Flights	£25

GB/Pre-1918

Barton Airship/Alexandra Palace 1905	£35
Beta/Gamma/Parseval etc.	£20

GB/1918-1939

R-100/R-101 etc.	£18

French/German

Pre-1918	£15
1918-1939	

Zeppelins

Early Chromo embossed etc.	£25+
World War 1/ Close-up	£18
/Combat sketches	£5
Wreckage/GB Locations	£10

MISCELLANEOUS

Airfields	£8-12
R.F.C. Interest	£5-8

Commemorative Cards

First/Historic Flights	£25+

Croydon Airport

C.H. Price Series	£20

ROYAL AIR FORCE

Halton Camp	£8
Airmen/Photographs Identified	£6
/Unidentified	£1.50

BALLOONS

At named locations	£65
Photographic	£35+
Printed	£20
Military/Printed	£8
Swiss/Meetings Posters	£75+

THE LATEST AIRSHIP. "THE PARSEVAL"

MILITARY AIRCRAFT

Tucks 'in the air' series £5

Artist Drawn	
Tuck R. & Sons In The Air	£4/6
Celesque Series	£4/6
Mack W.E.	£4
Salmon J.	£5
Real Photographic	
Flight	£3
Aircraft Manufacturing Co. Series R/P	£8
Valentines	£5

WW2 Artist drawn Spitfire c.1942 £6

Airships	
Nulli Secundus Pr.Photo c.1907	£6
Beta/Gamma	£12/£15
Zeppelins Close-up	£12
Combat sketches	£3/5
Wreckage/GB Locations	£8
Aircraft	
Royal Flying Corp1912-18	£10-£30
Royal Flying Corp silk badge	£40
Royal Naval Air Service 1914-18	
Pilots/Machines	£10/12
Groups/Machines named Sqdn.	£15/20
Aces/Machines	£20
Portraits	£12-£30

R.F.C. & R.N.A.S. amalgamated in 1918 to become the Royal Air Force.

1918-1939	£5
1939-1960	£3

Miscellaneous	
Airfields/Hangers	£8
Bombers/Fighters	£3
Flying Boats	£5
Gliders	£3

MODERN COMMERCIAL AIRLINES

Modern aviation is a well collected topic, cards range from as little as £1 for some of the later issues, to £10 -£30 for some of the better 1930s-50s advertising cards.

1970s airline £3

1950s airline £10

SPACE

Above: Man on the Moon Apollo 11 £4

Left: Commander Scott Carpenter in space suit with his spacecraft Aurora 7, 1962 £5

CHILDREN

One of the most popular themes for the early publishers of picture postcards, reflecting the tastes of our Edwardian forbears. Cards of Children and related subjects were published by the thousand. Perhaps the best known series is the `Queen's Dolls House', published by Tuck, while many of the early chromo-litho art studies, in their design and execution represent some of the most beautiful cards ever printed.

Market Report

Mabel Lucie Attwell is still collected and will sell if sensibly priced. Real photographic cards of Edwardian children with toys or dressed as angels have their followers.

CHILDREN

Angels

Art studies	£4
Photographic	£3

Babies	£1
Perambulators	£5

Fairies

Art Studies	£6-£20

Named artists can command a considerable premium

Photographic	£3

Nursery Rhymes

Art Studies	£4-£12
R. Caldecott	£1.50

Named artists can command a considerable premium

Chromo-Litho studies

These range from quite ordinary types to spectacular cards, again with named artists at a premium. (see Artists Section)

Prices range from £3 - £18

Photographic Studies	£1-£3

Tuck R. & Sons

Fairy Tales/Art Series 3472	£25
Ping Pong in Fairyland/ Art Series 1156	£35

Frederick Warne & Co.

Caldecott R./8 sets of 6/ Nursery Rhymes	£1.50

DOLLS

Close-up photos	£6
Early Art cards	£8
Greetings type	£2

Mirror Grange

Tuck R. & Sons	£3

Queen's Dolls House

Tuck R. & Sons/Set 48	
Price per card	£1
Complete Set	£60
Wembley Exhibition	£3

Titania's Palace

Tuck R. & Sons/ Two sets of 8 cards	£3
Gale & Polden	£2

TOYS

Bramber Museum	£1.50
Diabolo sketches	£5
Golliwogs	£15+
Close-up photos	£6
Greetings type	£2

Teddy Bears

Art Studies	£10
Photographic	£8
Pullouts	£15
Roosevelt Cartoons	£30

Nursery rhymes by Phyllis Cooper £12

Photographic study, hand tinted £3

"NEVER A LASS BUT LOVED A SOLDIER BOY."
"Je ne suis plus une enfant, j'aime un soldat."

Children artist, patriotic theme, £4

Comic children Deco style, signed £4

Early card signed by M. Sowerby £8

CINEMA

Not a subject much in evidence during the hey-day of the picture postcard, the majority of Film Stars collected today date from the 1920-1939 period. While other collectors look for individual Stars from the 40s to the 60s, which are also very popular,

Market Report
The middle period 1930's and 1940's is still struggling. Prices have come down generally but there are deals to be done if the price is right. 1950s and 1960's artists sell better than their earlier counterparts and there is a stirring of interest in the silent movie stars.

FILM STARS

This is a select list of names, whom because of scarcity or demand, are currently fetching prices in excess of Catalogue valuation.

Abbott and Costello	£12
Astaire, Fred	£4
Ball, Lucille	£6
Bardot, Brigitte	£10
Bergman, Ingrid	£8
Bogart, Humphrey	£4
Brando, Marlon	£8-£12
Brooks, Louise	£20
Cagney, James	£4
Chaplin, Charlie	£6
Comic sketches	£5
Red Letter Stills	£3
Cole, Nat King	£12
Doris Day	£4
Davis, Bette	£6
Dean, James	£12
Dietrich, Marlene	£6
Dors, Diana	£10
Durante, Jimmy	£8
Fields, W.C.	£8
Flynn, Errol	£6
Formby, George	£8
Gable, Clark	£3
Garbo, Greta	£3
Garland, Judy	£10
Betty Grable	£5
Harlow, Jean	£6
Hepburn, Audrey	£12
Holliday, Judy	£6
Howerd, Frankie	£8
Jolson, Al	£8
Karloff, Boris	£6
Kelly, Grace	£6
Lamour, Dorothy	£5
Lanza, Mario	£8
Laurel & Hardy	£20
Leigh, Vivien	£8
Lloyd, Harold	£4
Lombard, Carole	£5
Loren, Sophia	£5
Mansfield, Jayne	£6
Marx Brothers.	£15
Monroe, Marilyn	£25
Presley, Elvis	£9
Paul Robeson	£15
Robinson, Edward G.	£4
Rogers Ginger	£4
Temple, Shirley	£4
Valentino, Rudolph	£3
Wayne, John	£6
Welles, Orson	£8
West, Mae	£10
Wisdom, Norman	£6

Foto: Sam Lévin/Ufa
Brigitte Bardot
Ufa/Film-Foto
Reproduktion verboten

Beautiful Brigitte Bardot Bargain at £10

Series

Dave and Dusty	£3
Pictures Portrait Gallery	£2
Cinema Chat	£2
Picturegoer/1921-1939	£2
/1940-1962	£3

The Picturegoer Series ran to 6600 cards, published from 1921 to c.1962.

Film Sets/Stills

Pre-1939	£4
1940 onwards	£6

Picturegoer and other firms also produced six-card sets of scenes from individual films. Prices for the most part follow those of the respective Stars.

Miscellaneous Publishers

Pre-1939	£2
1940 onwards	£3
Continental Stars	£2
Coral-Lee 1980	£1

With all Film Star postcards, the value is determined by the name of the artist. Cards of the 1940's,1950's and some from the 60's are in most demand, and a price of £4 would be realistic for the majority of artists from this period. For cards of the 1920's and 1930's, a corresponding figure would be £2. But there are exceptions as given in our select list, and including certain other names of significance, or with a cult following. As a rule of thumb, the well-known Star is worth more than the unknown.

Please note that plain back cards carry the same value as postcard backs.

This card could possibly be in the wrong section, but this young Ronald Reagan is still in the 'B' movie business, price £4

1940s Picturegoer series £3

Charlie Chaplin comic sketch £5

Autographs / Ink Signed

Value is determined by the individual Star. Certain names are worth more than others. See pages 210 to 215 of this catalogue for a more in depth guide

Early real photo of Green's Bioscope £50

MISCELLANEOUS

Bioscopes	£50
Cinemas Exterior close up	£35
Felix the Cat	£12

Cinema Organists

Dixon, Reginald	£5
Others	£4

Disney

Mickey Mouse/Picturegoer Series Nos. 452, 452a, 452b	£50
Foreign published/France/Holland	£10+
Other Disney issues	£8+

Elvis Presley £9

Early close up of the Electric Cinema building in Highgate, North London, easily worth £35

COMIC

The Comic postcard is a British institution. It is the yardstick by which most non-collectors judge our hobby! Everyone recognises the Comic card, with its bygone images of hen-pecked husbands, red-nosed drunks, saucy jokes, and embarrassed Vicars! It has been the subject of learned dissertations by authors as varied as George Orwell to Ronnie Barker. And yet, with the exception of a few named Artists or themes allied to other subjects, Comic cards are not as popular today as in former times.

Market Report

Town names will boost the price of any comic card. Themes are important – cricket, golf, military, political, photography and wireless are popular. McGill and the non-pc humour of the 1960's are always wanted.

SERIES

Bamforth & Co.

Pre 1918	£3
1918-1939	£2
1940 onwards	£1-£3

Tuck R & Sons

Write Away/Early Vignettes	£10
Write Away/Later Issues	£4

Fragments from France/

B. Bairnsfather	
Numbers 1 - 48	£4
Numbers 49-54	£10

Sketches of Tommy's Life/

F. Mackain	
Set 10/In Training	£4
Set 10/Up the Line	£4
Set 10/Out on Rest	£4
Set 10/At the Base	£4

Black Humour

Happy Little/Tuck R. & Sons/	
Oilettes/H.D. Sandford	£10
Other Black Humour	£4

Other Series

Write Off Series/Valentine	£5
Other 'Write-Away' Series	£5

Early Tuck write away by Thackeray £10

WW1 Military comic Henry Sayer £5

WW1 Bruce Bairnsfather £4

GENERAL

All unsigned cards of general interest may be grouped together into the periods listed below, with this suggested price structure.

Pre-1918	£2
1918-1939	£1.50
1940-1960	£1

Early/Chromo-Litho

Undivided back	£8
Divided Back	£3

Double up, Political and football comic £6

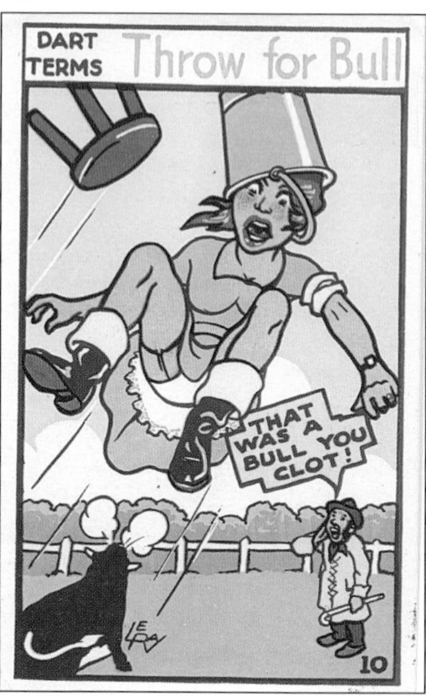

Bullseye theme makes this comic £4

Jewish comic £15

Politically incorrect humour £12

TYPES

Listed below are suggested minimum prices, bearing in mind that certain Artist signed may be worth considerably more.

Angling	£4
Anti-black, racist humour	£8-£12
Aviation	£4
Barbers	£4-£10
Billiards/Snooker	£9
Cameras	£8
Card Games	£5
Cats	£3
Chess	£15
Cigarette Packets	£8
Corkscrews	£8
Cricket	£9
Crossword Puzzles	£5
Cycling	£3/£6
Dentistry	£10
Diabolo	£3
Dialect	£1
Drinking/Drinks etc.	£2
Erotic	£5
Fitness	£3
Fleas	£1.50

Golf comic by Tom Browne £10

Football	£6-£10
Golfing	£8- £12
Got Any Cigarette Cards	£10
Gramophones	£8
Horoscopes	£5
Hatpins	£2
Hunting	£2
Jewish	£15 - £25
Lavatorial	£2
Limericks	£4
Maps	£3
Masonic	£20
Match Boxes	£6
Strikers	£15
Military	
Pre-1914	£3
World War 1	£3-£6
World War 2	£5-£20
Miscellaneous	£3
Motorcycling	£8
Motoring	£5
Obscene/Sexual	£3
Pawnbrokers	£5
Ping Pong	£20
Playing Cards	£5
Police	£4
Postal	£4
Postcards	£5
Postmen	£6
Prehistoric	£2
Pussyfoot	£3
Racing	£5
Railways	£3
Rinking	£3
Rugby football	£6
Scouts	£12
Smoking	£3
Suffragettes	£25
Telegrams	£3
Telephone	£3
Television	£4
Tennis	£8
Trams	£3
Wireless/Radio	£8
Irish	£3
Scottish	£3
Welsh	£3

Horoscope plus WW2 comic £5

EARLY CARDS

Postcards were first introduced by Austria in 1869, the first British postcard appearing on 1st October 1870. These were officially issued plain cards with a printed stamp and without a picture, and came to be known as postal stationery. The idea spread rapidly, and within a few years many countries were issuing these novel plain cards. On the Continent, shortly after their introduction, privately issued picture cards came into being, published in varying sizes, but it was not until 1st September 1894 that similar picture cards were permitted in Great Britain, being accepted by the Post Office one month later. These early British cards were known as Court Size. They were smaller and squarer in shape, being issued from 1894-1902, and led to an Intermediate Size from 1898-1902. Until 1902 all cards had to carry the message on the front and the address on the back, thus restricting the design on the card to that of a small picture, or `vignette', with the rest of the surface left free for writing. But on 1st January, 1902, after mounting pressure from commercial interests, Britain became the first country to divide the back, thus permitting both message and address on this side, leaving the front of the card free for a picture. This move saw the adoption of a universal Standard Size of 5.5 x 3.5in, and heralded the real beginning of picture postcards as a major collecting pastime. Other countries quickly followed, and the resultant explosion in picture postcard production world wide lasted until 1914, when the First World War brought an end to this `Golden Age'. This is the most complex heading in Postcards, impossible to catalogue in any depth, covering as it does many millions of undivided back cards published throughout the world from 1869-1907, by which latter date all countries had divided the back and adopted the Standard Size. The entries below will form a general guide to type and price for all Early Cards.

Market Report

This was a very popular subject amongst the older school of collectors and dealers but seems to have limited appeal these days. Clean cards or early postal usage are important.

GREAT BRITAIN

POSTAL STATIONERY/PRE-1894

First Day of Issue Postcard

p.u. 1st October 1870	£400
Unused	£5

Penny Postage Jubilee/Red Card

p.u. May 1890/Guildhall	£50
Unused	£25

Penny Postage Jubilee/& Cover

p.u. July 1890/S. Kensington	£25+
Unused	£8

COURT SIZE/1894-1902

Gruss Aus type	£25

Early Vignettes

Coloured	£10-£25
Sepia/bw	£5-£12

Postally Used

When the above cards are found postally used before 1897, this consideration of early usage would usually over-ride other factors. The prices given below may be taken as a general guide:

1896	£40
1895	£60
1894	£250
September 1894	£400

With all cards from 1895 onwards, certain rare types may fetch prices in excess of those given above.

INTERMEDIATE SIZE/1898-1902

Early Vignettes

Coloured	£10-15
Sepia/bw	£6

GB Views

Sepia/bw	£2

STANDARD SIZE/1899-1902

Gruss Aus type	£20

Early Vignettes

Coloured	£12
Sepia/bw	£4

GB Views

Sepia/bw	£2

If postally used, a small premium may be added to the above prices. It will be seen that some over-lapping occurs in the periods of usage for these cards. This is because there are examples of different sizes known. With regard to the entry for GB Views, it may be added that the majority of these published before 1902, were mass produced common scenes of large cities, towns and holiday areas, and consequently of little interest to Topographical collectors.

Early Chromo-litho British Court card, £15

FOREIGN

POSTAL STATIONERY/PRE-1894

First Day of Issue Postcard

p.u. 1st Oct. 1869	£400
Unused	£12

GRUSS AUS/EARLY VIGNETTES

Anniversaries	£25
Festivals	£20
Heraldic	£10
Parades	£18
Souvenirs	£15

Early Vignettes

Coloured	£5-£10
Sepia/bw	£2

For postally used cards a modest premium may be added, in keeping with the scale printed under `Gruss Aus/Topographical'.

1897-1900 £6

GRUSS AUS/TOPOGRAPHICAL

A difficult area to catalogue, for prices are governed by country of issue, design, condition, and if used date of postmark. The prices given below may be taken as a general indication of value for cards issued in Germany, Austria, Italy and Switzerland, although cards from the smaller towns here are usually worth more than those from large cities.

Fewer Gruss Aus cards were issued by other countries, and as a general rule, the more obscure the country, the higher the value of its cards, with those from places such as the German Colonies, Greece, Palestine, Singapore, and small islands forming the top price bracket of perhaps three times above our base rate.

Prices given apply to postally used cards, although this factor has little significance with later issues from 1896 onwards. Before this date, however, considerations of early usage leading to the field of postcard history may be felt to be of primary importance.

1869-1879	£60
1880-1884	£45
1885-1889	£40
1890-1895	£20
1896-1900+	£6-£12

Early Gruss aus vignette P.Used.1897 £7.50

Sepia/Black & White

From 1896 onwards the production of Gruss Aus (Greetings From) cards increased dramatically.

Those listed above are usually printed chromo-litho in solid colours from 1896 onwards, and in colour and shades of sepia before this date.

From 1896 we find a great many sepia and black & white cards bearing the legend `Gruss Aus', but these are not worth anything like the superb coloured examples. Their average price would be £2.

ETHNIC

Dealing with the races and peoples of the world, this subject was not much in evidence during the early days of collecting, this subject heading covers a fairly broad spectrum of topics mainly showing people in action throughout the world, similar to Social History in Britain. Although before photographic representation of the European Nude became permissible in France during the latter years of World War 1, the many similar studies of native girls offered a culturally acceptable, if hypocritical alternative.

Market Report

There is strong demand from foreign dealers for good ethnic studies which feeds through to the domestic market. Unusual countries and primitive types are what are wanted. Most of the southern hemisphere is collected.

ETHNIC GLAMOUR

Cards in this section show girls either topless or semi-clothed.

Ceylon	£10
Ethiopia	£6
South Africa	£5
Sudan	£8
West Africa	£8
India	£10
Japan	£10

Egypt

Tuck R. & Sons/Oilette 7200/	
Egypt - The Sphinx	£3
Miscellaneous types	£5

Senegal

Fortier/Dakar	£8

Reproduction interdite
Collection Générale Fortier, Dakar
1059. - Afrique Occidentale - Sénégal. - Cérère None
Jeune Fille - Chez les Nones, les filles ne portent
qu'un rudiment de vêtement, le " Guembé "

Senegal £8

North Africa

The source of the great majority of Ethnic Glamour cards, depicting mainly Arab or Bedouin girls. The leading publisher was Lehnert & Landrock of Cairo and Tunis.

Lehnert & Landrock

Coloured/Numbered on front	£6
/Other series	£6
Sepia/Numbered on front	£4
Real Photographic	£6
Black & White	£3

Other Publishers

ELD/LL/ND/Geiser	£10
Real Photographic	£6
Miscellaneous types	£3

The following cards show girls fully clothed, but are different to the usual National Dress or Trades and Workers types in that they are specifically intended as glamour studies of beautiful girls in the context of their Ethnic background.

Europe	£2
Far East	£3
North Africa	£2

Cards may be found in both categories from certain other countries - Java, Indo China, Japan etc. Depending upon the image, such cards may be rated slightly higher than the above figures.

Chinese Mining boys in South Africa £15

Printed study of a man in traditional costume, from Dakar £10

MISCELLANEOUS

American Indians photo	£10
American Indians printed	£4+
Cowboys	£5
Fakirs/Snake Charmers	£4
Hats	£2
Opium Smokers	£5

Contemporary Fashion

c.1910 Family Portraits	£3

Great Britain

Portraits of People/Groups	£2

Ireland

Irish Humour	£1.50
People/Costume/Life etc.	£2-£10

Japan

Geisha	£6
People/Costume/Life etc.	£1.50
Temples/Cherry Blossom etc.	£1

National Dress

Misch & Stock/Stengel etc.	£1.50
Miscellaneous types	

Native Races

South American Indians	£6
Other Native Tribes	£6
Local Industries	£4
People/Costume/Life etc.	£2+

Russia

Types of Russian Life	£8+
People/Costume/Art	£4

Scotland

Types of Scottish Dress/Castle Series	£5
Scottish Humour	£1.50
Highland Washing scenes	£1
People/Costume/Life etc.	£1.50+

Wales

Welsh Humour	£1.50
People/Costume/Life etc.	£2

See also `Ethnic' listing under individual countries.

JEWISH POSTCARDS

The subjects of Jewish postcards ranged from New Year's greeting cards, Synagogues & Palestine, to those featuring specific Jewish themes like Jewish Holidays, famous Jewish people and Rabbis.

SYNAGOGUES

This is a very collectable subject.
The synagogues of Germany, Austria and East Europe are very much in demand especially photographic cards showing those destroyed during the Pogroms & Second World War.(£30 - £40)
Northern American & French Synagogues are more common and therefore less desirable.(£8 - £15)

PALESTINE

Most of the postcards of Palestine are topographical or historical. There are mainly cards of towns and street scenes. Some postcards mark special occasions like a visit of an important person etc.
(£5 - £10) For general views see overseas section.

NEW YEARS GREETING CARDS

Sending Jewish New Years cards has always been very popular. Most of the cards had no specific Jewish motive but the pictures were taken from different sources. Many of the images were staged, often featuring models that made multiple appearances in different settings but they faithfully represented realistic elements of daily life.
"Happy New Year" in Hebrew, English and Yiddish, and a short poem was often added.
(£5 - £10)
The New Years greeting cards that were published in Poland & Russia are rare and therefore more valuable. (£30 - £60)

CURIOSITIES

Houses/Models etc.	£2
Natural/Trees etc.	£2

CEREMONIAL

Masonic

Are You a Mason?/24 cards	
Millar & Lang	£20
Regalia/Miscellaneous	£8
Oxford University Robes	£1.50

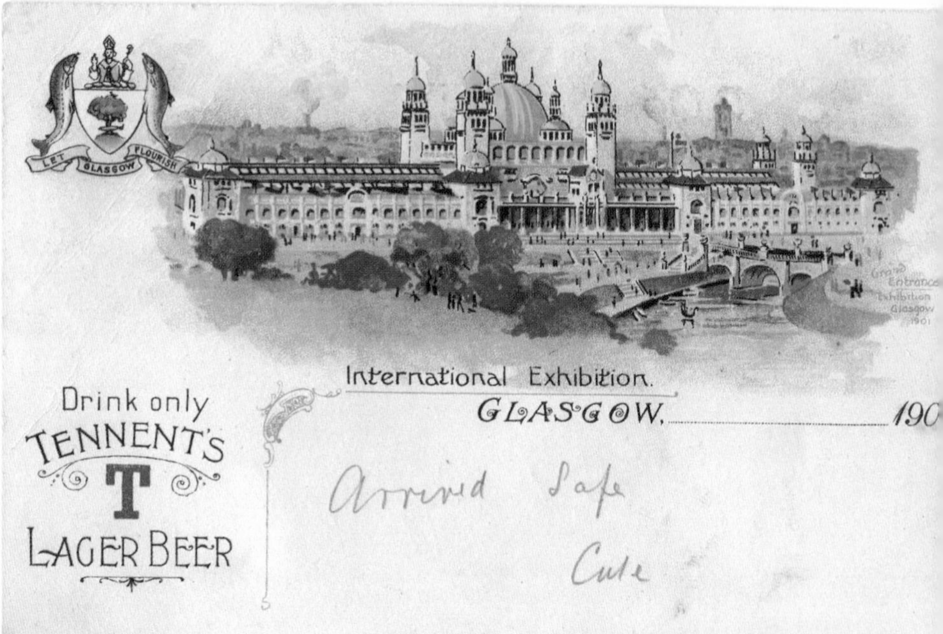

Advertising adds to the value of these 1901 Glasgow exhibition cards, pushing them to £20 for the Tennent's beer above and £40 for the Mitchell's cigarettes below

EXHIBITIONS

A vast and complex field with many Exhibitions well able to support their own specialised Catalogue. All the events listed below had picture postcards issued, some of which were sold at retail outlets throughout the country, quite removed from the Exhibition itself. All one can do here is to list the main events, and give a suggested minimum price per card, bearing in mind that certain cards may be worth more if depicting Trade Stands, carrying Advertisements, or bearing an Artist's signature. This whole section needs to be re-done by an expert in the field

Market Report
This section is still exhibiting signs of a revival. If you can plough your way through the common material there is now strong demand for anything unusual. Postmarks and Olympic history add to the interest and value. Foreign exhibitions carry on to be difficult.

GREAT BRITAIN

Royal Naval Exhibition/S.W.	
Eddystone Lighthouse	
p.u.1891/Violet postmark	£75
p.u. 1891/Blue postmark	£75
Gardening & Forestry Exhibition	
Eddystone Lighthouse	
p.u. 1893/Earls Court	£150
Unused	£75
Victorian Era 1897	
Earls Court	£50
Women's Exhibition 1900	
Earls Court/Dinka Village	£5
Glasgow 1901	
Cassiers H.	£8
bw views	£4
Military 1901	
Earls Court	£6
Cork 1902	£5
Wolverhampton 1902	£6
Highland & Jacobite 1903	
Inverness	£5
International Fire 1903	
Earls Court	£5
Scottish Home Industries 1903	
Manchester	£5

Illinois Building, Earls Court Exhibition 1908 Oilette type view card, £2

Latin-British Exhibition, White City 1912 £1.50

Bradford 1904	£3
International Gas 1904	
Earls Court	£5
Italian 1904	
Earls Court	£3
Nottingham 1904	
Fire scenes/General views	£3
Colonial 1905	
Crystal Palace	£5
Imperial Austrian 1906	
Earls Court	£1.50
Balkan States 1907	
Earls Court	£3
Irish International 1907	
Dublin	£3
South African Products 1907	
Poster Advert Card	£12
Crystal Palace 1908	£5
Hungarian 1908	£2
Scottish National 1908	
Edinburgh	£2-£4
Worlds Mining 1908	
Olympia	£5
Franco-British 1908	
Mucha	£150
Woven Silk	£80
Trade Stands	£10

Poster Adverts £20+
Hagenbeck Circus/Stadium £8
Comic/Patriotic £4
Views £2

Imperial International 1909
Trade Stands £8
Patriotic/Tartar Camp £5
Views £1.50

C.M.S. Africa & The East 1909
Islington £3

Golden West 1909
Earls Court £3

Japan-British 1910
Trade Stands £8
Comic/Patriotic £3
Views £2

Coronation 1911
Trade Stands £8
White City Views £3

Festival of Empire 1911
Oxo/Patriotic £8
Crystal Palace/Views £4

Scottish National 1911
Glasgow £2

Jubilee International Stamp 1912
Victoria S.W./Ideal Stamp £10

Latin-British 1912
White City £1.50

Shakespeare's England 1912
Earls Court £1.50

Building Trades 1913
Olympia £3

Imperial Services 1913
Earls Court £3

Liverpool 1913 £3

Russian Village 1913
Olympia £3

Anglo-American 1914
Band/Patriotic/Wild West £5
White City/Views £2

Anglo-Spanish 1914
Earls Court £3

Bristol International 1914 £3

Newcastle upon Tyne 1929 £3

Empire 1938
Glasgow £1.50
Advertising £20+

Festival of Britain 1951
Signed Watercolours £8
Far Tottering & Oyster Creek Railway £5
Views £3

Entrance to the amusement park at the British Empire Exhibition, Wembley 1924 £4

Miscellaneous Exhibitions

Daily Mail/Flower Shows etc.	£2
Cards printed on Stands	£8

BRITISH EMPIRE 1924/25

Advertising Cards

Cope Bros/Poster Adverts	£60
Tuck R. & Sons by C.E. Flower/ APOC/North British Rubber/ Bryant & May/Sharp's etc.	£12
Anchor Line/HMV etc.	£12

Court & Pavilion cards

Australia/Bengal/Bombay etc.	£3
Falklands Court	£50

Exhibition views

Tuck R. & Sons/Coloured	£4
Fleetway/Sepia	£1.50
Other Publishers/RP & Coloured	£3
/Sepia	£1.50

Colonial views

Tuck R & Sons/RP	£3
/Coloured	£3
/Sepia	£2

PAGEANTS U/K £2

For full listings of UK and overseas Pageants see Picture postcard values 2003

Glasgow 1938, superb Deco advert £20

Expo 1967 £1.50

Other Publishers/Sepia	£1.50

Queens Doll's House

Tuck R. & Sons	£3

OVERSEAS EXHIBITIONS

With hundreds of overseas Exhibitions held world-wide during the past century, it is neither realistic nor practical to attempt to list every single one, let alone give prices for all their cards. Many of these Exhibitions could support their own Catalogue! As for pricing, any attempt at this is dependent upon knowing exactly what was published, and this information is not yet in the public domain. As a general guide the following price structure may be of some help:

1881-1895	**£20/£40**
1896-1900	**£10/£20**
1901-1905	**£2/£12**
1906-1918	**£1/£5**
1919 onwards	**£1/£3**

Any pre-1907 card of Gruss Aus design would be worth at least £10, but other early bw or sepia cards such as those from Paris 1900 would be valued at around £1.50. It must be further pointed out that the unusual or spectacular card, such as a Poster Advert, from any Exhibition may be worth considerably more than its range given above while at the same time some Exhibitions may be more popular than others.

PAGEANTS/OVERSEAS

Quebec 1908	£3
Hudson-Fulton 1909	£5
Capetown 1910	£2
National Fetes	£3

EXPLORATION

The explorations and expeditions of the Edwardian Age were well covered by the picture postcards of the time, albeit in smaller production runs than the more popular themes. For this reason the cards which remain are difficult to find and consequently highly priced.

1893 Nansen (Norway) Aus Nansen in Nacht und Eis/Set 12/Meissner & Buch/Series 1016 £

Market Report
Much sought after but seldom found. Prices tend to be determined at auction as very little is discovered in dealers stocks. Prices are generally strong.

1907-09 SHACKLETON

S.S.NImrod was the ship used by Ernest Shackleton in his 1908 Antarctic Expedition for the South Pole.
£25

POLAR

All prices are for unused cards; beware modern reproductions.
Cards sent from expeditions carry a large premium.

ANTARCTIC

1897-99 de Gerlache (Belgium)
Set 12 pub. Nels each £25
Return of expedition 1899 £40
Various cards £30

1901 Drygalski (Germany)
Set 5 Artist drawn cards each £125

1901-04 Nordenskjold (Sweden)
Set 10 'S.Y.Antarctic' exp. each £60
Argentine rescue cards various £50

1901-04 Scott
Set 4 Wrench Links of Empire
p.u. from ports of call each £150
Set 24 Canterbury Times each £45
Set 12 Weekly Press each £80
Ship 'Discovery' various £25

1903-05 Charcot (France)
Set 6 for subscribers (Tuck) p.u. each £100
Launch of 'Francais'1903 £40
Set 20 Expedition cards each £50
Various cards of ship 'Francais' £30

1904 Scottish National Expedition
Set 12 pub W.Ritchie each £50
Various pub. in Argentina £40
Ship 'Scotia' various £35

1907-09 Shackleton
Set 12 expedition views each £20
With printed adverts £30
Ship 'Nimrod' various photos £25+
Shackleton various photos £20

1908-10 Charcot (France)
Launch of 'Pourquoi-Pas?' £40
Various ship cards pub ELD, ND £30
Expedition cards £50

1910-12 Amundsen (Norway)
Set 5 chromo-litho pub Mittet each £20
Amundsen photo £25

1910-13 Scott
Set 12 Ponting photos each £25-£35
Memoriam cards Rotary / Batchelder £15/30
Various NZ pub ship 'Terra Nova' £50
Advertising cards Fry, Shell, etc £60
Memorials to Scott, statues, cairns etc £8
Expedition memorial cards, various £25

1914-17 Shackleton
Set 8 sepia expedition photos each £20
With Spratts dog food advert each £30
Ship 'Endurance' in port £40
Various Return of Expedition cards £50

1921-22 Shackleton –Rowett Expedition
'Quest' at Portsmouth £70
Various departure, crew members etc £50
Shackleton's grave 1929 £15

1928-30, 1933-35 Byrd (USA).)
Set 17 sepia photos 1929,
each p.u.1934 £20
Set dog teams pub Neill NZ 1928 each £60
1933 Fair 'City of New York' ship £5
Expedition dogs, various £10

1954 Australia research expedition
Map card £10
Set 5 photos pub Seven Seas each £10

1955-58 Trans-Antarctic Expedition
Set 7 b/w photos each £10+

ARCTIC

1893 Nansen (Norway)
Composite Set 4/Price per Set £400
On board the `Fram' £40
Aus Nansen in Nacht und Eis/Set 12/
Meissner & Buch/Series 1016 £20

1897Andree (Sweden)
Hot Air Balloon
Set 25/Bergeret, Nancy £60
Portraits etc/1930 discovery £15

1899 'Princesse Alice'
Prince Albert of Monaco etc in Spitzbergen / set 24 each card £20-£35

1899 Abruzzi /Cagni (Italy)
On board the `Stella Polare' £50
Rome Conference 1901/
Subscription Cards £40
Various cards £35

1901 Otto Sverdrup
Various cards £40

1903-1905 Ziegler/`America'
Various cards £40

1903 Swedish South Polar Expedition
'SY Antarctic' Expedition views / set 12 £60
Argentine rescue pub La Nacion / 16 £40
Various Argentine rescue £50

1899-1900 ABBRUZZI/CAGNI

Duke of the Abruzzi was an Italian mountaineer and explorer, and member of the royal House of Savoy. He is known for his Arctic explorations and for his mountaineering expeditions. **Umberto Cagni** was a polar explorer and an admiral in the Royal Italian Navy. Best known for his leadership in a probe, by dogsled, northward over the surface of the Arctic Ocean in 1900 Cards sell for £35

LA SPEDIZIONE NOBILE - 11 - Esplorazioni di Alpini (Fot. Istituto L. U. C. E.)

1908 Robert Peary (USA)

N.Pole Gravure /Hampton's mag/ set 13	£12
Kawin & Co./Chicago/Set 50/bw photos	£8
Taggart/Series of sepia photos	£6
Tuck R. & Sons/Oilettes/Operati A.	£8
Ullman North Pole Series 162/Wall B.	£8
S.S. `Roosevelt'/Inset Peary portrait/ Set 3 Official/p.u. 12.9.09	£75
Peary & Cook/Comic sketches	£5

1911 Filchner (Germany)

Views of 'Deutschland', various £50

Hot Air Balloon/`Princess Alice'

Set 24/Alfonso XIII & Prince of Monaco etc. in Spitzberg £30

1925-26 North Pole flights in Airships/ Dirigibles by Amundsen, Bennett, Byrne, Ellsworth, Nobile

Various cards £30

1936 J.B.Charcot (France)

Shipwreck 1936	£35
Funeral 1936	£60
1954 Australian Antarctic Bases Pub. Seven Seas stamps / set 5	£8
1957 Trans-Antarctic Expedition bw photos / set 7	£8

EVEREST

1922 Expedition

Group photo/RP £15

1924 Expedition

p.u. from Rongbuk Base Camp £20

SAHARA

1921 Capt. Angus Buchanan

Set 12/Portraits & Events R/P £8

CAMPAGNE SCIENTIFIQUE DE LA " PRINCESSE ALICE "
Le Prince de Monaco surveillant le gonflement d'un ballon sonde.

Left: 1899 Princesse Alice, Prince Albert of Monaco £35

GLAMOUR

One of the stalwarts of the Edwardian picture postcard industry as shown by the great numbers handed down to us. Glamour cards in one form or another are to be found in almost every original album, although the top of the range Artists and photographic Nudes are none too common. These were to be collected mainly in France, or by our troops during the First World War.

Market Report

Many dealers around the world are sitting on expensive glamour cards which are not selling as collectors tend to be very discriminating these days. Prices being asked are far too high. The best Kirchners still command high prices but the market needs a readjustment. The slightest blemish will seriously affect the value of any card.

ART STUDIES

Chromo-Litho

Meissner & Buch	£15
Other publishers	£10

Nudes/Semi-Nudes

Pin-up type	£6
French Salon/Coloured	£4
/Sepia/BW	£2
Classical Art	£1

Pretty Girls

Better cards/Pre-1914	£3
Miscellaneous	£1.50

USA Post-War Pin-Ups

Machine cards/Plain back	£5

BATHING BEAUTIES

Embossed/Artist drawn

Chromo-Litho	£10
Other types	£5

Photographic/Portraits

Miscellaneous	£3

Bathing portrait Art repro £3

Stocking up on nudes? this one will be £15

PHOTOGRAPHIC

Nudes

Prices given both for Nudes and Lingerie apply equally to plain back cards as these formed the bulk of publishers' output during this period.

France c.1916/RP	£15
Germany/Italy etc.c.1916/RP	£12
c.1916/Coloured/Hand Tinted	£18
Printed/Bw & Sepia	£6
Stage Acts/The Seldoms	£8
Couples	£8
Between the Wars	£6
Post-War studies	£4
Body Stocking types	£4
Private photographs	£2
Modern reproductions	£1.50

SM Interest
Numbered RP series c.1920 £25
Bondage/Spanking etc. £20

Lingerie Studies £10

Pretty Girls
Better cards/Pre-1914 £3
Miscellaneous £1

MISCELLANEOUS

Pornographic/Postcard back
Art/Photographic £18
Plain back cards have a much lesser value

Lesbian interest £20+

Erotica
Photographic £20+
Art £6
Comic Sketches £6

Bedroom Scenes
Art/Photographic £4

Miss Europe Competition
RP studies of contestants £3

Nude glamour by Penot £15

1960s Glamour model £4

Riding high, Harrison Fisher at £10

Saucy sofa by Ribas £10

Well drawn, Art nouveau glamour £20

Artist Mela Koehler, Winter-fashion £50

French glamour published by Tuck £10

GREETINGS

Greetings Cards in one form or another provided the bulk of the Edwardian publishers' output. Birthday and Christmas cards of all types were produced in their millions, while the better Embossed cards remain as superb examples of the printer's art. Coin and Stamp Cards were published in long series, although these have never been too popular in today's market. Other themes have been grouped together to make this heading.

Market Report
This category tends to suffer from an over supply of mundane material but which can hide hidden gems. Worth a rummage as prices are low for the quality of some of the cards here.

COIN CARDS

National Coinage

Embossed	£8
Printed	£5

Banknote Cards

Embossed	£8
Printed	£5

DATE CARDS

Turn of the Century/Postally used

Sent 31.12.99/Received 1.1.00	£30

Year Dates/Up to 1903

Embossed	£10
Printed	£3

Year Dates/1904 onwards

Embossed	£6
Printed	£4

Calendar Cards £4

Valentine greeting comic, £5

EMBOSSED

Grade A	£12
Grade B	£5
Grade C	£1

These are as difficult to describe as they are to illustrate! At the top of the range are the superb chromo-litho cards of ornate design, in the middle are the great bulk of nice Embossed, while below these come the common, run of the mill types.

FANTASY

Enlarged Objects	£4
Erotic	£12
Faces in Smoke etc.	£4
Fantasy Maps	£15
Multi-Babies	£2-£4

Fantasy Heads

Coloured	£18
Black & White	£8

Faces in Mountains

Pub. Killinger	£12
Later issues	£4

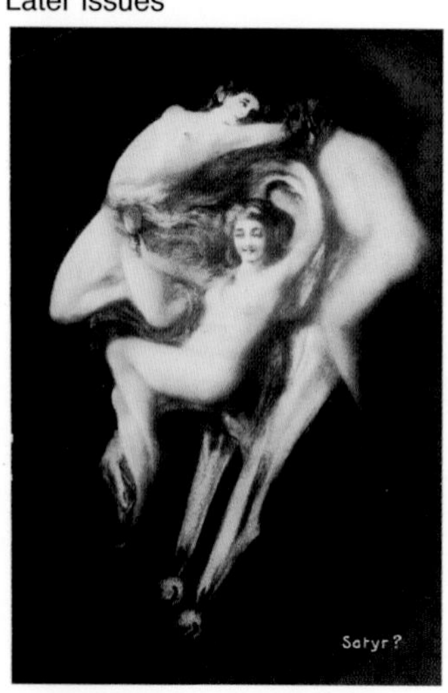

Fantasy head, black & white of Satyr £8

Father Christmas greeting Tuck oilette £6

FATHER CHRISTMAS

Hold to Light type	£75
WWI Silk type	£25
Tuck Oilette	£6
Coloured	£5
Photo type	£2
Snowmen	£3

Early embossed

Red robes	£12
Other Coloured Robes	£15

Prices are for good full-length or full-face Santas. Small designs or those with Santa forming part of a larger picture are worth less.

LANGUAGE

Deaf and Dumb Alphabet	£5
Language of Fruit	£2
Language of Stamps	£2
Language of Vegetables	£2

Esperanto

Tuck R. & Sons/Oilette series	£8
Miscellaneous issues	£3/£5

Language of Flowers

Welch J & Sons	£1.50
Miscellaneous issues	£1.50

RECREATIONAL

Casinos	£1.50
Playing Cards	£8
Roulette Wheel Cards	£2

Romance

Cupid's Darts/Welch J. & Sons	£1.50
Proverbs/Welch J. & Sons	£1.50
Miscellaneous Comic Types	£1.50
Greetings/Sentimental/Lovers	£1

LARGE LETTER

Names of People	£2
Names of Places	£2
Numbers	£2

Cherubs

Tuck R. & Sons	£12
Other series Embossed	£8
Printed	£4

Initials

Colour embossed	£8
Coloured	£4
B/W & Sepia	£2

Large Letter, £2

Easter Greeting, £1

SEASONAL GREETINGS

Christmas	£1-3
Decoration Day	£6
Easter	£1
Halloween	£8+
Independence Day	£4
New Year	£1
Poisson d'Avril	£1
St. Patrick's Day	£3
Thanksgiving Day	£3
Valentine's Day	£5

These are prices representing the average card found in any section, but the spectacu lar item will fetch considerably more.

Birthday

Deckle-edge c.1930	.50
Miscellaneous	£1-£4

STAMP CARDS

Embossed	£8
Printed	£5

Certain countries, realise a considerable premium.

MISCELLANEOUS

Champagne Bottles	£5
Davis Message Cards	£2
Fireworks	£6
Flowers	£1-£8
Fruit	£1-£8
Hands Across the Sea	£1.50
Moonlight	£1
Mottos/Sayings	£1
Rough Seas	£1
Swastikas/Greetings type	£1

Faith, Hope and Charity

Set 3	£5
Single cards	£1.50

Silhouettes

Camp Silhouette Series/ 25 cards/Photochrom Co.	£4
Cut-out types	£6
Printed types	£2
Children	£3-£10

Smoking

Cigarette Card Comics	£20
Cigarettes/Pipes/Tobacco	£4

Miscellaneous Greetings

Better cards/Pre-1914	£3-£6
General Types	£1

With the lower value Greetings cards, Christmas and Birthday etc., anything Embossed, or printed Chromo-Litho, or carrying an unusual design, would certainly be worth more.

Silhouette style greeting £8

Birthday greeting £2

HERALDIC

Originally far more popular than they are now, Heraldic cards of all kinds were published in profusion by the Edwardians. Perhaps the sense of identity with a particular town or city was stronger then than it is now, certainly this would account for the enormous numbers of cards left to us.

Market Report
Not much wanted but the topographical element will help to sell the better designs. Maps are still popular.

FULL OUT CRESTS

Faulkner C.W. & Co. £3

Ja-Ja- Heraldic Series
Stoddart & Co. £2

School/University Arms
Robert Peel Postcard Co £1.50

Reliable Series
W. Ritchie & Sons £1.50

Multi-crest cards £1

Special Crests
Sports/Occupations £1.50

Miscellaneous Publishers
Better cards/Pre-1914 £2
General issues £1

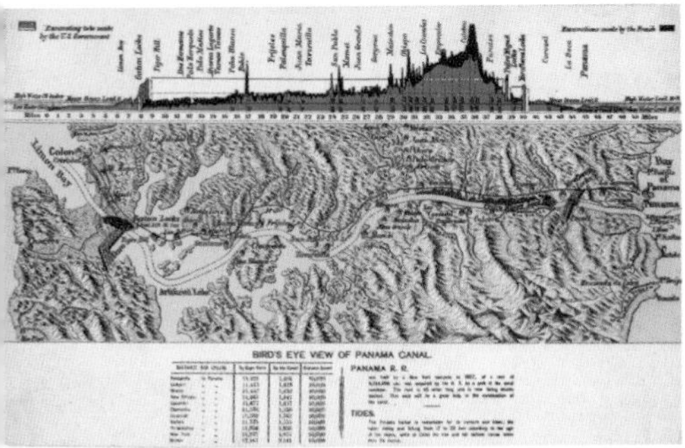

Map showing the Panama Canal, Embossed £10

CRESTS WITH VIEWS

B & R's Camera Series
Brown & Rawcliffe £1.50

Faulkner C.W. & Co.
Cathedrals/Stately Homes £1.50

Favourite Series
W.E. Byers £1

F.S.O. Heraldic Series £2

Ja-Ja- Heraldic Series
Stoddart & Co. £3

Jarrold's Series £1

Robert Peel Postcard Co. £1.50

Reliable Series
W. Ritchie & Sons £1

Tuck R. & Sons
Heraldic Series £12
Heraldic View £2

Valentine's Series £1

Miscellaneous Publishers £1

MISCELLANEOUS

Papal Series
Ferloni L. £5

FLAGS/NATIONAL ARMS

Aristophot Flag Series £1.50

E.F.A. Series
Excelsior Fine Art £1.50

Faulkner C.W. & Co.
Early series £6

Arms of the Nations
Kohl/Tuck R. & Sons £12

Flags of the Nations
Valentine & Sons £4

Miscellaneous Publishers
Embossed/Chromo-Litho £8
Printed/Coloured £1.50

TARTANS

B.B.
Tartan View Series £1

Brown & Rawcliffe
Arms, Views & Tartans £1
B & R's Camera Series £1

Cynicus Co. £1

Johnston W. & A.K.
Tartan & Arms Series £3

Stoddart & Co./Ja-Ja
Clan Tartan Heraldic Series £3

Tuck R. & Sons
Scottish Clans Series £3

Valentine & Sons
Tartan Series £1.50
Valentine's Series £1

Wildt & Kray
Badge & Tartan £2

Miscellaneous types £1

MAP CARDS

Early Chromo /Embossed £6/ £25
Mountain Charts £1.50
Romantic/Comic types £2

Walker John & Co.
Geographical Series £8

LITERARY/MUSIC

Judging from the diverse range and numbers remaining, cards of Literary and Musical interest would appear to have been quite popular in the pre-television days of our forebears. A good subject to collect, reflecting as it does, a wide spread of artistic endeavour.

Market Report
Not much activity in this sector. Various types of musical instruments on cards will sell and autographed musicians are worth looking out for.

Wrench series comic illustration of Rudyard Kipling's book 'The Days Work' £5

DICKENS

Cassell & Co./Barnard F.
Character Sketches from Dickens £4

Chapman & Hall
Dickens Novels/Set 13 £6

Faulkner & Co.
Pickwick Series/244 £4

Hildesheimer/Manning E.F.
Dickens Characters £4

Jones A.V.N./Reynolds F.
Dickens Characters £5

Stewart & Woolf/Crowquill A.
Dickens Characters/3 sets £4

Tuck R. & Sons
Early Numbered Series £12
Dickens Postcard Series/Kyd £12
Dombey and Son/
Set 6/Oilette 6050 £3
Nicholas Nickleby/
Set 6/Oilette 6052 £3
With Famous Authors & Painters £4
In Dickens' Land/Oilettes £2
Dickens Characters £4

Valentine
Dickens Characters £4

Portraits/Sites/Events £1.50

MISCELLANEOUS

Alice in Wonderland
Nixon K./Set 6/
Faulkner & Co./Series 1819 £12
Tenniel/Set 8/
Fuller & Richard £12
Folkard C./Set 6/
A&C Black/Series 80 £12

Literary Personalities
Early Chromos £8
Later Portraits £1.50

Lorna Doone
Scenes from Lorna Doone/
Set 12/Photochrom Co. £1.50
Characters from Lorna Doone/
Valentine £1.50

Poetry
Patience Strong cards £1
Verses/Miscellaneous £1

Sherlock Holmes £15

SHAKESPEARE

Ackermann/Munich
Silhouettes/Set 12 £5

Faulkner & Co.
Shakespeare Series £5

Hildesheimer/Carter S.
Sketches from Shakespeare £4

Nister E.
Scenes from Shakespeare/ub £8
Later series/Divided back £2

Tuck R. & Sons
Early Numbered Series £12
Hamlet/Set 12/Copping H. £5
Merry Wives of Windsor/
Series 466-477 £5
In Shakespeare's Country/Oilettes £2

Valentine
Characters from Shakespeare £2

Portraits/Sites/Events £1

BANDS

Brass Bands	£6
Dance Bands	£10
Military Bands	£6
Pipe Bands	£5
Dagenham Girl Pipers	£3
Champion Bandsmen	£4
Band Leaders	£5

OPERA

Gilbert & Sullivan

Savoy Co.	£12
Other Publishers	£8

Breitkoff & Hartel/Set 60

Wagner Series	£12

Faulkner & Co./Series 1401

Wagners Operas/Set 12	£15

Meissner & Buch

Wagner series	£18

Ricordi

Chromo-litho ub/Japanese style	£18
Madame Butterfly	£18
Tosca	£18

Tuck R. & Sons

Wagner series	£18

Opera Houses £5

Opera Singers

Butt Clara	£5
Caruso Enrico	£20
Chaliapin	£20
Farrar Geraldine	£8
Melba Dame Nellie	£10
Patti Adeline	£10
Tetrazzini	£10
Other Singers	£6

POP STARS

Beatles	£7-£15
Others 1950's/70's	£3-£8+
Modern	.50
Elvis	£9

Actor and singer Sammy Davis Jnr £5

Opera singer Sandraz £6

SONG CARDS

BAMFORTH

Set 3	£4.50
Set 4	£6

Prices are for complete sets

Odd cards	£1.50

OTHER TYPES

Miscellaneous Types	£1

Tuck R. & Sons

Illustrated Songs Series	£1.50

MISCELLANEOUS

Bandstands	£5
Bells	£1.50
Bellringers	£8
Hymns	£1
Musical Instruments	£3
Advertised by musicians	£6
Musicians	£3
Orchestras	£6
Singers	£3

Composers

Art Studies	£3
Photographic	£4

Gramophones

Art/Photographic	£8
Comic types	£5

Jazz

Bands/Groups	£12
Instrumentalists/Singers	£12

Organs

Church	£2
Cinema/Theatre	£5

Song Cards/Musical Notation

Embossed	£5
Printed	£1.50

MILITARY

The Military conflicts of history from the Boer War to the present day have always been covered by the picture postcard. In a variety of styles ranging from actual battle scenes to the personalities, patriotic and propaganda issues of the period, the postcard was not slow to reflect current tastes and national sentiment. The many issues relating to the First World War form the largest catalogue.*For Political Cartoons in all sections please see POLITICAL classification.*

Market Report The Centenary of the First World War has stimulated demand. Regimental historians and the family history lobby are all actively seeking relevant material. Humour and patriotic themes are in demand. Artist drawn material is suffering a bit though with Harry Payne out of favour at the moment.

SPANISH AMERICAN WAR 1898

Miscellaneous types	£25

BOER WAR 1899-1902

Jamestown Raid	£40
St. Helena/Camps etc.	£25
War Photographs	£15
Sites & Events/Historic	£5

City Press

C.I.V./bw Vignettes	£15

Collectors Publishing Co.

Personalities/Photographic	£15

Koumans P.J.

Personalities/Photographic	£15

Picture Postcard Co.

War Sketches/Caton Woodville etc.	£20
Personalities/Vignettes	£20

Tuck R. & Sons

Peace Card/Coloured Vignette	£25
Souvenir of 1900	£25
Empire Series/Art Sketches/bw	£18
Overprinted for Victories	£30

Other Publishers

Early Vignettes/Coloured	£18
Early Vignettes/bw	£15

Early Boer War comic Vignettes £15

BOXER REBELLION 1900-1901

The Boxer Rebellion was an uprising by members of the Chinese Society of Right and Harmonious Fists against foreign influence in areas such as trade, politics, religion and technology. The campaigns took place from November 1899 to 7 September 1901, during the final years of Manchu rule in China under the Qing Dynasty.
The members of the Society of Right and Harmonious Fists were simply called "Boxers" by the Westerners due to the martial arts and callisthenics they practised.

War Photographs	£30
Caricature	£40-45
Publishers include Eysler, Bruno Burger, Kunzli freres	
Troops, ships and railways	£25
Publishers include Franz Scholz, E.Lee, Brun et cie (Expedition de Chine).	
Notable artist Willy Stower (ships)	
Villages,towns,forts etc	£15
publishers as below, Max Wolff.	

RUSSO-JAPANESE WAR 1904-1905

Military Review 1906

With Kobe Handstamp	£10
With Tokyo Handstamp	£8
Without Handstamp	£6

Japanese troops 1904, £10

Japanese Official
Post Office 1904 issue £8
Photo montage/Art borders £8-£12
Communications Dept/Post War issue £5

Peace Conference
Knight Bros./Multi-view £8
Miscellaneous issues £5

Russian Outrage on Hull Fleet
Real Photographic £5
Valentines/Other Publishers £3

Tuck R. & Sons
Real Photographic Series 5170 £8
Russo-Japanese Series 1330 £8
Russo-Japanese War Photographs/
Set 6/Silverette 6534 £8
The Russo-Japanese War/
Set 6/Oilette 6484 £6

WarPhotographs/Sketches
Hildesheimer/War Series 5224 £6

Other Publishers £5

ITALIAN-TURKISH WAR 1911-1912

War Photographs
Traldi/Milan £12
Miscellaneous issues £8

CHINESE CIVIL WAR 1911-1917

War Photographs £20
Art Studies £15

BALKAN WARS 1912-1913

War Photographs £12

WORLD WAR 1 1914-1918

FUND RAISING CARDS
Anglo-Russian Hospital Fund £5
Asiles de Soldats Invalides Belges £2
Belgian Relief Funds £3
Bovril/Lord Roberts £5
British Ambulance Committee £5
British Committee of the
French Red Cross £3
British Gifts for Belgian Soldiers £3
National Egg Fund £5
National Fund for Welsh Troops £3
National Institute for the Blind £2
National Relief Fund £3
Performer Tobacco Fund £6
Red Cross £4
War Bond Campaign/Set 12 £3
Y.M.C.A. Hut Fund £5

YMCA Hut £5

National War Bond Tank
Trafalgar Square £6
In G.B. locations £18

War Bond Campaign Postcard
Trafalgar Square £5
In G.B. locations £15

Weekly Dispatch Tobacco Fund
`Arf a Mo' Kaiser/Thomas B. £5

War Loan/Patriotic Designs
France £5
Germany £6
Italy £5
Russia £8

NAVAL ACTIONS
Bombardment of Britain 1914 £12

Scapa Flow
German Fleet/Sinking etc. £9

Zeebrugge
WW1 Actions/Interest £1

OFFICIAL STATIONERY/ FIELD SERVICE CARDS
Great Britain £2
France £2
Germany £3
Other Countries £3

British Ambulance shattered by shell-fir
at the French (Verdun) front.

WW1 Ambulance £5

SAY GOOD-NIGHT, DADDY, NOT GOOD-BYE!
Dis-moi bonne nuit, papa, et pas adieu!

Patriotic Greeting by Nash £4

PATRIOTIC

Admirals of the British Navy
Francis Dod £3

Britain Prepared Series
24 cards/Photochrom Co. £3

Butterfly Girls
Published Geligne/Marotte £6

Generals of the British Army
Francis Dodd £3

Heroes of the War
Cuneo, Cyrus £10

Leurs Caboches/Nos Allies/Nos Poilus
Dupuis Emile £5

Les Femmes Heroiques
Dupuis Emile £4

Out for Victory
Hill L. Raven- £5

Series 1021
Vivien Mansell £5

The Allies Series
James Henderson £4

United Six Series
Inter-Art Co. £4

Types
Bulldogs £10
Comic £4-£12
Flags £5
Poems £2
Royalty £3

Miscellaneous Types
Great Britain £3
France £3
Germany £6
Other Countries £3

PERIOD SENTIMENT
Great Britain £2
France £1.50
Germany £2
Other Countries £2

PERSONALITIES

France £2
Other Countries £3

Germany
Generals/RP Portraits £8
Art Studies £5
Other Generals/Leaders £3

Great Britain
Kitchener Memorial Card £3
Other Generals/Leaders £2

PRISONERS OF WAR
Allied in German Camps
Art sketches £10
Photographic £5

German in Allied Camps
Photographic £8
Isle of Man £60

WELFARE ORGANISATIONS
Church Army £3
Salvation Army £3
St. Dunstans £3
Y.M.C.A. £3

Red Cross
There are many cards issued by Red Cross Organisations dealing with aspects of WW1 in their respective countries,
A guide to price may be inferred by reference to similar themes in the WW1 section and a premium added for the presence of the Red Cross symbol. We would suggest £5 as a basic price.

WAR PHOTOGRAPHS
Chicago Daily News £4
E.L.D/N.D. etc. £4
Hildesheimer & Co. £4
Imperial War Museum £2
In the Balkans/E.L.D. £3
L.V. Cie £3
Official Photograph/Censored at GHQ £3
Photochrom Co.

Hun prisoners help wounded Frenchmen Daily Mail series, £2

Bw series	£4
On Active Service/Set 48	£3
Sketch The	£4
Sphere The	£4
French Edition	£4
Sport & General Press Agency	£3
Tit-Bits	£3
War Photogravure Publications	£3
The War Series	£3
World War Series	£3
Yes or No	£3
Special Cards	£5

Daily Mail Battle Pictures

Numbers 1 - 96	£2
Numbers 97-144	£2.50
Numbers 145-160/Anzac Series	£6
Numbers 161-176	£4

This famous series was published in 22 sets of 8 cards each.

Real Photographic series	£6

Daily Mirror

Canadian Official Series/RP	£6
Coloured	£3
Sepia	£3

Newspaper Illustrations	£3
Black & White series	£3
Coloured series	£3
Sepia series	£3
Shell damage Series	£1

Regent Publishing Co.

The War Series	£3

Tuck R. & Sons

At the Front	£4
The European War 1914	£3
Types of Allied Armies	£4

Miscellaneous

Great Britain	£3
France	£3
Germany	£5
Other Countries	£5

MISCELLANEOUS WORLD WAR 1

Allied Occupation/Germany 1919	£4
Armoured Cars	£6
Campaign Maps	£5
Cemeteries/Memorials	£1.50
Conscientious Objectors	£20
German proclamations issued in French towns	£4
Greetings Cards/Regimental	£6
Mesopotamia Campaign	£4
Palestine Campaign	£8
Recruiting Parades/Departures	£25
Refugees in G.B.	£25
Salonika Campaign	£3
Shell Damage/Foreign	£1
Tanks	£6

Christmas Cards

From POW Camps	£8
Miscellaneous	£3

Dardanelles Campaign

Gallipoli/Anzac Cove/Suvla Bay etc.

Troops/Action	£12
RP Landscapes	£6

Dogs

Major Richardson's War Dogs	£8
Red Cross War Dogs	£8

Victory Parades

GB	£1.50
Paris 1919	£1.50

War Wounded

Brighton	£10
Miscellaneous	£4

Women on War Work

For the Cause/Tuck R. & Sons	£8
La Femme et La Guerre/Leroy	£8
Our Own Girls/Arthur Butchur	£8
Photographic scenes	£8-£25

Military barber shop, £3

RUSSIAN CIVIL WAR 1917-1921

Allied Expeditionary Forces £15
Red Propaganda £18
White Russian Propaganda £20
Miscellaneous Issues £10

GRAECO-TURKISH WAR 1919-1923

War Photographs
Smyrna £15
Miscellaneous issues £8

SPANISH CIVIL WAR 1936-1939

Gen. Franco £15
Republican Propaganda £20
War Photographs £20
Military Personalities £15

ITALIAN-ABYSSINIAN WAR 1938

War Photographs £12
Coloured Cartoons £20

Regimental badge £6

MILITARY ART

Gale & Polden
History & Traditions £8
History & Traditions/Rates of Pay £18
Regimental Badges £6
Miscellaneous Coloured £6

Knight Bros. £3

Lavauzelle C./Paris
Early Vignettes £8

Valentine
The Kings Army £3

Italian Regimental
Chromo-Litho £12
Sepia/Black & White £4

Early Tuck vignette £20

Miscellaneous Art/Coloured
Early Vignettes £12-£40
Later Issues £3

Photographic Studies
Coloured £3
Black & White £1.50

Tuck R. & Sons
Oilette Series
3100 Cavalry on Active Service/ Harry Payne £15
3105 Our Fighting Regiments/ The RoyalArtillery/Harry Payne £10
3113 Comrades/ Harry Payne £20
3159 The US Army on the Western Front /Harry Payne £20
3160 Colonial Badges and their Wearers/ Harry Payne £12
3163 Our Fighting Regiments/ 1st LifeGuards/Harry Payne £12
3165 Our Fighting Regiments/ 1st Dragoon Guards/Harry Payne £12
3204 Badges and their Wearers/ Harry Payne £65
3205 Badges and their Wearers/ Harry Payne £65
3546 Military in London/ Harry Payne £5
3642 Scots Pipers/ Harry Payne £6
6412 Military in London/ Harry Payne £4
8491 Badges and their Wearers/ Harry Payne £45
8625 The Scots Guards/ Harry Payne £10
8635 The 21st Lancers/ Harry Payne £10
8637 17th Lancers/ Harry Payne £12
8731 Our Territorials/ Harry Payne £10
8732 Wake up England/ Harry Payne £12
8738 Types of the British Army £25

8761 Defenders of the Empire/ Harry Payne	£10
8762 The Red Cross Series/ Harry Payne	£30
8763 The Royal Horse Artillery/ Harry Payne	£10
8770 Regimental Bands/ Harry Payne	£5
8807 16th Lancers/ Harry Payne	£12
8831 1st Royal Dragoons/ Harry Payne	£12
8835 1st Life Guards/ Harry Payne	£12
8848 11th Hussars/ Harry Payne	£12
8871 Badges and their Wearers/ Harry Payne	£12
8890 6th Dragoon Guards/ Harry Payne	£10
9081 Military in London II/ Harry Payne	£5
9132 Deeds of British Heroism	£8
9134 British Battles	£8
9139 Military Life & Military Tournaments/ Harry Payne	£5
9478 The British Army	£5
9527 Life at Aldershot/ Harry Payne	£12
9587 Military in London III/ Harry Payne	£5
9762 Scotch Pipers/ Harry Payne	£8
9883 Queens Own Cameron Highlanders/ Harry Payne	£10
9884 Gordon Highlanders/ Harry Payne	£10
9885 Seaforth Highlanders/ Harry Payne	£10
9934 For Home and Empire/ Harry Payne	£12
9937 Argyll and Sutherland Highlanders/ Harry Payne	£10
9980 Royal Scots Greys/ Harry Payne	£10
9993 Coldstream Guards/ Harry Payne	£10
9994 Black Watch/ Harry Payne	£10

Tuck R. & Sons

Military in London/Oilettes	£2
Unsigned Oilettes	£3

MISCELLANEOUS

Artillery	£2
Battlefields/Historic	£1.50
Battle of Waterloo	£1
Beefeaters	£1

Field camp at Shoreham £8

Joan of Arc	£2
Napoleon	£3

Army Camps

Field Camps/Named	£8
Field Camps/Un-named	£3
Hut Camps/Named	£5
Hut Camps/Un-named	£2
Barracks	£5

British in India

Military Life/Sites etc.	£4

Italian Regimental

Menus/Patriotic/Seals etc.	£4
Chromo-Litho designs	£12

Life in the Army

Gale & Polden	£3
Star Series	£1.50
Miscellaneous photographs	£3

Medals

Present Day War Ribbons/Rees H.	£4
V.C. Winners/Various issues	£10
Daring Deeds	£3

Military Tattoos/Displays

Aldershot	£1.50
Royal Tournament	£1.50
Miscellaneous Events	£1.50

Uniforms/Dress

Mrs. Albert Broom series/Guardsmen	£8
Regimental photographs	£3
Identified	£3
Unidentified	£1.50

Unknown Warrior

Cenotaph Services/Parades	£2

There are many photographic cards depicting aspects of pre-war Military Life in different countries, including Troops on exercise, Parades,Training etc. One may use a guide price of around £3 for such cards,bearing in mind that some will be worth more, some less.

Crown war photograph £4

WAR PHOTOGRAPHS/SKETCHES
Crown

War Office Photographs	£4

Photochrom Co.

Britain Prepared	£4

Salmon

Aviation sketches/A.F.D. Bannister	£5

The Times

"with the army" series (set 23)	**£5**

Valentine

Real Photograph series/Aviation	£2
Aircraft Recognition silhouettes	£2

WORLD WAR 2 - 1939-1945

OFFICIAL STATIONERY/FIELD SERVICE CARDS

Germany	£3
U.S.A.	£3
Other Countries	£2

PATRIOTIC

Great Britain	£8
France	£5
Germany	£12
Netherlands	£5
U.S.A.	£8

PERSONALITIES

France	£4
Germany	£10
U.S.A.	£4
Gen. Eisenhower	£5
Franklin D. Roosevelt	£5
Other Countries	£4

Great Britain

Churchill	£4/£8
Gen. Montgomery	£5
Other Leaders	£3-£6

BEWARE!
YOU ARE WARNED NOT TO TALK!
BUT THAT DOESN'T MEAN YOU CAN'T
WRITE !!
SO
WHAT ABOUT IT ?

Hitler comic by Tempest using the careless talk warning as a joke £10

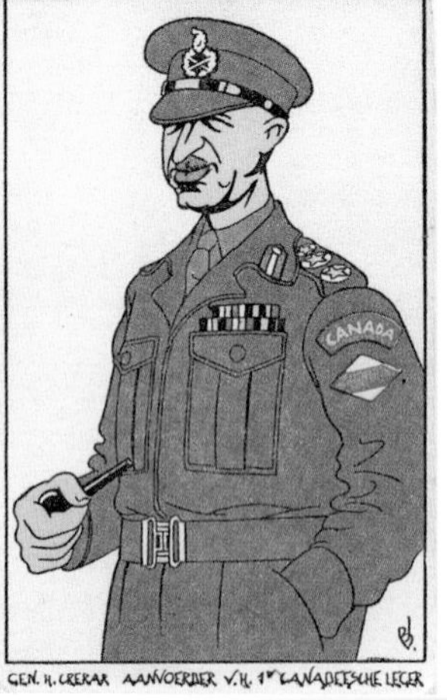

Cartoon of WW2 Canadian General H. Crerar £10

MISCELLANEOUS WORLD WAR 2

Prisoners of War	£10
Tanks/Guns/Vehicles	£5
V2 Rocket on display	£8
With The W.A.A.F./Set 24	£3
Sepia photos/Tuck R. & Sons	£20
Women on War Work	£12

Comic Sketches

Bizeth/Sets of 6/Price per set	£36
Dutch Troops	£4
U.S.A.Troops	£4
Maneken-Pis	£3
Tuck R. & Sons	£4

Germany

Erich Gutjahr Series	£8

Wehrmachte Panzer in action £6

This is an extensive numbered series of superb RP studies of the German Army in WW2.

Wehmacht-Bildserie,	*£6*

Germany/6x4 size

Generals/RP Portraits	£12
Patriotic Posters	£12
Hitler/Portraits	£12
Luftwaffe propaganda	£10

Posted from Canada 1941, £8

Peace Celebrations

Amsterdam Victory Parade 1945	
6x4 size	£5
VE Day	£6
VJ Day	£6

Red Cross

As with WW1 there were many cards issued by Red Cross Organisations in WW2 dealing with aspects of war in their respective countries,A guide to price may be inferred by reference to similar themes in the WW2 section and a premium added for the presence of the Red Cross symbol. We would suggest £5 as a basic price.

Shell Damage

London Blitz	£4
London under fire Photochrom.co.	£5
Foreign	£1.50

USA

Troops/Action	£5
Pre-war Camp Life	£3

Indian troops in France £6

There are many photographic cards, particularly those issued by Germany, France and Belgium depicting different aspects of World War 2, including Troops in Action, At Rest, Anti-Aircraft emplacements, Ammunition Transport, Convoys, Gun Crews, Machine Gun Nests,Vehicles etc. One may use a guide price of around £5 for such cards, bearing in mind that some will be worth more, some less

King George VI in France, on his visit to B.E.F. £6

NAVAL

A vast and complex section where we will attempt to give some idea of the types of Warships in HM's service.
Publishers produced large quantities of cards relating to capital ships where crews often numbered 1000-1200+. These are common and so priced. Other R/P's of named ships in exotic ports and harbours are of more interest and priced according to location.

Market Report:
There is a steady demand for WW1 battleships although material is plentiful Campaigns and exotic foreign locations help lift values considerably.

HMS Norfolk, County-class heavy cruiser launched in 1928 £4

HMS Courageous converted into an Aircraft Carrier in 1928. Sunk by U-Boat in September 1939 making this card £12

Pretty ladies? Entertainment on board £6

BATTLESHIPS/CRUISERS

Tuck R. & Sons	
Empire Series	£20
Oilette Series	£3/5
Artist drawn	£3/5

Foreign Types

Early Vignettes	£15
Visit of US Fleet to Melbourne	
1908 / Embossed / Inset Ship	£18
Japanese Official/Inset Ship	£10/15
Pre - 1939	£3/10
1939 Onwards	£3/5

LIFE IN THE NAVY

Social Real Photo	£5-£12
Gale & Polden	£2/4
Nelson Victory Cards	£2/5

Miscellaneous

Shotley Barracks/HMS Ganges	£4
Ships moored off-shore	£4
Other Barracks etc.	£4
Wooden Walls (Training Ships)	£4-10
Fleet Reviews/Displays	£3
Naval Engagements/Sketches	£6/£8
Personalities	£2
Sailor's Photographs etc.	£2
Graf Spee sinking set of 12	£6

HMS Thames Mother of the submarine £7.50

The Imperial British Navy

Battleships	£3-£6
Dreadnought Cruisers	£4
Battlecruisers	£3/5
Cruisers	£4
Aircraft Carriers	£5-£15
Sea Plane Carriers	£6-10
Flotilla Leaders	£3/4
Destroyers	£3/4
Torpedo Boat Destroyers	£4
Submarines	£4-10
Sloops	£5-6
Mine Layers	£5
Mine Sweepers	£5
Depot Ships	£4-£6
Repair Ships	£5
Hospital Ships	£10-30
Surveying Ships	£5
Yachts.	£3/6

Small Craft & Auxiliaries

River Gunboats	£8+
Monitors	£6+
Patrol Boats	£5
Motor Torpedo Boats	£3-£8
1939-1950 R/Ps	£2/5

Hospital ship, HMS China £10

HMS Royal Oak, Revenge-class Battleship £5

OTHERS INCLUDE

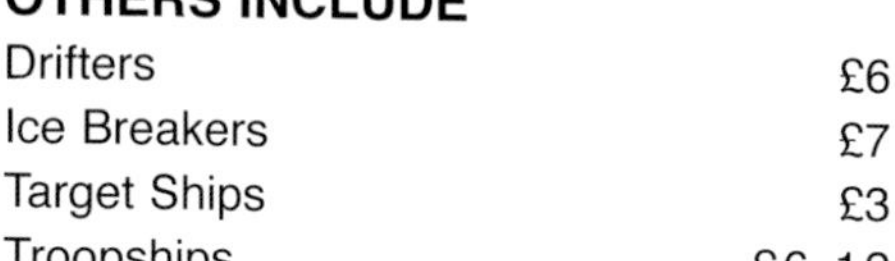

Drifters	£6
Ice Breakers	£7
Target Ships	£3
Troopships	£6-12
Tugs	£3

HMS Argamemnon, Battleship, £5

Troopship, HMT Dorsetshire £8

HMS Effingham, Hawkins-class heavy cruiser £4

Battleship "Rodney" R/P £4

Flotilla Leader "Keith" - Sunk 1940 R/P £5

Battlecruiser "Hood" R/P £5

Destroyer "Ambuscade" R/P £3

Cruiser "Gloucester" R/P £4

Submarine "E9" R/P £6

Aircraft Carrier "Hermes" R/P £5

Sloop "Dwarf" R/P £5

Minesweeper "Harebell" R/P £5

Depot Ship "Titania" R/P £5

Monitor and Destroyers R/P £8

Repair Ship "Assistance" R/P £4

Patrol boat "P.40" R/P £4

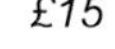

Hospital Ship "St.George" R/P £15

Motor Torpedo Boat R/P £4

Surveying Ship "Flinders" R/P £4

NOVELTY

Today, as in the past, a strong collecting area, where the original publishers vied with each other to produce the exotic and unusual cards which now make up this category. Novelty cards are those which do something, or have things attached to them, or which deviate in any way from the norm.

Market Report

Traditionally a popular introduction to the hobby, this section is regarded with something akin to horror by most dealers but which is due for a revival. Stamp montage and novelty santas and some pull-outs with named locations are about all that's moving at present.

APPLIQUED MATERIALS

Dried Flowers	£2
Feathered Birds	£6
Feathered Hats	£5
Glass Eyes	£4
Glitter Cards	£1.50
Jewellery	£3
Lace	£6
Matchbox Strikers	£12
Material	£2
Metal Models	£8
Mirror Cards	£2
Photo Inserts	£1.50
Real Hair	£8
Sand Pictures	£4
Seeds	£2

COMPOSITE SETS

Animals/Set 3/5	£30/£50
G.P. Government Tea/Set 6	£120
Jeanne d'Arc/Set 10/12	£75
Jesus Christ/Set 10/12	£75
Nansen/Set 4	£400
Napoleon/Set 10/12	£75
Samurai Warriors/Set 8/10/12	£96/£120/£144

Albert Memorial/Set 15

F.G.O. Stuart	£60

Map of London/Set 6

Tuck R. & Sons/Series 9352	£75

HOLD TO LIGHT

Exhibitions	£15
Father Christmas	£85
Flames	£18
Gruss Aus type	£10
Greetings/Churches etc.	£6
G.B. Views/W.H. Berlin	£4
Large Letter/Date cards	£15
Better Designs	£15

MATERIALS

Aluminium	£3
Celluloid	£3
Leather	£2
Panel Cards	£1
Peat	£2
Rice Paper/Oolong Tea	£8
Wood	£2

MECHANICAL

Blow Up	£18
Heat-activated	£4
Invisible Picture	£5
Kaleidoscopes	£20
Lever Change	£5
Moveable Hats	£4
Paper Chains	£10
Perfumed	£4
Push-Out Models	£15
Reversible Bottle/Sand etc.	£8
Squeakers	£2
Venetian Blinds	£5
Wagging Tails	£2

Cut-out Models

Tuck R. & Sons	£45+
Mack W.E./Henderson J.	£40
Star Series/Animals	£15
Later issues/Salmon J	£10

Bathing Mecha[…] Fold ou[…] card by artist E[…] rare to in good conditi[…] £12-£1[…]

Applique felt material £2

Gramophone Records

Ettlinger	£4
Tuck R. & Sons	£4
Other Publishers	£4

Jigsaw Puzzles

Tuck R. & Sons	£20
Other publishers	£12

Roller Blinds

Early type	£18
Later issues	£3

Rotating Wheels

Early type	£10-£20
Later issues	£2

Stand-up Models

Exhibition types	£50

Whitstable crab pull-out £3

PULL OUTS

Animals	£3
Artist/signed	£5
Beer Bottles	£5
Buses	£4
Cats	£4
Comic	£3
Dogs	£4
Father Xmas	£6
Fortune Telling	£6
Hop-Picking	£6
Irish Subjects	£2
Mail Vans	£4
Military	£5
Motor Cars	£5
Postmen	£5
Railway Tickets named	£5
Shamrocks	£2
Teddy Bears	£9
Town views/multi-view fronts	£3
Trams	£6
Welsh Ladies	£2

SIZES

Folded	£3
Giant	£5
Midget	£3
Panorama	£5

Book Marks

Art type	£3
Actors/Actresses	£2
Egyptian Scenes	£1.50
Other types	£2

TRANSPARENCIES

Angels/Greetings	£6
Continental subjects	£10
Exhibitions	£15
Father Christmas	£12
GB Views/Hartmann	£8
GB Views	£3
Meteor	£10
Puzzle Type	£5

MISCELLANEOUS

Bas Relief	£3
Puzzle Cards	£4
Stamp Montage	£6

Shapes

Circular/Leaf etc.	£6

Three Dimensional

Pre-1914/With eye-piece	£6
Modern/Nudes etc.	£1

POLITICAL

This section covers a wide collecting field, reflecting perhaps a greater awareness of current affairs at the time. This is a major collecting area, covering Wars, Political satire and Social events, Campaigns and Strikes, etc. For more on this subject see our Military Section.

Market Report
Irish political, Masonic, anti-Kaiser and comic cards generally are popular. Prices for Suffragette material continue to be extremely volatile.

Boer War Transvaal series No.8 £15

CARTOONS/WAR

BOER WAR 1899-1902

Antiquariat Bremen	£18
Bruno Burger	£18
Friedello	£18
Kunzli Freres/Thiele A	£25
Regel & Krug	£18
Ropke & Woortman	£18
Vlieger J.G.	£18
Zieher Ottmar/Thiele A	£20
Leaders/Personalities	£15

BOXER REBELLION 1900-1901

Bruno Burger	£25
Kunzli Freres	£25

RUSSO-JAPANESE WAR 1904-1905

Hildesheimer/Hardy D	£15
P.L. Paris/Muller E.	£15
M.M. Paris	£1

WORLD WAR I/1914-1918

Great Britain

The Hun/E. Sachetti/ Set 6/Geo. Pulman & Sons.	£8
Davidson Bros./Ludovici A.	£5
Jarrold & Sons/Punch Cartoons	£3
Tuck R. & Sons/Aesop's Fables Set 6/Oilette 8484	£8
Miscellaneous Publishers	£4

France

Les Monstres des Cathedrales	£6
Miscellaneous Publishers	£4

Germany £6

Italy

Sculpture Montage types	£5
Miscellaneous Publishers	£5

Edith Cavell

Corbella T.	£10
Mourning Cards	£6
Portraits	£3
Grave	£2

See also Silk Cards

Other Types

Human Butterflies/WWI Leaders	£10
Raemaekers, L	£4

OTHER CAMPAIGNS

Alsace Lorraine

Hansi	£15
Miscellaneous Cartoons	£5

Bulgaria 1903 £12

CARTOONS/SOCIAL

GREAT BRITAIN

Anti-Semitic	£20
National Insurance Acts	£5
Shops Act	£4
Worker's Compensation Acts	£5

Fiscal

Tuck R. & Sons/Game Birds	£8
Bradshaw P.V.	£8
Premier Series-The Fiscal policy	£8
Fiscal Series 217 Stewart & Woolf	£10

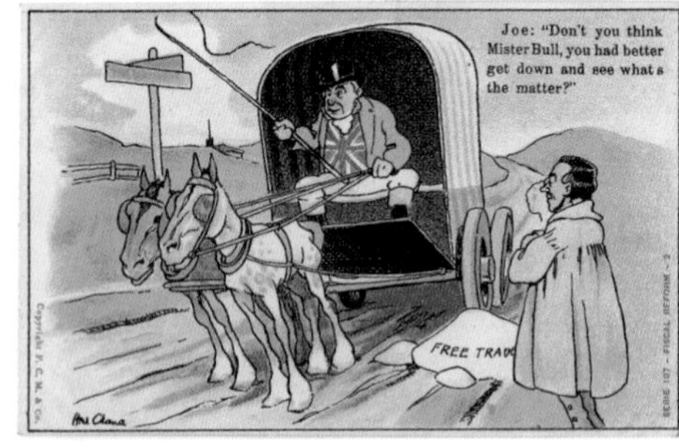

Series 107 Fiscal Reform Card No.2 £8

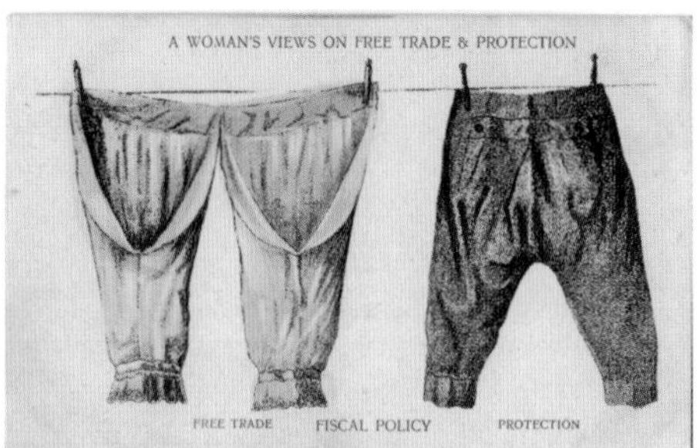

Woman's view of Free Trade, £5

Masonic

Are You a Mason?	
24 cards/Millar & Lang	£15

Tariff Reform

Free Trade/Family in Kitchen	£1
Other Types	£8

Other types

Westminster Cartoon Series	£6
Davidson Bros/Ludovici A.	£5
Faulkner & Co./Moreland A.	£6
Morning Leader Series	£6
Walker J. & Co./Furniss H.	£6
Wrench E./Punch Cartoons 1901	£8
Miscellaneous Publishers	£5

FRANCE

Anti-Royalty/KE VII Debauchery	£10
Russia/Czar Nicholas etc.	£18

Orens D./le Burin Satirique

& other Limited Edition Series	£18

ITALY

Fascist Cartoons	£12
Mussolini/Portraits	£10
/Hanging	£8

DREYFUS AFFAIR

Miscellaneous issues	£8

ELECTIONS

Candidates	£8
Canvassing Cards	£8
Poll Declarations	£10

IRISH HOME RULE

ULSTER CAMPAIGN

Sir Edward Carson/Portraits	£15
Meetings/U.V.F.	£25
Political Cartoons	£15/ £25

EIRE CAMPAIGN

Easter Rising 1916	£15-£30
Gun Running	£100
Leaders	£35+
Mourning Cards	£30
Troubles 1920	£25

CORNELIUS COLBERT
(Who took a prominent part in the Rebellion),
Executed May 8th, 1916.

Irish rebellion leader £35

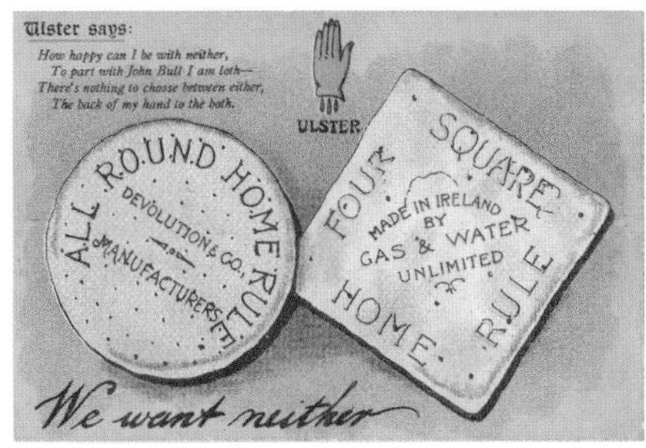

Home Rule cartoon £20

POLITICAL EVENTS

Meetings/Treaties	£6
Mourning Cards	£6
Funerals	£6

Visits

Czar Nicholas to France 1896	£25
Miscellaneous visits	£6

WW2 Nazi party £20

WORLD WAR 2/1939-1945 (ALLIES)

All my own work by Grimes	£4
Anti-Nazi (Hitler Photo type)	£15
Bamforth Comic series	£5
ITMA comic	£5
Our Modern Army Reg Carter	£8
Military Photo propaganda	£6
Miscellaneous Cartoons	£4/8
Patriotic	£8
U.S. Armed forces	£4
'What a war' by G.Wilkinson	£4
War-office Photo propaganda	£6

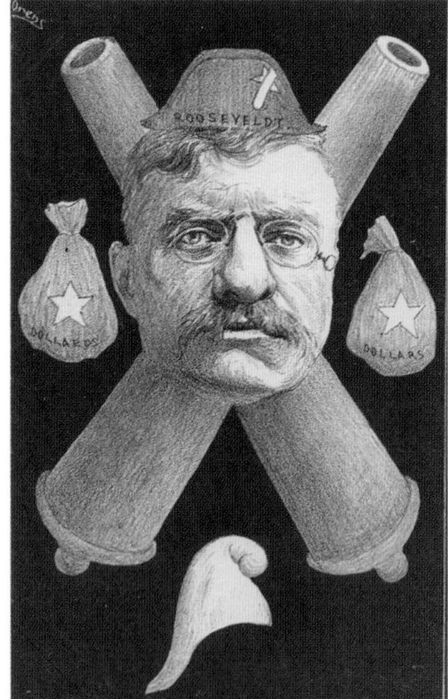

Political caricature by Denizard Orens £18

NATIONAL SOCIALIST PARTY

Nationalist Socialist Party	£15-£25
Hitler portraits	£12-15
Other portraits	£10
Mosley period	£20

PERSONALITIES

Tuck R. & Sons/Empire Series	£20
Sir Winston Churchill	£6/15
Lloyd George	£8
Prime Ministers	£3/6
Cabinet Ministers	£3
Governor Generals	£3
M.P.'s Memorial Cards	£6
Foreign Personalities	£2 / £8
De Gaulle	£6
J.F.Kennedy	£8
Martin L King	£8-£12

Faulkner C.W./Series 41

British Statesmen	£15

Great Britain

Early Vignettes	£15
Portraits/Art	£3
Portraits/Photographic	£2
House of Commons/Lords	£1.50

US President £5

UK P.M. £4

Spy Cartoon £8

P.M. Asquith £5

Votes for Women comic £35

Churchill £12

SUFFRAGETTE CAMPAIGN

Events/Demonstrations	£85
Leaders/Portraits	£70
Publicity Cards	£70
Misc. comic Non cartoon	£20

Cartoons

Davey Geo/Suffragette Series	£30
Valentine & Sons	£30
Nat Union of Women's Suffrage Soc.	£45
Artist's Suffrage League	£45
Other Publishers/comic	£25

FIRE! FIRE!! FIRE!!!

Great Salvage Sale.

Bargains in

WOMEN

Come early and have your choice.

LOT 1.—Splendid assortment of Fat Cooks, would suit a copper. Once round their waists, twice round the Gasworks.

LOT 2.—Several good old Gin Tasters, slightly imperfect.

LOT 3.—Cheap line of Old Maids, (we don't think) who have never known the meaning of a good night's kiss Samples on approval.

LOT 4.—A few Suffragettes just arrived from Pentonville.

LOT 5.—A good collection of Tarts, Old Sports, Relics, Pursuers and some who never but wished they had, none over 99, Some with wooden legs, can speak 5 Languages, 7 when they have been indulging, would suit a cabman.

All goods delivered tree, packed in Sawdust.

All goods must be paid for at time of purchase, as we expect the Brokers by the end of the week.

Love, Cupid & Co., Ltd.

Paradise Court, Love Lane, N.S.

Copyright.

Politically incorrect comic poster card which mentions 'Suffragettes just arrived from Pentonville' and 'good collection of tarts'. £20

National Insurance Act £5

Iron workers strike Frodingham, Lincolnshire, April 1909 £50

STRIKES/MARCHES/UNREST

Seathwaite Navvy Riot 1904	£40
Leicester March to London 1905	£25
Belfast Strike 1907	£25+
Laxey Miner's Strike 1907	£50
Winchester Riots 1908	£40
South Wales Coal Strike 1910	£40
Liverpool Strike 1910/11	
Carbonara Co.	£20
W. & Co.	£20
Cardiff Strike 1911	£30+
Llanelly Strike/Riots 1911	£35+
Thirlwell Strike 1911	£50
Ilkeston Strike 1912	
Coal Picking Scenes	£75
Sydney Street Siege 1911	£8
Smethwick 1913	£50
Tonypandy Riots 1913	£40
General Strike 1926	£25
London Dock Strike	£30-£45
Worcester Railway Strike	£50
Strikes/Demonstrations/Meetings	£15-£60

When we're socialists cartoon £6

Womens Suffrage cartoon £45

RAILWAYS

As the dominant mode of transport in the Edwardian years, this subject was very well covered by the publishers of the time. The Railway Companies themselves led the way with a great number of sets and series extolling the virtue of travel on their own particular lines, and here the less common cards, or those from the smaller Companies, are highly sought after. As well as the correspondence cards listed here, many ordinary set cards were overprinted for advertising use. These command a premium of no more than a couple of pounds.

Market report.

In all categories of railway cards the best and rarest cards continue to sell. Prices of the cheaper, more common cards have fallen as many collections bulky in this material have appeared on the market. Many dealers need to cut their asking prices to more realistic levels to get stocks rolling and to entice the next generation of collectors.

OFFICIAL CARDS

A term used to describe postcards issued/sold by railway companies to gain revenue and to promote all aspects of their business. Subjects depicted include hotels, ships and buses.

PRE-1923 COMPANIES

BARRY

Paddle Steamers £10
Barry Island/coloured view £30
Barry Docks/correspondence £40

BELFAST AND COUNTY DOWN

Slieve Donard Hotel/Jotter £10
Hotels/black & white £12

BIDEFORD, WESTWARD HO AND APPLEDORE

Views/Trains £25

CALEDONIAN

Engines/Rolling Stock

Sepia £4
Coloured £5

Hotels

General views £5
Interiors/Black & White £6
Interiors/coloured £8
Poster Adverts £15

Views

Coloured (Valentines) £4+
Coloured (other) £6
Black & White £10
Tartan Border £8
Caledonian Steamers £10+
Clyde views £5+
Early Multi-view/vignette Pic both sides £15
Green or Brown artwork/1903 £30+

Poster Adverts

Shipping (coloured) £30
Other types £100+

CALEDONIAN AND LNWR

West Coast Joint Stock/Coloured £8
Sleeping Car/Reservation card £40

Royal Mail Route

Coloured £15
Black & White £15

CALLANDER & OBAN

Ballachulish Hotel £10
Sepia views (from booklet) each £10+
Complete booklet £80+

CAMBRIAN

Views £6
Holiday Advertising/Correspondence £12
Maps £22
Vignette/PicturePostcard Co. £25

CAMPBELTOWN & MACHRIHANISH

Poster Advert 3 versions £100+

CENTRAL LONDON

Celesque Series £8
Maps/Rolling Stock £20
1911 Strike £50
Poster Adverts £40

Exhibitions

Pillar Box Pullout £35
Blow Card £75

CHESHIRE LINES

Views/Correspondence £30

CORK BANDON & SOUTH COAST

Views/Oilettes £4

CORK BLACKROCK & PASSAGE

Paddle Steamer `Audrey' £40

CORRIS

Views

Corris Railway Series (photographic) £8
(printed) £12
As above but Georges £5

DISTRICT RAILWAY

Vignettes

Court size(Pictorial Postcard Syndicate) £40
Intermediate(Pictorial Postcard Company)£35

DUBLIN & SOUTH EASTERN

Hotel/Jotter £10
Views/Correspondence £30

DUBLIN, WICKLOW & WEXFORD

Peacock Series/Correspondence £35
Views/Undivided Back £35

DUMBARTON & BALLOCH JOINT LINES
Views
Sepia £6+
Coloured £12

EAST COAST ROUTE
Flying Scotsman/Hildesheimer £4
Views/Rolling Stock/Stations £12
Vignette(Write Away) £10

FESTINIOG
Views(Photochrom) £8
Views(Valentines) £10
Poster Adverts £90

FRESHWATER YARMOUTH & NEWPORT
Vignette(Picture Postcard Co.) £40

FURNESS
Engines & Rolling Stock/Series 18-19 £6
G. Romney Art/Series 12-13 £24
Exhibitions £45
Poster Adverts/Series 21 £90
Views
Furness Abbey/Series 14-15 £1
McCorquodale £2
Tuck/Series 1-7 £2
Tuck/Series 8 £2
Furness Abbey Hotel/Series 16-17 £4
HHH Series £20
Sankey/Tours through Lakeland £30
Vignettes/McCorquodale £45

Steamers
Lake Steamers/Series 9-11 £5
Barrow & Fleetwood Steamers/Ser. 20 £15

GLASGOW & SOUTH WESTERN
Poster Adverts £75
Steamers
McCorquodale £3
Other publishers £10
Hotels
General views & multi-view £4
Tuck/Chromo-litho £10
Views
Oilettes £5
Vignettes (crest on front) £20

GREAT CENTRAL
Immingham Docks £4
Hotels £6
Engines/Rolling Stock £18
Restaurant Car £15
Poster Adverts £65
Perforated Engine Card/
Central Advertising Co. £90
Shipping
Overprints on other company cards £20
Printed £14
Photographic £16
Turner C.E. £12
Steam Ship Department £40
Tuck £30
Views
Faulkner Series 545 & 546 £8
as / panel cards £4
HHH Series £20
Vignettes/Picture Postcard Co. £30

GREAT EASTERN
Stations./Trains £6
Hotels £7
Underground Railway Maps of London £6
Southwold Bus £15
Poster Adverts £100
Views
Crest on Picture/Oilettes £3
Crest on Picture/bw £4
Shipping
Black & White £8
Coloured £10
Black & White/Correspondence £12
Correspondence
General types £25
Jarrold £35
Oilette type £25
Vignettes
Greetings from Harwich £12
Tuck cathedrals £75
Cathedrals
Faulkner/Series 118 £60
Faulkner with crest £75

GREAT NORTH OF SCOTLAND
Views/Porter £25
Cruden Bay Golf Tournament £80
(Named players) £100
Hotels
Palace Hotel Series £15
Multi-view £25
Multi-view/Pictures both sides £30

GREAT NORTHERN
Hotels £6
Correspondence £25
Panoramic/Skegness & Sheringham £30
Poster Adverts £90
Engines
Photochrom £2
Locomotive Publishing Co. £5
Views
Photochrom/Coloured £3
Black & White £30

Vignettes

London views/Picture Postcard Co.	£25
Coloured	£40
Intermediate/Picture Postcard Co.	£35

GREAT NORTHERN & CITY

Views/bw Poster style	£35
Map	£50

GREAT NORTHERN/IRELAND

Correspondence	£15
Views/Overprint on picture	£25
Hotels/Multi-view	£18
Milroy Bay Motor Bus	£40

GREAT NORTHERN PICCADILLY & BROMPTON

Railway scenes	£10
Map	£25

GREAT SOUTHERN/IRELAND

Hotels	£6

GREAT SOUTHERN & WESTERN/ IRELAND

Views/Oilettes	£4
Joint with MGW/Wembley 1924	£25
Parknasilla Hotel/Motor Bus/ Stage Coach Tours	£15
Poster Adverts/Parknasilla/	£70

Hotels

Jotter	£6
Lawrence/Correspondence	£12
Hotels in the Kingdom of Kerry	£20

GREAT WESTERN

Docks Series	£10
Fishguard Harbour/Route	£8
Motor Bus/Slough	£12
Restaurant Car/En Route	£18
Maps/with GWR crest	£40

Engines

Series 6	£2
Others	£4

Shipping

Photographic	£5
Coloured	£12

Views

Coloured or Sepia	£4

Hotels

General types	£4
Vignette	£8

Correspondence

General	£20
Wyndhams	£18

Poster Adverts

General types	£50
Series 3	£90

Vignettes

Intermediate/Picture Postcard Co.	£25
/London views	£30
Court Size/London views	£30

HAMPSTEAD TUBE

Views

Last Link	£6
Multi-view/Map on reverse	£12

HIGHLAND

Map/Correspondence	£75

Hotels

Inverness	£5
Others	£10

Views

Black & white (circular crest)	£12
Straight line inscription	£15
Highland Railway photos	£40
Early coloured/Red circular crest	£40

HULL & BARNSLEY

Scenes at Alexandra Dock etc.	£35
Views	£35
Train	£40

INVERGARRY & FORT AUGUSTUS

Views (Highland Railway series)	£30

ISLE OF WIGHT

Vignettes/Picture Postcard Co.	£35

ISLE OF WIGHT CENTRAL

Vignettes/Picture Postcard Co.	£35
Views	£40

JOINT SOUTH WESTERN & BRIGHTON

Vignettes/Picture Postcard Co.	£35

KENT & EAST SUSSEX

Engines/Correspondence	£8
Views/1-6	£7
Other Correspondence cards	£35

LANCASHIRE & YORKSHIRE

Correspondence	£30
Vignettes/Picture Postcard Co.	£25

Engines/Rolling Stock

General issues	£3
Overprinted French	£6

Views

1905 &1907 series	£3
New series	£4
Overprinted French/All series	£5

Shipping

1907 series	£4
New series	£6
Overprinted French/All series	£7
Liverpool and Drogheda Steamers	£35

LIVERPOOL OVERHEAD
Dock views £25

LONDON, BRIGHTON & SOUTH COAST
Correspondence £40
Poster Adverts £90

Views
Waterlow/Series 1-6 £4

Vignettes
French vignettes/Red overprint £15
Picture Postcard Co. £25

LONDON, CHATHAM & DOVER
Vignettes/Court Size
Black/White £25
Coloured £35

LONDON & NORTH WESTERN
McCorquodale
Engines/Rolling Stock 50p-£2
Views 50p+
Hotels £4
Shipping £1-£1.50
Buses/Lorries etc. £10
/Horse drawn £5
Exhibitions £20
Poster Adverts £100
Maps/Correspondence £100

Tuck
Coloured/Royal Trains etc. £1
Engines/Rolling Stock £2
Views £2
Shipping £4
Hotels £4

St. Louis Exposition/Undivided back
Exhibits/Multi-view £6
Tuck/bw £10
Tuck/Coloured £15

LONDON & SOUTH WESTERN
Orphanage £4
View with crest/Correspondence £40

Shipping
Black/White £6
Coloured/Early £18

Poster Adverts
Southampton Hotel £45
Other Posters £80

Vignettes
Pictorial Postcard Syndicate £35
Intermediate/Picture Postcard Co. £22
London views/Picture Postcard Co. £22

LONDON UNDERGROUND ELECTRIC
Poster Adverts
W.H.S. £40
London Nooks and Corners £40
Other types £35

LONDONDERRY & LOUGH SWILLY
Map/Correspondence £60

LYNTON & BARNSTAPLE
Views/Stations/Trains £18

MARYPORT & CARLISLE
Map/Correspondence £90

MERSEY
Views/Stations/Lifts/Trains £12
Poster Advert £80

METROPOLITAN
Correspondence £12
Maps £12

VIEWS
Sepia/1-30 £5
Black/White £15

METROPOLITAN DISTRICT
Engines/Rolling Stock £5

MIDLAND
Engines £2
Rolling Stock £8
Midland Express/St. Pancras £5
Ships £6
Carriages £10
Exhibitions £18
Maps £20
Heysham Electric Train £25

Views
Photochrom £4
Nearest Station/Coloured £12

Hotels
General types £4
Vignettes/Coloured £6
/Travel & Entertainment £30
/BW & Sepia £18
Midland Grand Hotel/Business Lunch£90

Vignettes
Black/White £15
Coloured/Andrew Reid £20

Poster Adverts
General types £25
Series £75

MIDLAND & GREAT NORTHERN JOINT
Views/Correspondence £40

MIDLAND GREAT WESTERN
Hotels £6
Wembley Exhibition/Trade Stand £15

MIDLAND/NORTHERN COUNTIES COMMITTEE
Trains £12
Views/Correspondence £35

NEWPORT GODSHILL & ST.LAWRENCE
Vignette/Picture Postcard Co. £35

NORTH BRITISH

Ships/Coloured	£6
Ships/BW with crest	£12
Scottish Exhibition/Poster overprint	£40

Hotels

General types	£3
Poster Adverts	£8

Views

Coloured Caledonia series 129	50p
Black & White & Coloured (no crest)	£12
Black & White with crest	£10-£12
Sepia real photo(imprint on reverse)	£15

NORTH EASTERN

Hotels/ York & Newcastle	£2
Hotels/ Others	£5
Riverside Quay/Hull	£5
Newcastle Electric Trains	£6
Brussels Exhibition	£12
Steam Goods Lorry	£50

Views

Photo Panoramic/1-40	£25
/Maps below picture	£30

Poster Adverts

General types	£75
Industrial Poster Reproductions	£90

NORTH STAFFORDSHIRE

Correspondence	£15

Views

McCorquodale/W&K	£4
W&K and W&TG/White border	£7
Golf	£30
Glossy anon.	£15

PORTPATRICK & WIGTOWNSHIRE JOINT

Ships	£18
Views	£35

SNOWDON MOUNTAIN RAILWAY

General types	£4
Snowdon Series/1-90	£8
Maps	£40
Poster Adverts	£60

Court Cards

Advertising/Hotel & Railway	£65

SOMERSET & DORSET JOINT

Views/Correspondence	£60

SOUTH EASTERN AND CHATHAM

Views/McCorquodale	£3
Engines/Rolling Stock	£3
Stations/Trains	£4
Hotels	£6
Ships	£4
London-Paris/English or French	£12
Bologne views/Stevenard	£12
Exhibitions	£8
Views/Correspondence	£25
Maps	£22
Poster Adverts	£90

SOUTH EASTERN & CHATHAM & DOVER

Vignettes

London views/Picture Postcard Co. etc.	£20
Intermediate/Picture Postcard Co.	£25
Pictorial Postcard Syndicate	£35

STRATFORD-ON-AVON & MIDLAND JUNCTION

Poster Advert	£100

VALE OF RHEIDOL

Views/Advertising overprints	£15

WEST CLARE

Views	£25

WEST HIGHLAND

Views	£15

WESTON, CLEVEDON & PORTISHEAD LIGHT

Train	£35

WICK AND LYBSTER

Views/Highland Railway Series	£35

WIRRAL

Views/Correspondence	£60
Map/Correspondence	£80

POST 1923 COMPANIES

GREAT WESTERN

Engines	£3
Views	£4
Hotels	£4
KGV/Folded locomotive card	£75
Poster Adverts	£60

LONDON MIDLAND & SCOTTISH

Engines	£3
Hotels	£4
Ships	£6
Camping Coaches	£12
Views/Holiday tickets	£12
Container services/Removals	£35
Poster Adverts	£30

LONDON & NORTH EASTERN

Engines/Trains	£4
Hotels	£2+
Ships	£8
Views	£8
Camping Coaches	£10
Paddle Steamers	£6
Poster Adverts	£90

Northern Belle Cruise Train

Unused	£25
Used on Train with Cachet	£75

SOUTHERN

Engines/Trains	£3
Ships	£5
Poster Adverts/LBSCR	£90
Views	
Coloured/L. Richmond	£25
Correspondence	£35

POST 1947 (BRITISH RAILWAYS)

Hotels	£3
Ships	£3
Trains	£3
Gleneagles/Turnberry Golf Courses	£10
Seaspeed/Hovercraft	£1.50
Birmingham/New St. Station	£4
Correspondence	£4
Kyle of Lochalsh Station	£5
Poster Adverts	£15

NON-OFFICIAL CARDS

ACCIDENTS

Cudworth	£6
Grantham 1906	£4
Shrewsbury 1907	£6
Salisbury 1906	£6
Witham1905	£4
W. Gothard (In Memoriam type)	£15/£75
Miscellaneous	£10-£40

OVERSEAS RAILWAYS

Engines	£3
Rolling Stock	£3
Stations	£1.50+
Views	£3
Official Cards (crest or title)	£4
Japanese Official	£5

FRENCH POSTERS/OFFICIAL ISSUES

Orleans post-1920	£8
Artist signed	£12
Chemins de Fer de l'Ouest	£8
Chromo-litho/Undivided back	£25

FUNICULAR & CLIFF RAILWAYS/LIFTS

Lynton-Lynmouth	£2
Other UK	£5
Overseas	£3

LOCOMOTIVES

Oilettes	£1.50
OJ Morris	£2
E.Pouteau	£2
Locomotive PublishingCo. / F.Moore	£1.50
Real Photographic	£1.50
France/F. Fleury	£3
Other Artist Drawn cards	£2.50

MINIATURE RAILWAYS

Ravenglass & Eskdale	£5
Romney, Hythe & Dymchurch	£3
Volk's Electric Railway	£3
Other Railways	£7

MISCELLANEOUS

Animated Scenes	£10
Bridges/Tunnels/Viaducts	£4
Level Crossings	£20
Locomotive Works	£12
Locomotive Sheds	£6
Motor buses/ road vehicles	£20
Railway staff	£10+
Signal boxes	£20
Hospital trains	£1

Locomotive Publishing Co.

Vignettes/Coloured	£30
Vignettes/Monochrome	£25

MOUNTAIN RAILWAYS

Snowdon/Non-Official	£1.50
Overseas	£2

NARROW GAUGE

Vale of Rheidol	£3
Others	£6

RAILWAY STATIONS

Large City Stations

Interior	£8-£15
Exterior	£4-8
Others	
Interior Real Photo	£40+
Interior Printed	£25-£35
Exterior Real Photo	£20-£40
Exterior Printed	£12-£30

UNDERGROUND RAILWAYS

London Transport	£10
Interior Real Photo	£20
Interior Printed	£18
Exterior	£10-30
Station names comic series	£10
Foreign/U. Bahnes/Metros	£6-12

RAILWAY STATIONS

Railway station with train crash, close-up, real photo £60

Real photo interior, Highgate Station £40

Exterior of Clacton on Sea Station, printed £18

Exterior view, real photo £35

Shepherds Bush Tube Station, real photo £25

ROAD TRANSPORT

Many of these cards were the work of the town or village photographer and produced for the local topographical market and issued in limited numbers. There is an insatiable demand for unusual photographic studies, particularly where there is an added topographical element. which sometimes sets town collectors against transport collectors and this pushes the price up accordingly and is why they are so highly rated today.

It is pointed out that for all relevant entries e.g. Buses, Lorries,Traction Engines, Trams etc. the stated prices are for cards, either real photo or printed, fully identified and showing a 'Close-up at a named location' with real photographic cards generally being the most desirable. Unlocated cards and middle or far-distance views should be priced as topographical cards.

Market report.
Good quality close-up real photos of cars, buses, trams, military vehicles, ambulances etc. sell quickly to the serious collectors who understand the rarity of the material they are looking over. At the same time many transport collections have hit the market in recent years as collectors move on in one way or another and combined with the transparency offered by so much material being on the internet, prices for many of the more ordinary and printed cards have either flatlined or dropped. Again you need to price this material realistically to get it moving.

BUSES

STEAM	£40
Horse-drawn	
Real Photographic (close up)	£30/£50
Printed	£15
London horse-drawn/Coloured	£10
MOTOR BUSES	
Real Photographic	£40-£60
Printed	£20
CHARABANCS	
Whole Vehicle (identified location)	£10
Part Vehicle	£2
COACHES/SINGLE-DECK	£12/£20
TROLLEY BUSES	
Pre-1939	£25
1940 onwards	£12

There are in circulation many privately produced, postcard-size, plain back photographs of Buses and Trams.
Most of these have been printed in quantity from an existing negative and consequently have only a nominal value.

London Motor Bus No.24 to Hampstead £45

Real photo, motor lorry, *£50*

LORRIES

Petrol Tankers	£15-£30
Vans	£25
Coachbuilders' advertising cards/ RP studies of Lorries/Removal Vans	£8-£18
HORSE-DRAWN WAGONS AND CARTS	
Commercial R/P Close-up	£20-£45
Private R/P Close-up	£5-£15
STEAM	
Commercial	£40
Military	£25
MOTOR	
Lorry Fleets/Groups/RP	£50
Commercial	£30
Military	£25
ADVERT CARDS	
Poster type	£35
Adverts (other types)	£12
Adverts *(post 1960)*	*£6-8*

Where applicable, prices are for trade vehicles sign-written with company name and location.

Printed advertising card *£35*

Traction engine accident, this type crosses into social history and topographical and would sell at the top of the price range £60

Real photo view of motor cycle shop £25

MOTOR CYCLES

Close-up photo	£15-£25
Photo other	£8-£15
Printed	£20

Advert Cards

Poster Type (Colour)	£35
Other Adverts	£12

MOTOR RACING
MOTOR CYCLE RACING

See Sport Pages 158-163

TRACTION ENGINES

Showmans	£50
Commercial	£40-£50
Agricultural	£30
Military	£20
Steam Rollers	£30
Repair Gangs	£25
Accidents	£40-£60

There are in circulation many privately produced, postcard-size, plain back photographs of Fairground and Showman's engines.
Most of these have been printed in quantity from an existing negative and consequently have a nominal value of maybe £5

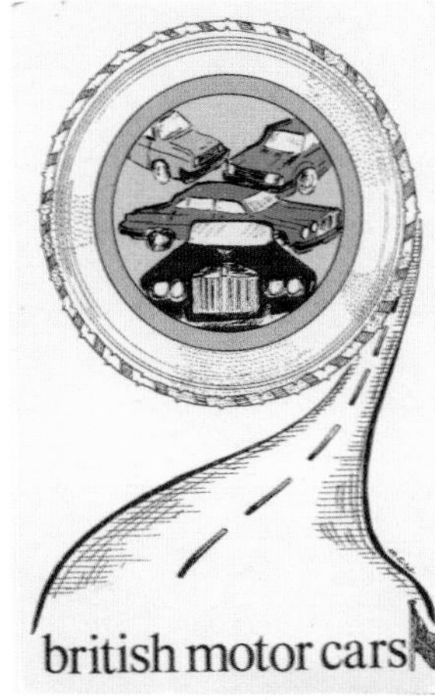

Left: Modern advert for the British motor industry £2

Early motor car and tricycle R/P £50

MOTOR CARS

(*If the Registration plate/No. can be read, this will enhance the value of the card, putting it towards the top end of the price band shown*)

Pre-1918	£10-£20
1918-1939	£10-£15
1940 onwards	£6-£12
Garages	£30-£45
Exhibitions/GB and Foreign	£6
Factories and Works/Interiors	£12
Celebrities of the Motoring World/ Set 6/Tuck Oilette 9017	£6

Advert cards

Poster Type	£35
Other Adverts/Pre-1939	£15
/1940 onwards	£5

OTHER TRANSPORT

AMBULANCES

Horse-drawn	£35
Motor	£25

ROYAL MAIL VANS £35

FIRE ENGINES

Close-up, real photo (motor, horse drawn & steam)	£20-£50

TRAMS

Steam Trams	£35
Electric Trams close-up	£35+
Horse-drawn Trams	£30+
Track-laying/Removal	£10-£30
Opening Ceremonies	£35
First Tram	£35

Real photo view of electric tram £35

Last Tram	£20
Commemorative Cards	£25
In Memoriam Cards	£15
Tram Graveyards Early	£35
Decorated Cars	£4
Depots	£35
Works Vehicles	£30
Douglas S.E. Tramway	£6

Real photo of Lewisham tram £30

Superb real photo view of a1950s garage, £45

ROYALTY

The British Royal Family, and the many European dynasties at the turn of the century, must have been looked upon as a commercial goldmine by Edwardian publishers. The vast numbers of cards handed down to us bears testimony to their popularity at the time, when all types of Royal personages and events both British and foreign were subject to volume output by the picture postcard industry. The same is true today, as interest in this field has continued unabated through the years.Yet the wide public interest in Royalty and their doings is not reflected in current price levels for historical picture postcards, for while the more unusual portraits and events will always sell, as will the many superb chromo-litho foreign commemorative issues, the bulk of the category consisting of the more common GB types has always proved difficult.

Market Report
British Royalty is suffering from a huge over supply of common material. If you can tiptoe through it there is a steady market for the better earlier commemoratives and minor royalty. In the foreign sections Thailand, Russia and Albania can command high prices and are worth looking out for.

GREAT BRITAIN

QUEEN VICTORIA

Diamond Jubilee 1897

p.u. 1897	£125
Unused	£65
Mourning Cards 1901	£15
Portraits	£8

KING EDWARD VII

Royal Tour 1901/`Ophir'

Wrench/Links of Empire/Set 20	
p.u. from Ports of Call	£30
Unposted	£15

Coronation of King George V *£3*

Tucks Empire series, Queen Victoria, £15

Tuck R. & Sons/Empire Series 1649	
p.u. from Ports of Call	£30
Unposted	£15

Coronation 1902

Tuck R. & Sons/Coronation Series/ Embossed	£10
Stewart & Woolf/Set 10	£10
H.Cassiers/London View Series	£8
Other Souvenir Cards	£6
Coronation Souvenir/bw	£4
Coronation Procession	£2

Visits to Paris 1903

Tuck R. & Sons/Set 10	£6
Voisey Chas./Set 15	£8

Death 1910

Mourning Cards	£2
Funeral Procession	£1

Visits

GB	£12
Foreign	£8
Portraits	£1.50

KING GEORGE V

Coronation 1911

Souvenir Cards	£3
Coronation Procession	£1
Delhi Durbar 1911	£3

Silver Jubilee 1935

Souvenir Cards	£3
Procession	£1

Death 1936

Mourning Cards	£3
Funeral Procession	£1.50

Visits

GB	£6-£12
Foreign	£6
Portraits	£1

KING EDWARD VIII

Investiture as Prince of Wales 1911	£3
Coronation Souvenir	£6
Wedding Souvenir	£35

King George V at RAF brigade inspection £10

With Mrs Simpson £40

KING EDWARD VIII (cont'd)

Visits

GB	£20
Foreign	£15
Portraits	£2

KING GEORGE VI

Coronation 1937

Souvenir Cards	£4
Coronation Procession	£2

Visit to France 1938 £10

Victory Celebrations 1945 £5

WW2 period patriotic card showing George VI with Queen Elizabeth, £4

Tuck 'Royal postcard' No.389 c.1901, £15

Mourning Cards 1952 £10

Visits

GB	£12
Foreign	£8
Portraits	£1.50

QUEEN ELIZABETH II

Marriage 1947

Souvenir Cards	£5
Betrothal Souvenir Cards	£3

Coronation 1953

Souvenir Cards	£2
Coronation Procession	£1

Prince of Wales Investiture 1969 £1.50

Silver Wedding 1972 £1

Silver Jubilee 1977 £1

Visits/Pre-1970

GB	£6
Foreign	£4
Portraits	£1/£4
Princess Diana	£1-£4
Prince Charles	£1-£2
Prince William	£1

MISCELLANEOUS EVENTS

Coronation Bonfires	£20
Proclamations	£10
Royal Gatherings	£2
Royal Weddings	£3

N.B. Portraits include family groups. Less photographed members of the Royal Family, e.g. Prince John, together with other examples of minor Royalty, would be worth around £1.50+.

SERIES

Kings & Queens of England

Tuck R. & Sons/Set 42

Price per card	£12
King Insurance Co.	£6
Faulkners Series	£8

OVERSEAS

It will be seen that an equivalent list to the foregoing could be produced for every country in the world which has had a Monarchy at any time since 1869! This remains a vast, uncharted field, where much research is yet to be done. I give below a general guide to price for the Commemorative Souvenir cards already known.

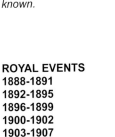

The Czar with Russian soldiers £20

ROYAL EVENTS

1888-1891	£50
1892-1895	£35
1896-1899	£25
1900-1902	£20
1903-1907	£15
1908-1914	£10
1915 onwards	£5

PORTRAITS

Balkans/Eastern Europe	£8-£12
Belgium/Spain	£3
Other Countries	£6-£10
Weddings	£6

Russia

Russian published cards	£25-£35
Continental Publishers	£20-£30
Cartoons	£25
British Publishers	£20-£25

THE ALEXANDRA AGENCY CO. H.M. QUEEN VICTORIA OF SPAIN. PHOTO W. S. STUART, RICHMOND.

Queen Victoria of Spain £3

Her Majesty Queen Elizabeth II

Queen Elizabeth II £2

Art of Hamburg-Sūdamerika Line

Here is a fine selection of artist-drawn cards from the same shipping company

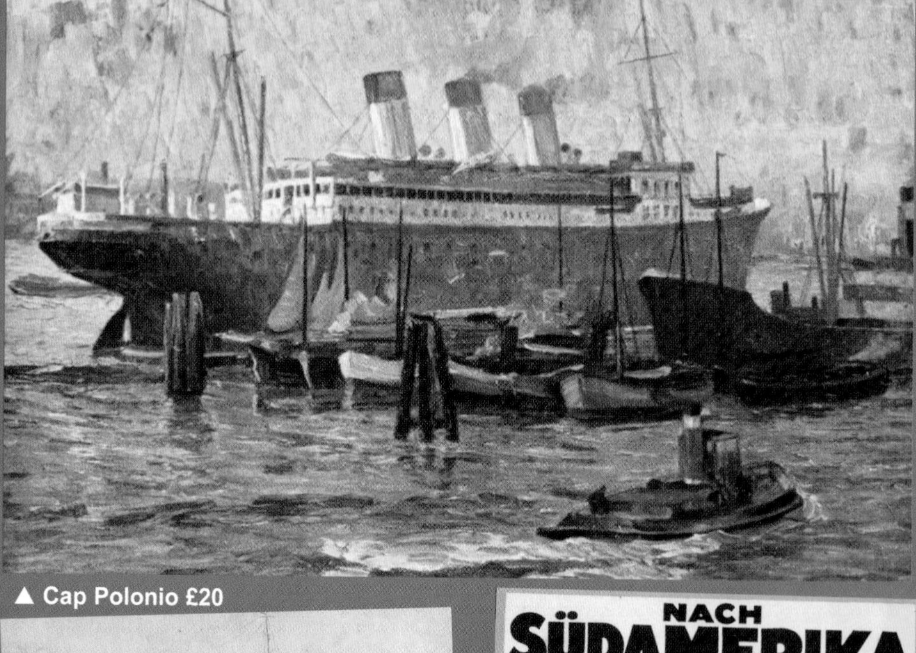

▲ Cap Polonio £20

NACH
SÜDAMERIKA
ATLANTISCHER OCEAN
STILLER OCEAN
NORD-
AMERIKA
VEREINIGTE STAATEN
SÜD-
AMERIKA
SAHARA
AFRIKA
CAP POLONIO
HAMBURG-SÜDAMERIKANISCHE
DAMPFSCHIFFFAHRTS-GESELLSCHAFT
HAMBURG 8 - HOLZBRÜCKE 8.
REGELMÄSSIGE ABFAHRTEN VON HAMBURG
über spanische und portugiesische Häfen nach Brasilien,
Uruguay und Argentinien
Anschluß nach Paraguay, Patagonien und Chile

▲ Poster advert Sud-Amerika line £25

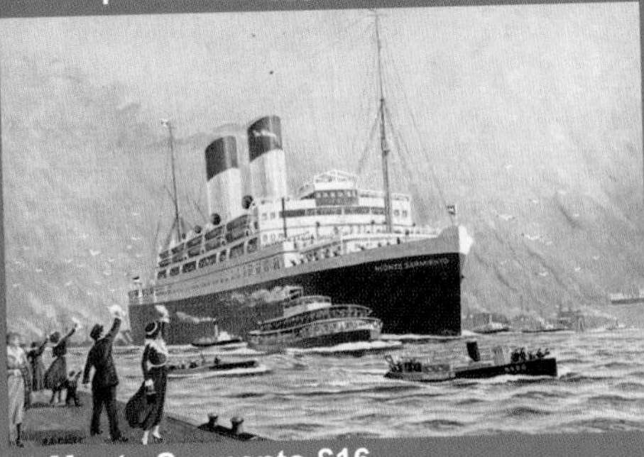

▲Monte Sarmento £16

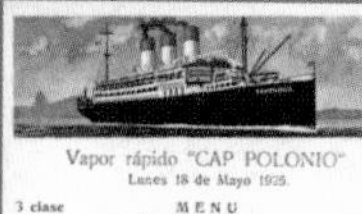

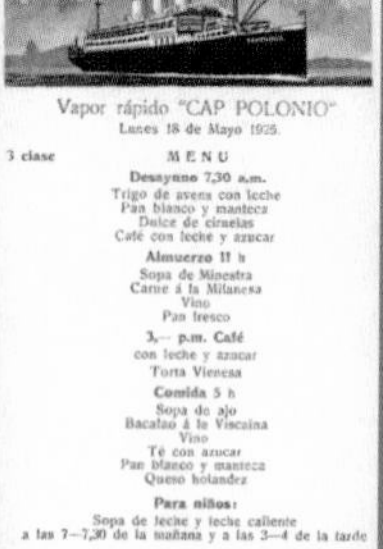

Vapor rápido "CAP POLONIO"
Lunes 18 de Mayo 1925.

3 clase

MENU

Desayuno 7,30 a.m.
Trigo de avena con leche
Pan blanco y manteca
Dulce de ciruelas
Café con leche y azucar

Almuerzo 11 h
Sopa de Minestra
Carne á la Milanesa
Vino
Pan fresco

3,— p.m. Café
con leche y azucar
Torta Vienesa

Comida 5 h
Sopa de ajo
Bacalao á la Viscaina
Vino
Té con azucar
Pan blanco y manteca
Queso holandez

Para niños:
Sopa de leche y leche caliente
a las 7—7,30 de la mañana y a las 3—4 de la tarde

▲ Menu card £20

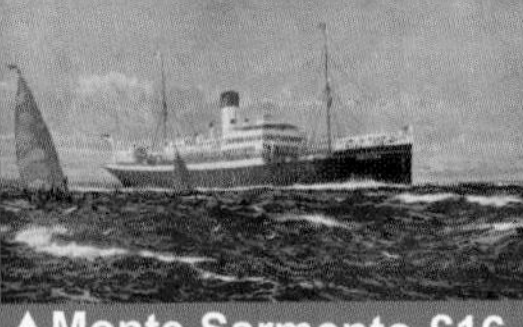

▲Monte Sarmento £16

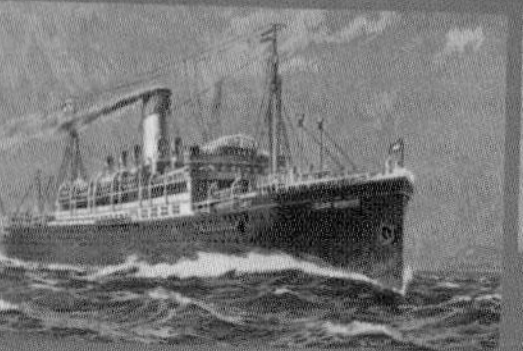

▲Cap Norte £20

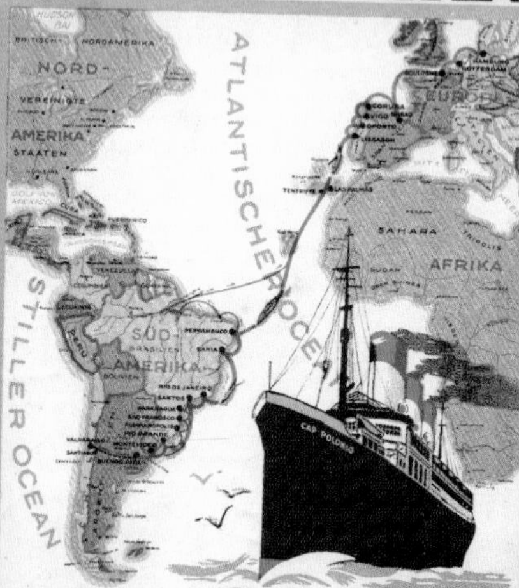

SHIPPING

A great number of cards were issued during the early years of the century, and indeed later, perhaps reflecting the dependence which an island nation placed upon the sea. Always a popular theme with collectors, there has been a steady supply of new cards issued on this subject, thanks largely to the many Shipping Companies, who continued publishing throughout the depressed inter-war years, when the flow of more general cards abated.

Market Report; There are an awful lot of remaindered cards on the market but this is a strong collecting subject with serious collectors prepared to pay good prices for unusual cards. Demand is stimulated by new collectors looking for certain artists, but photographic cards are on the up and the family history enthusiast is always looking for ships that have a family link.

This is a list of all the shipping Companies known to have published postcards of their ships and routes. This list is not complete, and probably never can be, and will be added to as more information becomes available.
To list each Company along with the types of postcards produced by each has therefore become impractical. It would become a catalogue in itself - remembering that there were thousands of shipping companies, that some had hundreds of vessels and that some ships had many postcard images published (of varying scarcity). The result is that it is only practicle to suggest general guide lines as to values in this catalogue. Some ships, like the "Titanic" and "Olympic", will always have more interest.
The popular artist-impression postcards are best viewed in Christopher Deakes's "A Postcard History of the Passenger Liner" which has short biographies of many artists. Values of postcard by specific artists are included in the main Artists Section of this Catalogue. Shipbuilding companies from around the world have also published postcards of ships that they have built and, in general these are not so easy to find.
The suggested values are as follows:

Canadian Pacific poster advert £30

Price guide: No star = low range, 1 star = Mid range & 2 star = Top of range

Chromolithographic advertising	**£25-£80**
Poster advertising	**£20-£60**
Japanese inset types	**£15**
Artist Impressions	**£5-£20**
Real photographs (officials)	**£6-£12**
Real photographs	**£4-£15**
Printed photographs (officials)	**£2-£10**
Printed photographs	**£1-£8**
Interiors (artist impressions)	**£5-£20**
Interiors (photographic)	**£3-£8**
Japanese ship-launch cards (post war)	**£5**

How the star system works-
No star, One star and two stars - with 2 stars being the higher value. The cards are presumed to be Pre-1939 and in good condition.
Readers should be aware that the rating will depend on the popularity, not necessarily the scarcity, of a company - many people will not have even known that some companies produced cards therefore they do not necessarily have a scarcity value - but good art cards, for example, could influence this. Obviously many cards will be much more common but within these companies there are likely to be ships worth more.

Price guide: No star = low range, 1 star = Mid range & 2 star = Top of range

THE ABERDEEN LINE T.S.S. "MILTIADES."
Managers GEO. THOMPSON & CO., Ltd.,
7, Billiter Square, London, E.C.

Aberdeen Line* Mid range, £12

*ABC Steamship Line (GB)**

Aberdeen & Commonwealth Line (GB)

*Aberdeen Direct Line (Rennie) (GB)*8*

*Aberdeen Line (GB)**

Aberdeen Steam Navigation Co (GB)

*Aberdeen, Newcastle & Hull (GB)**

*Adelaide Steamship (Australia)**

Adler Linie (Germany)

Admiral Line (USA)

*Adria Co (Austria/Italy)**

African Steamship Co (GB)

Afrikanische Frucht-Comapgnie (Germany)

Alaska Cruises Inc (USA)

Alaska Steam Ship Co (USA)

*Albion Steamship Co (GB)**

Alcoa Steamship Co (USA)

Alexandria Navigation Co (Egypt)

*Allan Line (Canada)**

American Banner Line (USA)

American Export Lines (USA)

American Hawaii Cruises (USA)

American Hawaiian Line (USA)

*American Line (USA)**

American Mail Lines (USA)

American Merchant Lines (USA)

American Pioneer Line (USA)

American President Lines (USA)

American South African Line (USA)

Amsterdam, Reederij, (Holland)

Anchor Line (GB)

Anchor-Donaldson Line (GB)

Anek Lines (Greece)

*Anglo-American Nile & Tourist Co (GB)**

*Anglo-Egyptian Mail Line (GB)**

A-O Lines (GB)

*Apcar Line (GB)***

*Argo Reederei (Germany)**

Arosa Line (Panama)

Athel Line (GB)

Atlantic Steam Navigation Co (GB)

*Atlantic Transport Lines (USA)**

Atlanttrafik, AB, (Sweden)

Austasia Line (GB)

*Australasian United Steam Navigation (AUSN) (GB)**

Australian Commonwealth Line (Australia)

Australian-Oriental Line (GB)

Australia-West Pacific Line (Norway)

Australind Steam Navigation Co (GB)

*Austrian Lloyd (Austria)***

Avenue Shipping (GB)

Aznar Line (Spain)

*Bailey & Leetham (GB)***

*Baltic American Line (Denmark)***

Baltic State Shipping Line (USSR)

Baltimore & Carolina Steamship Co (USA)

British India Steam Navigation Co* £10

Price guide: No star = low range, 1 star = Mid range & 2 star = Top of range

Baltimore Insular Lines (USA)

Baltimore Mail Line (USA)

*Baltimore Steam Packet (USA)_*

Bank Line (GB)

Barber Lines (Norway)

*Barry & Bristol Channel (GB)**

Batavier Line (Holland)

Bateaux ?Moulettes? (France)

Belfast Steamship Co (GB)

Belgian Fruit Lines (Belgium)

Belle Steamers (GB)

Ben Line (GB)

*Bennett Line (GB)***

Bergen Line (B&N Line) (Norway)

Bermuda Star Line (USA)

*Bibby Line (GB)**

Birkenhead Corporation Ferries (GB)

Black Ball Line (Canada)

Black Sea Steamship Line (USSR)

Black Star Line (Ghana)

*Bland Line (Gibraltar)**

*Blue Funnel Line (GB)***

*Blue Star Line (GB)**

*Bombay Steam Navigation Co (India)***

Booker Line (GB)

*Booth Line (GB)**

Bore Line (Finland)

Bornholm Line (Denmark)

British Rail GB

British Rail £3

Botel Cruises (Holland)

Bournemouth & South Coast SP Co (GB)

Bowater Steam Ship Co (GB)

Bristol Steam Navigation Co (GB)

British & African Steamship Co (GB)

British Columbia Ferries (Canada)

*British India Steam Navigation Co (GB)**

British Petroleum (BP) (GB)

British Tanker Co (GB)

Brodin Line (Sweden)

Broere NV, Gebr., (Holland)

Brostrom Shipping (Sweden)

Brugge-Sluis (Du)

Bruns, W., & Co (Germany)

*Bucknall Steamship Lines (GB)**

Bull Lines (USA)

Buries Markes Ltd (GB)

Burns Line (GB)

*Burns, Philp & Co (Australia)**

*Cairn Line (GB)**

Caledonian Steam Packet Co (GB)

Caltex (World)

Campbell, P&A., (GB)

Canada Steamship Lines (Canada)

Canadian Australasian Line (Can/NZ)

Canadian National Steamships (Canada)

Canadian Northern Steamship (Canada)

*Canadian Pacific Steamships (Canada/GB)**

Canguro Linee (Italy)

Cape Cod SS Co (USA)

Caribbean Cruise Lines (USA)

Carnival Cruise Lines (USA)

*Carron Line (GB)**

*Cassar Co (Malta)***

*Castle Line (GB)***

Cawston (GB)

Central Hudson Steamboat (USA)

Chandris Lines (Greece)

Price guide: No star = low range, 1 star = Mid range & 2 star = Top of range

Clyde shipping Co.* Chromo-litho advert £25

*Chemin de Fer du Congo Superior (Belgium)***

Chia. Nacional de Navegacao (Portugal)

*Chia. Nacional de Navegacao Costeira (Brazil)***

Chicago Duluth Transit Co (USA)

China Mail Steamship Co (USA)

*China Navigation Co (GB)**

Cia. Anonima Venezolana de Navegacion (Venezuela)

Cia. Argentina de Navegacion Dodero (Argentina)

Cia. Maritima Frutera (Spain)

*Cia. Transoceanica Argentina (Argentina)**

*Cia. Trasatlantica (Spain)**

*Cia. Trasmediterranea (Spain)**

Cie. Auxiliaire de Navigation (France)

Cie. de Affreteurs Reunis (France)

Cie. de Navigation Charles le Borgne (France)

Cie. de Navigation Fraissinet & Cyprien Fabre (France)

Cie. de Navigation Mixte (France)

Cie. de Navigation Paquet (France)

Cie. de Navigation Sud-Atlantique (France)

Cie. de Transports Maritimes de l?AOF (France)

Cie. des Chargeurs Reunis (France)

*Cie. des Messageries Maritimes (France)**

Cie. Fraissinet (France)

Cie. Generale Transatlantique (France)

Cie. Havraise de Navigation (France)

Cie. Havraise Peninsulaire (France)

*Cie. Maritime Belge du Congo (Belgium)**

Cie. Nationale de Navigation (France)

Cie. Nationale de Navigation de Grece (Greece)

Cities Service Tankers (USA)

*CITRA (Italy)**

*City Line (GB)**

City of Cork Steam Packet Co (GB)

*City of Dublin Steam Packet Co (GB)**

City Steamboat Co (GB)

Clan Line (GB)

*Clarke Steamship Co (Canada)**

Clarkson's Cruises (GB)

Cleveland & Buffalo Line (USA)

Clipper Line (Sweden)

*Clyde Line (USA)**

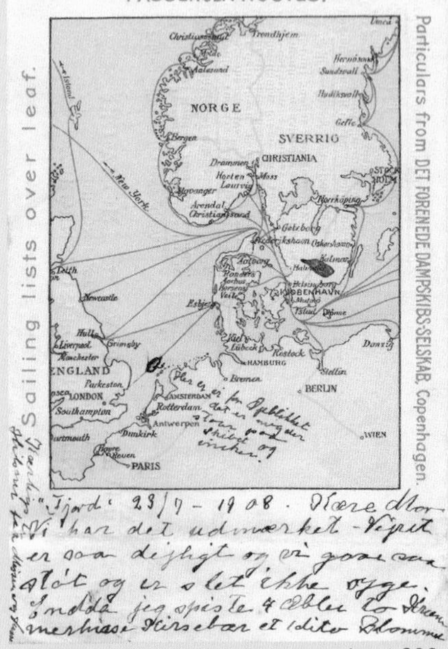

DFDS Lines map and poster advert £30

Cunard Line, Queen Elizabeth, £3

*Clyde Shipping Co (GB)**

Clyde-Mallory Line (USA)

Coast Lines (GB)

Cogedar Line (Italy)

*Colombian Line (USA)**

Colonial Navigation Co (USA)

*Colwyn Bay & Liverpool SS Co (GB)***

Common Brothers (GB)

Commonwealth & Dominion Line (GB)

Concordia Line (Norway)

Constantine Line (GB)

Cook's Tourist Steamers (GB)

Corsica Ferries (Italy)

Cory, William, & Son (GB)

Cosens & Co (GB)

Costa Line (Italy)

Crescent Shipping Lines (Pakistan)

Cunard Line (GB)

Cunard White Star (GB)

Currie Line (GB)

*Cusolich Line (Austria/Italy)**

*Dairen Kisen Kaisha (Japan)**

Dalen, Rederi, (Sweden)

Dansk-Statsbaner (DSB) (Denmark)

De la Rama Lines (USA)

Deilmann, Peter, (Germany)

Delta Line (USA)

Denholm, J&J, Ltd (GB)

Detroit & Cleveland Line (USA)

Deutsche Eisenbahn (Germany)

Deutsche Levante Linie (Germany)

*Deutsche Ost-Afrika Linie (Germany)***

Deutsche Seereederie (East Germany)

DFDS (Denmark)

*Di Giorgio SS Line (USA)**

*Direct Line (GB)**

Doeksen, Reederij,

Dollar Steamship Lines (USA)

Dominion Far East Line (GB)

Dominion Line (GB)

Donaldson Line (GB)

Drake Shipping Co (GB)

*Dublin & Manchester Line (GB)**

*Dublin & Silloth Line (GB)**

Dubrovacka Parobrodska Plovidba (Yugoslavia)

*Dundee & Newcastle Steam Shipping (GB)**

*Dundee, Perth & London Shipping Co (GB)***

*East African Railways (GB)**

*Eastern & Australian Line (GB)**

*Eastern Mediterranean Express Line (GB)**

Eastern Shipping Corporation (India)

*Egyptian Mail Steamship Lines (GB)***

Egyptian Shipping Co (GB)

Elder Dempster Lines (GB)

*Elders & Fyffes(GB)**

Ellerman & Bucknall Steamships (GB)

*Ellerman & Papayanni Lines (GB)**

Ellerman Lines (GB)

Ellerman's City Line (GB)

Ellerman's Hall Line (GB)

Ellerman's Wilson Line (GB)

ELMA (Argentina)

Empresa Insulana de Navegacao (Portugal)

Enkhuizen-Stavoren (Holland)

Enterprise Transportation Co (USA)

Epirotiki Line (Greece)

Epirus Line (Greece)

Erste Donau (Austria)

Ertslijn (Holland)

Esso Petroeum (international)

Europe Canada Line (Panama)

Europe-Australia Line (Greece)

Euxine Shipping (GB)

Everard, F.T.., & Sons (GB)

Fabre Line (France)

Fall River Line (USA)

*FANU (Argentina)**

Far-Eastern Steamship Co (USSR)

Farrell Lines (USA)

Fearnley & Eger (Norway)

*Federal Steam Navigation (GB)**

*Ferrovie dello Stato (Italy)**

*FHS (Federal-Houlder-Shire) (GB)**

*Finland Steamship Co (Finland)**

*Finska Angfartygs Aktiebolaget (Finland)**

Fisher, Renwick & Co (GB)

*Flota Argentina de Navegacion de Ultramar (FANU) (Argentina)**

*Flota Mercante del Estado (Argentina)**

Flotta Lauro (Italy)

Flushing Line (Holland)

Fragline (Greece)

MOTOR VESSEL "SUPREMITY" PROCEEDING DOWN PRINCES CHANNEL

Everard line (no star), Artists impression of 'Supremity' in Princes Channel, £10

Federal Line*, Photographic £12

*France, Fenwick & Co (GB)**

Fratelli Grimaldi Armatori (Italy)

Fraternitas, Rederi, (Sweden)

French Line (CGT) (France)

Fritzen & Sohn, Johs., (Germany)

Furness Bermuda Line (GB)

*Furness Lines (GB)**

*Fyffes (GB)**

Gdynia-America Line (Poland)

General Steam Navigation Co (GB)

*Glen Line (GB)**

Goodrich Transit Co (USA)

Gorthon Lines (Sweden)

Gota Kanal Rederi (Sweden)

Goteborg-Frederikshavn Linjen (Sweden)

Gothabolaget (Sweden)

Gotland, Angfartygs Ab, (Sweden)

Grace Line (USA)

Grand Trunk Pacific Steamship (Canada)

Grangesbergsbolaget (Sweden)

Great Lakes Transit Corporation USA)

Great Northern Pacific SS Co (USA)

Greek Australian Line (Greece)

Greek Line (Greece)

Grimaldi-Siosa Line (Italy)

*Gulf Line (GB)***

Haaland (Norway)

Hadag (Germany)

Furness Line* £10

Hafen Dampschiff. AG (Germany)

*Haj Line (India)***

Hall's Line (GB)

Hamburg & Anglo-American Nile Co

*Hamburg-Amerika Linie (Germany)***

Hamburg-Atlantic Linie (Germany)

Hamburg-Bremer-Afrika Linien (Germany)

*Hamburg-Sudamerika Linie (Germany)**

Hansa, Deutsche Dampfschiff, Gesell. (Germany)

HAPAG (Germany)

Hapag-Lloyd (Germany)

Harrison, T&J., Line (GB)

Havenlijn (Holland)

Hawaiian Steamship Co (USA)

Hellenic Mediterranean Lines (Greece)

Helsingborg, Rederi Aktiebolaget, (Sweden)

*Henderson Line (GB)**

Holland Afrika Line (Holland)

Holland Friesland Lijn (Holland)

Holland Ireland Line (Holland)

Holland Steamship Co (Holland)

Holland Veluwe Lijn (Holland)

Holland West-Afrika Lijn (Holland)

Holland-Amerika Lijn (Holland)

Holt, John, Line (GB)

Home Lines (Panama)

*Hong Kong, Canton & Macau Steamboat (GB)***

Horn Linie (Germany)

*Hough Line (GB)**

Houlder Line (GB)

*Howard Smith Ltd (Australia)**

Huddard, Parker (Australia)

Hudson Navigation Co (USA)

Hudson River Day Line (USA)

Iberian Star Line (Panama)

Imperial Department Railways (Japan)

*Imperial Direct West India Mail (GB)***

*Incres Line (USA)**

Independent Gulf Line (Holland)

Indiana Transport (USA)

Indiana Transportation Co (USA)

*Indo-China Steam Navigation Co (GB)**

*Instone Line (GB)**

Inter-Island Steam Navigation Co (USA)

Intourist (USSR)

Irish Shipping Ltd (Ireland)

*Irrawaddy Flotilla Co (GB)***

Isbrandtsen Lines (USA)

Island Tug & Barge (Canada)

*Islands Steamship (Iceland)**

Isle of Man Steam Packet Co (GB)

Isles of Scilly SS Co (GB)

Italia Line (Soc. Per Azioni di Navigazione) (Italy)

Glen Line* Colour artwork £10

Jamaica Direct fruit Line* £15

Ivaran Lines (Norway)

Jadranska Plovidba (Yugoslavia)

Jakob Lines (Finland)

*Jamaica Banana Producers SS Co (GB)**

Japan Line (Japan)

Japanese Railways (Japan)

*Jardine Mathison (GB)**

Johnson Line (Sweden)

Johnston Warren Lines (GB)

Jugoslavenski Lloyd (Yugoslavia)

Karageorgis Lines (Greece)

Kavounides Line (Greece)

*KdF (Germany)**

*Khedivial Mail Line (GB)***

*Kingsin Linie (Germany)***

Kinkai Yusen KK (Japan)

Knutsen Line (Norway)

*Kokusai Kisen Kaisha (Japan)**

Koln-Dusseldorfer (Germany)

Khedivial Mail Line** Photographic £15

Lloyd Austria Line** Printed Photo £12

Koln-Dusseldorfer Rheindamfschiffahrt (Germany)

Kolokotronis Lines (Greece)

Koninklijke Hollandsche Lloyd (Holland)

Koninklijke Java-China Pakepvaart Lijnen (Holland)

Koninklijke Nederlandsche Stoomboot Maats (KNSM) (Holland)

*Koninklijke Paketvaart Maats (KPM) (Holland)**

Koninklijke Rotterdamsche Lloyd (Holland)

*Kosmos Linie (Germany)***

Kreisschiffahrt (Germany)

Kriton Shipping (Greece)

*La Veloce (Italy)**

Laegterkompaniet (Norway)

Laeisz, F., (Germany)

Price guide: No star = low range, 1 star = Mid range & 2 star = Top of range

Lamey Tugs (GB)

*Lamport & Holt Line (GB)**

Langlands & Sons (GB)

*Lassman (Russia)***

Lauritzen, J., (Denmark)

Lauro Lines (Italy)

Leonhardt & Blimberg (Germany)

*Leyland Line (GB)***

Libra Maritime (Greece)

Lindblad Travel (USA)

Linea 'C' (Italy)

*Lineas Maritimas Argentinas (ELMA) (Argentina)**

*Liverpool& North Wales Steamship Co (GB)**

*Lloyd Austriaco (Austria)***

*Lloyd Brazileiro (Brazil)***

*Lloyd Genovese (Italy)**

Lloyd Italiano (Italy)

*Lloyd Royal Belge (Belgium)**

*Lloyd Sabaudo (Italy)**

Lloyd Triestino (Italy)

London & Edinburgh Shipping Co (GB)

London & Overseas Freighters (GB)

London County Council (GB)

London Missionary Society (GB)

Los Angeles Steamship Co (USA)

Lubeck Linie (Germany)

*Lund's Blue Anchor Line (GB)***

Isle of Man Steam packet Co. £6

Lund's Blue Anchor Line ** £30

Lykes Bros. Steamship Co (USA)

Lyle Shipping Co (GB)

MacAndrews & Co (GB)

*MacBrayne, David, Ltd (GB)**

MacIver Line (GB)

Maersk Line (Denmark)

Manchester Liners (GB)

Metcalf Motor Coasters (GB)

Marittima Italiana (Italy)

*Matson Navigation Co (USA)**

McIlwraith, McEarcharn Line (Australia)

Mediterranean Sun Line Lines (Greece)

Melbourne Steamship Line (Australia)

*Merchants & Miners Transportation Co (USA)**

Mersey Docks & Harbour Board (GB)

Messina, Ignacio, &Co (Italy)

Meyer Line (Norway)

Miami Steamship Co (USA)

Military Sea Transportation Service (USA)

*Mitsui Line (Japan)**

Mitsui OSK Lines (Japan)

Mobil (international)

*Mogul Line (India)**

Monticello SS Co (USA)

Moore-McCormack Lines (USA)

Morgan Line (USA)

*Morocco, Canary Islands & Madeira Line (GB)**

Mory & Cie (France)

Moss Hutchinson (GB)

Price guide: No star = low range, 1 star = Mid range & 2 star = Top of range

*Moss Steamship (GB)**

Muller, Wm.H., & Co (Holland)

Munson Steamship Co (USA)

Murmansk Shipping Co (USSR)

Muskoka Navigation Co (Canada)

Naias Shipping (Greece)

*Natal Line (GB)**

National Hellenic American Line (Greece)

Nautilus Steam Shipping Co (GB)

Naviera Aznar (Spain)

Naviera de Exportacion (Spain)

*Naviera Pinillos (Spain)**

*Navigazione Generale Italiana (NGI) (Italy)**

Navigazione Libera Triestina (Italy)

Navigazione sul Lago di Garda (Italy)

Nederland Line (Holland)

Nederlandse Tank & Paketvaart Maats (Holland)

*Nelson Line (GB)**

Neptun Dampfs. (Germany)

New Bedford, Martha's Vineyard etc (USA)

New Medway Steam Packet Co (GB)

New Palace Steamers (GB)

*New York & Cuba Mail (USA)**

*New York & Porto Rico SS Co (USA)**

New Zealand Shipping Co (GB)

Niagara Navigation Co (Canada)

Nicholson Erie-Dover Line (Canada)

Nelson Line* GB £10

Niederland Dampfs. Rhederei (Holland)

Nihonkai Kisen Kaisha (Japan)

Nippon Enkai Ferry (Japan)

*Nippon Yusen Kaisha (Japan)**

Nobiling, Reederei, (Germany)

Nomikos Lines (Greece)

*Norddeutscher Lloyd (Germany)***

Nordenfjeldske Damps. (Norway)

Nordsee Linie (Germany)

Norfolk & Washington Steamboat Co (USA)

*Norske Amerikalinje (Norway)**

North Coast Steam Navigation Co (Australia)

*North of Scotland, Orkney & Shetland Shipping (GB)**

Northern Michigan Transportation (USA)

Northern Navigation Co (Canada)

Northern Steamship Co (New Zealand)

Northland Shipping Co (Canada)

Northland Steamship Co (USA)

Norwegian Asia Line (Norway)

Norwegian Caribbean Lines (Norway)

Ocean Steamship Co of Savannah (USA)

Oceanic Steamship Co (USA)

Old Bay Line (USA)

*Old Dominion Line (USA)**

Oldenburg-Portugiesische Damps (Germany)

*Olsen, Fred., & Co (Norway)**

Olympic Cruises (Greece)

Orient Lines (GB)

Orient Overseas Line (Hong Kong)

Orient Steam Navigation (GB)

Orient-Pacific Line (GB)

Orient-Royal Mail Line (GB)

Orkney Islands Shipping Co (GB)

*Osaka Shosen Kaisha (Japan)***

Ostasiatiske Kompagni (Denmark)

Price guide: No star = low range, 1 star = Mid range & 2 star = Top of range

Orient Line poster advert Chromo £25

Ostend-Dover Line (Belgium)
*Ozean Linie (Germany)**
P&O (GB)
P&O Branch Service (GB)
PAAK (Pakistan)
Pacific Coast Steamships (USA)
Pacific Far East Line (USA)
Pacific Mail Line (USA)
Pacific Shipowners
*Pacific Steam Navigation Co (GB)***
Pacific Steamship Co (Admiral Line) (USA)
Pacific Transport Line (USA)
*Palm Line (GB)**
Panama Mail Steamship (USA)
*Panama Railroad (USA)**
*Panama Steamship Line (USA)**
Panama-Pacific Line (USA)
*Pan-Islamic Steamship Co (Pakistan)**
Peninsular & Occidental Steamship (P&O) (USA)
Peninsular & Oriental Steam Navigation (P&O) (GB)
*Plant Line (Canada)**
Polish Ocean Lines (Poland)
*Polish-British Steamship Co (Poland)**
*Polytechnic Cruising Association (GB)**
Port Jackson & Manly Steamship Co (Aus)
Port Line (GB)
*Porto Rico Line (USA)**
Poseidon Schiffahrt (Germany)
*Powell Line (GB)**
Presthus Rederi, Johs., (Norway)
Primorsk Shipping Co (USSR)
Prince Line (GB)
Princess Cruise Lines (USA)
Prinzenlinien (Germany)
Provinciale Stoomboot (Holland)
Prudential Lines (USA)
Puget Sound Line (USA)
Purfina (France)
*Quebec Steamship (GB)***

Royal Mail Steam Packet Line poster ad £25

Queensboro & Flushing Line (Holland)

R&O Navigation (Canada)

Ragne, Rederiaktiebolaget, (Sweden)

*Rankine Line (GB)***

*Red Funnel Line (GB)**

*Red Star Line (Belgium/USA)**

Regency Cruises

*Rennie Line (GB)**

Reut, Rederi AB, (Sweden)

*Rickmers Linie (Germany)**

Ropner & Co (GB)

*Roumanian State Service (Roumania)***

Royal Cruise Line (Greece)

*Royal Hungarian River & Sea Navigation (Hungary)**

Royal Line (Canada)

Royal Mail Steam Packet/Lines (GB)

*Royal Netherlands West-India Mail (Holland)***

Svenska Amerika Line £8

Royal Viking Line (Norway)

*Russian Volunteer Fleet ***

*Russian Steam Navigation & Trade (Russia)***

*Russian-American Line (Russia)**

Sachsisch-Bohmischen Dampfs. Ges (Germany)

Sacor Maritima (Portugal)

Salenrederierma (Sweden)

Saltash, Three Towns & District Steamboat

Salter (GB)

San Francisco & Portland Steamship (USA)

Saturnus, Rederi, (Sweden)

Savannah Line (USA)

*Scandinavian American Line (Denmark)**

Schuppe, Victor, Reederei, (Germany)

*Scottish Shire Line (GB)**

Seas Shipping (USA)

Sessan Line (Sweden)

Setsuyo Shosen Kaisha (Japan)

SGTM (France)

Shaw, Savill & Albion Co (GB)

Shin Nihonkai (Japan)

Sidarma Line (Italy)

Silja Line (Scandinavia)

*Silver Star Line (USA)***

Siosa Line (Italy)

*SITMAR (Soc. Italiana de Services) (Italy)**

Sitmar Line (Italy)

Skou, Ove, (Denmark)

*Sloan & Co (GB)**

Smit, L., & Co's Internationale Sleepdienst (Holland)

Soc. 'Italia' (Italy)

Soc. Algerienne de Navigation (France)

*Soc. di Navigazione 'Puglia' (Italy)**

*Soc. di Navigazione 'San Marco' (Italy)**

Soc. di Navigazione 'Sicilia' (Italy)

Price guide: No star = low range, 1 star = Mid range & 2 star = Top of range

*Soc. di Navigazione a Vapore Italia (Italy)**

Soc. di Navigazione per Azione 'Italnavi' (Italy)

Soc. Generale de Transports Maritimes (Fr)

Soc. Geral de Comercio (Portugal)

Soc. Italiana de Servicei (Italy)

Soc. Italiana Servizi Maritime (Italy)

*Soc. les Affreteurs Reunis (France)**

Soc. Maritime Nationale (France)

*Soc. Misr de Navigation (Egypt)**

Soc. Napoletana di Navigazione e Vapore (Italy)

Soc. Navale de l'Ouest (Fr)

Soc. Partenopea di Navigazione (Italy)

Soc. per Azione di Navigazione 'Italia' (Italy)

Soc. per Azioni di Navigazione 'Tirrenia' (Italy)

Somerfin Passenger Lines (Israel)

South American Saint Line (GB)

*Southampton, Isle of Wight & South of England SP (GB)**

Southern Pacific Railroad (USA)

Southern Pacific Steamship (USA)

Soviet Danube Steamship Line (USSR)

*St. Petersburg Express Line (Russia)***

Stag Line (GB)

Standard Fruit & Steamship Co (USA)

State Shipping Service (Australia)

States Steamship Co (USA)

Stena Line (Sweden)

Stettiner Damfercompagnie (Germany)

*Stinnes, Hugo, (Germany)**

Stockholms Rederi AB Svea (Sweden)

*Sudan Government Steamers (Sudan)**

Sun Line (Greece)

Sun Tugs (GB)

Svea Line (Sweden)

Svenska Amerika Line (Sweden)

Svenska Lloyd (Sweden)

Svenska Orient Linien (Sweden)

Toyo Kisen Kaisha Line, Japan £20

Svenska Rederiaktiebolaget Oresund (Sweden)

*Swadeshi Steam Navigation Co (India)***

Swedish-Chicago Line (Sweden)

Taiyo Ferry KK (Japan)

Tasmanian Steamers (Australia)

*Taya Line (Spain)***

*Tedcastle, McCormick & Co (GB)***

Terukuni Kaiun Kaisha (Japan)

Testa, Bernadino, (Italy)

Thorden Line (Sweden)

Thule Line (Sweden)

*Tintore Line (Spain)***

Tirrenia Line (Italy)

Toho Kaiun Kaisha (Japan)

Tokai Line (Japan)

Tor Line (Sweden)

Torm Lines (Denmark)

Townsend Bros. Ferries (GB)

*Toyas, John, (Greece)***

Toyo Kisen Kaisha (Japan)

Toyo Yusen (Japan)

Transatlantic, Rederiaktiebolaget, (Sweden)

*Transatlantica Italiana (Italy)***

Transmarin Aktiebolaget (Sweden)

Transports Maritimes Est-Tunisien (France)

Traunsee Dampfschiffahrt (Austria)

Trinder, Anderson & Co (GB)

Turbine Steamers Ltd (GB)

SS Mokoia £10

Hall Line £12

Turkish Maritime Lines (Turkey)
Turnbull, Martin & Co (GB)
Turnbull, Scott & Co (GB)
*Tyne General Ferry Co (GB)**
*Tyne-Tees Shipping Co (GB)**
*Typaldos Lines (Greece)**
Ullswater Navigation & Transit Co (GB)
*Union Steam Ship(GB)***
Union Steamship Co (Canada)
*Union Steamship Co of New Zealand (GB/NZ)**
Union Sulphur Co (USA)
*Union-Castle Line (GB)***
United American Lines (USA)
United Arab Maritime Co (Egypt)
United Baltic Lines (GB)
United Fruit Lines (USA)
United States Forces (USA)
United States Lines (USA)
*Uranium Steamship Co (GB)***
USSR State Shipping Companies, Morflot etc
Vaccaro Line (USA)
Van Nievelt, Goudriaan & Co (Holland)
Van Ommeren, Phs., NV (Holland)
Vereeigde Nederlandsche Scheepvaart (Holland)
Vierwaldstatersee (Switzeralnd)
Viking Cruises (Italy)
*Viking Cruising Co (GB)**
*Villain & Fassio (Italy)**
Virginia Ferry (USA)
Volga Steam Navigation Co (Russia)
Vriesvaart Maats. (Holland)
Wagenborg's Scheep. (Holland)
Walleniusrederierna (Sweden)
*Ward Line (USA)**
Warnemunde-Gedser Linie (Germany)
*Warren Line (GB)***
Waterman Steamship Corporation (USA)
Watts, Watts & Co (GB)
Waxholms Nya Angf. (Sweden)
West Line (USA)
*White Star Line (GB)***
Wilhelmsen Lines (Norway)
Williamson's Turbine Steamers (GB)
*Wilson Line (GB)***
*Woermann Linie (Germany)**
*Ybarra & Cia (Spain)**
*Yeoward Line (GB)**
Zeeland Line (Holland)
Zim Israel Lines (Israel)

Yeoward Line GB* £10

FAMOUS LINERS

Lusitania R.M.S.	
Sketches of Disaster	£8
Art/Photographic	£8-20
In Memoriam	£15
Celebrated Liners/Tuck R.	
Oilette Series/20+ Sets	£6-12
MISCELLANEOUS LINERS	
Pre-1939	
/Coloured	£5-20
/Real Photographic	£4-15
1940 onwards	£4-10
Interiors	£3-10
Hoffman C./Southampton	£5-10
F.G.O. Stuart	£5-10

TITANIC R.M.S.

Building/Harland & Woolf	£250+
Ship's anchor in transport	£150+
Leaving Southampton 1912	£140+
Passengers in `Carpathia' lifeboats	£200+
Other related pre-disaster cards	£100+
'Nearer my God to Thee'/Set 3/4. Pub. Bamforth. Price per card	£25

The cards listed above are all genuine `Titanic' and mainly real photographic in style. As such they are worth considerably more than other `Titanic' cards listed below, which are usually re-titled versions of her sister ship `Olympic', often overprinted with details of the disaster. The reason for this is that the `Titanic' went down before the majority of publishers got round to photographing her, so they substituted existing pictures of the almost identical `Olympic'. One can tell the difference in that the real `Titanic' had a closed superstructure while that on the `Olympic' was open.

In Memoriam/Bragg E.A.	£60
National Series	£60
RP/Printed Photographic	£40+
Art Types	£30+

Associated Ships

Britannic (Sister ship/4 funnels)	£40
Carpathia	£50
Olympic	£20-£75

Card shows 'the Greatest six liners' including Olympic, Aquitania and Mauretania £10

The Olympic entering the Era dock, Belfast, 1911 £60

MISCELLANEOUS PHOTOGRAPHIC

Cable Ships	£5-10
Cargo Ships	£5-15
Cruise Ships	£1-6
Hospital Ships	£12-30
Houseboats	£5
Icebreakers	£10-15
Launchings	£15-30
Lightships	£12-5
On-board-ship scenes	£-10
Pleasure Boats	£3-7
Speedboats	£8-12
Tankers	£3-12
Troopships	£8-12

Convict Ships

At named locations	£10
Unlocated	£6
Interior Studies	£5

Divers

Naval	£5-15
Civilian	£15
Winchester Diver	£18
Docks/Harbours/Ports	
Construction/Southampton	£40
Construction/Immingham	£20
Spectacular RP Views	£30
General scenes	£3-10

Ferries

Cross Channel	£3-10
Steam Ferries	£3-10
Floating Bridges	£8
Rowing Boats	£5

Lifeboats

`Inland Launchings'	£35
Advertising Posters RNLI	£35
Lifeboat Saturday Parades	£35
Close-up Studies	£20
Crews/Portraits	£18

▲Cargo ship £6

▲GB Royal Mail Paddle steamer £15

Parades	£28
Coastguards/Stations	£10

Lighthouses

GB Locations	£2-10
Foreign Locations	£3-5

Paddle Steamers

GB	£4-15
Overseas	£4-10
Rhine Steamers	£3-10
Swiss Lake Steamers	£2-5

Royal Yachts

GB	£2-5
Foreign	£2-8

Sailing Ships

Barges	£5-15
Coastal	£5-10
Ocean	£5-10

Shipyards

Cammell Laird	£8+
Harland & Woolf	£5-15
Ship under construction	£10-20
Yards miscellaneous	£5-20

Tugs

Paddle	£7-12
Officials	£8-20
Others	£5-10
Whaling Industry	
Hebrides/Factory scenes	£45
Ships/General Views	£10-25
Stations/Factory Scene	£30
Washed up/Stranded	£5-18
Ships	£18

Wrecks

HMS Montagu	£5-25
Submarine at Hastings	£10-15
SS Mahratta	£5-15
Other Wrecks Real photo	£15-£30

▲Albatross, a four mast Schooner used in Tall-Ship racing £6

▲Convict ship unlocated £6

Yachts

Americas Cup	£5-10
Racing	£2-6
Private/Powered	£6

▲Shipwreck of the Fornjot at Lowestoft £20

SILK CARDS

The earliest cards of this type were Woven Silks which originated in Germany in 1898. The main manufacturers were H.M. Krieger and Rudolf Knuffman. Shortly afterwards in 1903 the Coventry based firms of Thomas Stevens and W.H. Grant began making similar cards in this country, while at around the same time Neyret Freres commenced manufacturing Woven Silks in France.

Embroidered Silks first appeared in 1900, although it was not until the First World War that they reached the height of their popularity. The basic difference between the two types is that Woven Silks were machine made, and consequently of uniform finish, whereas Embroidered silks were mainly produced on hand looms, leaving a raised surface where the threads may be clearly seen, with often irregular variations in design from card to card.

For more detail on Silk postcards "An illustrated history of the embroidered silk postcard" by Ian Collins is an excellent guide to this subject. Available from Brian Lund of Reflections.

Market Report

Rare regimental badges and unusual designs have been very popular at auction and generally the market is quite steady at the moment, with prices of patriotic designs holding up well. Condition is all important and the Centenary of WW1 is playing a part in stoking demand.

WOVEN

STEVENS T.

Experimental Types	£90
Portraits	£60+
Religious Subjects	£40
Views	£25+
General Subjects	£25+

Ships

Titanic	£750
Battleships	£90+
Transports	£60
Liners, Steamers and Landing Stages	£40+
Hands Across the Sea	£30+

Alpha Series

(Designs produced by Stevens for Alpha Publishing Co.)

Greetings	£25
Flags	£25+
Stevens Designs	£30+

Woven Silk Stevens T. £55

GRANT W.H.

Exhibitions	£40+
Portraits	£40+
Subjects	£35+
Hands Across the Sea / Ships and Greetings	£35+
Greetings from	£30+

Grant Houses of Parliament £20+

Greetings, Songs and Hymns	£35
Views	£20+

FRANCE

A. Benoiston

Paris Exposition 1900	£150
Others	£40

Neyret Freres

1903-1904

Art Nouveau/Paintings/Portraits	£50+

1905-1914

Art Nouveau/Portraits/Views	£50+

1907-1918

Religion/Paintings	£30+

1915-1917

WW1 Patriotic/Portraits	£25+

1917-1918

Embroidered butterfly £12

WW1 Patriotic/Portraits	£25+
1916-1919	
Flames	£20+
1917-1918	
Sentimental Greetings	£25
Bertrand and Boiron 1915-1916	
WW1 Portraits/Religion	£50+
Others 1930-1945	£12+

GERMANY

H.M. Kreiger	£30+
Rudolf Knuffman/1898-1905	£30+
Nazi Interest/1936-1938	£50+
Others/1899-1915	£25+

OTHER EUROPEAN

Austria/1900-1939	£25+
Switzerland/1900-1910	£25+
Czechoslovakia/1916-1938	£12+

JAPAN

Views and Portraits	£40
With Copy of Grant Mount	£50

U.S.A.

1904 Exposition	£200
Set 14	£2000
Others	£30+

British royalty £20

Irish greeting Embroidered silk £15

PRINTED SILK/SATIN

Flames//Edition Gabriel	£20
Kitchener Lord	£20
Stewart & Woolf Series	£15
Regiments/Countries	£15
Miscellaneous	£8

H.M. Krieger

Four Seasons Set	£200
Others	£30

Cavell Edith

In original D.M. envelope	£6
Card only	£4

Cinema Stars/Plain Backs

Transatlantic Films	£3

FAB PATCHWORK CARDS

W.N. SHARPE/BRADFORD

Actresses	£15
Royalty	£15
Views	£12
Heraldic	£12
Flowers	£12
PAT.735 (Gaunt Armley)	£12

EMBROIDERED/WW1

REGIMENTAL BADGES

Household Cavalry	£50+
Cavalry of the Line	£70+
Cavalry Special Reserve Units	£60+
Yeomanry Regiments	£60+
Royal Regiment of Artillery	
British Regiments	£35
Overseas Regiments	£50
Foot Guards	£50
Infantry of the Line	£50+
Territorial Force	
Independent Units	£50+
London Regiments	£40+
Expeditionary Forces	
Britain/France	£40
Australasia	£40
Canada/USA	£50
Divisional Corps	£40+
British Army Corps	
British Corps/ASC.RE.RFA, etc.	£12
Overseas Corps	£40
Overseas Regiments	£75
Royal Navy	
Units	£60+
Ships	£60+
Royal Navy	£40
Royal Naval Air Service	£50
Royal Air Force	
Royal Flying Corps	£50
Royal Air Force	£45
Independent Organisations	
Red Cross/Salvation Army etc.	£50+

The whole field of WW1 Embroidered Silk Cards is vast and complex, with literally thousands of different designs covered under the three columns of this listing. Many of these cards are very scarce, in some cases only one copy being known. This catalogue can only offer a general guide to type and price.

LEADERS/STATESMEN/ROYALTY

Inset Photos/Single	£20
Inset Photos/Doubles	£25
Names/WW1 Leaders	£25

HERALDIC

Overseas Towns	£40
Overseas Countries/Islands	£25
European Towns	£15
European Countries	£15
English Towns	£30
England/Scotland/Wales	£25
Ireland/Eire/Shamrock Isle	£25

Courtesy of Warwick & Warwick Auctions

London Artists Rifles, rare silk, *£200+*

Birn Brothers/With Printed Title	
Overseas Towns	£25
European Towns	£20
English Towns	£20

YEAR DATES

1914-1919	£10
1920-1923	£15
1925-1939	£18
1940	£10
1945	£15

SENTIMENTAL GREETINGS/ HEARTS & FLOWERS TYPE

Flag/Patriotic	£8
Sentimental Greetings	£5

Many cards of this type were made in the form of an Envelope. If such a card still contains its original insert, the following premium may be added to the prices above:

Silk Handkerchief	£3

Artist signed	£1
Celluloid	£1
War Scenes	£1
Perfumed	£1
BETTER DESIGNS	
Advertising	£60
Aircraft/Guns etc.	£20
Army Camps	£25
Buildings	£20
Cartoons	£25
Cathedrals	£20
Cathedrals in Flames	£15
Cats	£20
Colonial Exhibition	£40
English Buildings	£30
Father Xmas/Girls etc	£25
Flower Baskets	£8
Pan-Pacific Exhibition 1915	£40
Personal Names	£15
Saints	£15
Soldiers/Sailors/Medals etc	£25
War Destruction	£15
Zeppelins	£20

To qualify for listed price the image must be the dominant feature of the card. A tiny Cat or small Building will not do!

EMBROIDERED/ MISCELLANEOUS

Birn Bros.	
Printed Regimental Badges	£20
Flowers	£8
Tuck R. & Sons	
Broderie D'Art series	£6
Spanish Embroidery	
Early cards	£6
Later	£3
Modern	£1.50

Belgian royalty £20

Happy Xmas, Santa design silk £25

SPORT

One of the subjects which enjoys a popularity today at least equal to that of the Edwardian period, when Sporting cards filled every album. Always a good collecting area with a very wide variety of cards, where prices have been subject to continued and steady growth over the years.

Market Report

Bodybuilding, early Boxing, Tennis, Cycling, Swimming, Motor sports and some Olympics all have a good following and continue to sell, while the likes of Cricket, Golf and Football cards have to be quite scarce to make the higher prices.

ANGLING

Comic Sketches	£3
Miscellaneous	£4

ARCHERY

Competitions	£10
Miscellaneous	£5

ATHLETICS

Meetings	£15
Athletes/Named	£15
Stadiums	£12

BADMINTON

Miscellaneous	£8

BASEBALL

Players	£5/£15
Comic Sketches	£10/£18
Stadiums	£5/ £12

BASKETBALL/NETBALL

Miscellaneous	£4

BILLIARDS/SNOOKER

Players/Named Photographic Pro	£45
Players/General	£10
Billiard Halls	£8-£15
Comic Sketches	£8/12

World Lightweight Champion Freddy Welch, c.1907 Flett photographer, London, £15

Cricket, C.B.Fry, Photographic series £18

BOARD GAMES

Chess	£15-£20
Other games	£3

BOWLS

Miscellaneous	£4

BOXING

Famous Boxers/Beagles Ltd.	£15
Professional Boxing	£12-£20
Jack Johnson	£25
Amateur Boxing	£5

BULLFIGHTING

Art Studies	£2
Photographic	£3

CAVES/CAVING

Miscellaneous	£2

CRICKET

County/International Players	£18
W.G.Grace	£30
Donald Bradman	£25

County Grounds £15
Comic Sketches £8/£15

Teams

County Teams £15-20
International Teams £15-20
Star Series £6
National Series £15
Amateur Teams/ Identified £5

CROQUET

Miscellaneous £6

CURLING

Miscellaneous £3

CYCLE RACING

Tour de France/Portraits £20
Tour de France/Pre 1939 £25
Personalities/Events/Pre 1939 £20-£25
/Post 1939 £10

FENCING

Miscellaneous £6

FOOTBALL

LEAGUE TEAMS

Series

Rapid Photographic series £50
Famous Football Teams/
Wrench Series 107...(Names) £50+
Oxo Advertising Cards £55
London Football Teams/
B&B Series G11/Coloured £40
Ozograph Series/Bristol £50
Rotary Photographic/Series 3844 £50+
Health & Strength £45
Misch & Co "Football Teams" Series 4130 £40

Miscellaneous

Football League/Bw photographic £45-75
/Bw printed £40-50
Olympic Teams £15/£30

Prices for League Teams are governed largely by the popularity of the team itself. e.g. Man. Utd. is worth more than Barnsley.

Players

Wrench Series 21../29../c.1903 £45
Benefit Cards/Football League £30-£45
Bw photographic £35
Tuck Famous football players £40
Birmingham Novelty Co 'Football' series £50
C.W.Faulkner & co £35
"Herriot" series £45
Misch & Co "THE FOOTBALLERS" £15

MISCELLANEOUS

Wembley Cup Final 1923/Campbell Gray/

In memoriam cards can fetch £30 or more depending on the team shown.

Commemorative Set 3/With Packet £140
/Without packet £100
Arsenal Cartoon/Kentish Independent £45
International Teams £30+
Football Series 940/c.1903
Tuck R. & Sons £40
In Memoriam Cards/In Memory of/
b/w Comic Sketches £20-£35
Football League Stadiums £45-£75
Football Stadiums Overseas £15
Football Colours/Frank Reynolds/
Comic Sketches £15
Non-League Teams/Semi-Pro £15
Amateur Teams/Identified £6-12
/Unidentified £4
Crowd scenes/Brighton/F. Wiles £10-15

Football, Clapton Orient, Top quality real photo team group, 1907/08 season £45

GOLF

North Middlesex Golf Club £8

◀*Golf comic £8*

/Miscellaneous	£10
Comic Sketches	£8
Wrench Series/Players/	
Bw undivided back	£100-£150
Players Known/Named	£50 - £140
Pro Tournaments	£120+
Club Houses	£8/£20
Championship Courses	£15-£35
Courses	£5/£8
Comic Sketches	£8/£15
Golf Advert Cards	
Poster Type	£70
Product Advertising	£20-£40

GREYHOUND RACING

Tracks interior	£15-£20
Named Dogs R/P	£12

GYMNASTICS

Miscellaneous	£3

HOCKEY

International teams	£12-£15
Miscellaneous	£3-£8
Roller Hockey	£6

Scotland Ladies Hockey team c.1905 *£15*

HURLING

Team groups	£15

HORSE SHOWS/JUMPING

Int. Horse Show/Product Advert	£8
Show Jumping/Riders	£5
General Scenes	£3

HORSE RACING

Jockeys	£8-15
Race Horses	£7.50

Race Courses

Doncaster/York etc./	
Printed multi-view type	£4
In current use	£6-£8

Pre-1939

Gatwick	£70
Lewes	£50
RP studies	£20
Printed/Goodwood etc.	£8
Abandoned	£15

Horse Racing at Ascot *£6*

Courses where Racing was abandoned long ago are worth more than those in current use.

Series

B & D/Kromo Series	£12
Bird H./Everett's Series	£12
Meissner & Buch Series 1003	£15
Tuck R./Derby Winners	£15
Tuck R./Popular Racing Colours	£15
Walker J./Celebrated Racers	£15
Wildt & Kray/Racing Colours	£15
Wrench Series	£15

LACROSSE

Team groups UK R/P	£18

Early Brooklands motor racing, £15

Team groups OVERSEAS	£12

MOTOR RACING

Paris-Madrid Road Race 1903	£35
L'Hirondelle Series	£20
Peking-Paris	£20
French Drivers c.1905/ Pub. J. Bouveret/Le Mans	£20
European Circuits	£12-£20
Valentine's R/P racing car series	£7

Brooklands

Action/Portraits	£15-£25
Track Construction	£20

Gordon Bennett Races

Coloured	£18
RP/Printed	£10

Isle of Man

Motor Cars/RP Close-up	£50
Action/RP Middle distance	£25

Valentine & Sons

Autocar Series	£8

Action/Portraits

Pre-1939	£15
1940 onwards	£7
Art Studies	£7

MOTOR CYCLE RACING

Isle of Man

Pre-1939	£25
1940 onwards	£12-£18

Racing/Other Circuits

Pre-1939	£18
1940 onwards	£10

Action/Portraits

Pre-1939	£18
1940 onwards	£8

MOUNTAINEERING

Everest	£10
Miscellaneous	£3

OLYMPIC GAMES

Amongst the more collectable are those that capture real moments in sporting history whether it's Eric Liddell winning the 400 metres final in Paris (1924); Johnny Weissmuller at the Olympic pool in Paris (1924) or Amsterdam(1928); or Daley Thompson participating in Olympic Decathlon in the 1980s. Postcards of empty Olympic stadiums or poor photographs of competition in the distance will rarely draw the same interest.

SUMMER GAMES

1896 Athens	£10-£80

WINTER GAMES

1924/1928	£10-£50
1932/1936	£3-£12
1948/1956	£3-£10
1960/1968	£2-£8
1972/1988	£3-£5
Ancient Olympia	£2
Empty Stadiums	£8-£12
Crowded Stadiums	£10-£20
Torch Ceremony	£2-£5

For a more detailed price guide to the postcards of the Olympic games, please refer to the 2012 edition of PPV

POLO

Miscellaneous	£3

ROWING

Named Crews	£6-£12
Oxford Eights etc.	£6-£9
Henley Regatta	£4

Rugby Union,1900 Cartoon of a Springbok killing the dragon of St.George £25

RUGBY FOOTBALL

International Teams	£20-£35
Rugby League - pro teams	£15-£35
Rugby Union - pro teams	£20-£40
Players/Named	£15-£25
Amateur teams, local (both codes)	£6/£10
South African comic cards of internationals in UK 1907	£25

SAILING/YACHTING

Admiral's Cup	£5
Racing	£5
Kirk of Cowes/RP studies	£5
Powered Yachts	£5
General scenes	£3

SHOOTING

Scenes	£12
General Shooting	£5-£8

SKATING / RINKING

Miscellaneous	£3
Professional	£5

SPEEDWAY

Riders/Pre-1939	£18
Riders/Post-War	£12

SPORTS DAY/LOCAL SPORTS

Miscellaneous	£6

STADIA

British Football League	£45-£150
Overseas Football grounds	£5-£25
Amateur Grounds	£10-£20
Athletic Tracks UK	£15-£25
Athletic Tracks Overseas	£8

SWIMMING

Channel Swimming	£15-£25
Portraits of famous swimmers	£12
Miscellaneous	£6/12
Life Saving	£8/£20

The old Sheffield Wednesday ground £45

Old Trafford stadium interior £120

TABLE TENNIS

Players/Competition	£25
Players/General	£8
Comic/Early	£25
Comic Sketches	£15

TENNIS

Wimbledon scenes (early)	£18
Wimbledon scenes	£12
Tournaments/Miscellaneous	£8/£15
Tennis Courts Amateur	£5
Comic Sketches	£7/£15

Players

Portraits/Chaplain Jones	£20
Portraits/E.A. Trim early period	£18
Portraits/E.A. Trim pre 1939	£15
Competition/Pre-1939	£15
/1940 on	£8
Wimbledon series/c.1960	£5

Mens tennis published by Trim of Wimbledon £15

WALKING

London-Brighton	£10
Other Races	£6
Comic	£3
Long Distance feats	£10-£15

WATER POLO

Named Teams Photographic	£12
Miscellaneous	£8

WINTER SPORTS

Skating	£3
Skiing	£3
Climbing	£3
Tobogganing	£2
Art types	£4
Ice Hockey Teams Pre-1960	£20

WRESTLING/BODY BUILDING

Advertising poster type	£20-£30
Miscellaneous	£15-£30
Sandow	£15-£25
Hackenschmidt	£15-£20
Gymnasiums	£6-£15
Photographic Body Builders	£20

Rugby League team Wigan £35

Early motor racing, Paris to Madrid, £35

Winter sports, This card showing a ice hockey game in Montreal could sell for just £4

THEATRICAL

Part of the staple of the old publishers. Theatrical cards of all kinds filled the Edwardian albums, and have retained their popularity to the present day.

Market Report
There is plenty of material around which tends to keep prices low. Some of the Edwardian actresses have enthusiastic followers. This can be a very worthwhile hunting ground for the discriminating collector as there are plenty of bargains to be had.

ACTORS/ACTRESSES

Baker, Josephine	£50
Bernhardt, Sarah	£5
Coward, Noel	£15
Duncan, Isadora	£15
Hari, Mata	£25
Langtry, Lily	£8
Portraits/Miscellaneous	£1.50
Play Scenes	£1.50
Gaby Deslys	£5
Camille Clifford	£3

The predominant theme in this category is Edwardian Actors and Actresses of which vast quantities exist. Formerly little collected, they have now started to attract buyers, often looking for one or two named stars.
In the circumstances a price of £1.50 is considered reasonable for one card, but they can be picked up in bulk at auction, or from a dealer, at less than this figure.

ADVERTISING

POSTER TYPE

Coloured	£12+
Black & White	£6

▶*Theatre advert nice colour illustration £15*

▲ *Actresses Gladys Cooper and Gertie Miller can be bought for between £1 and £2*

▶*Ballerina Svetlana Beriosova, £8*

SVETLANA BERIOSOVA Le Lac Des Cygnes Act II.

Holloway Empire Real photo £25

The Strand Theatre audience laughing at "Fifty-Fifty," snapped unawares by Dominion Press

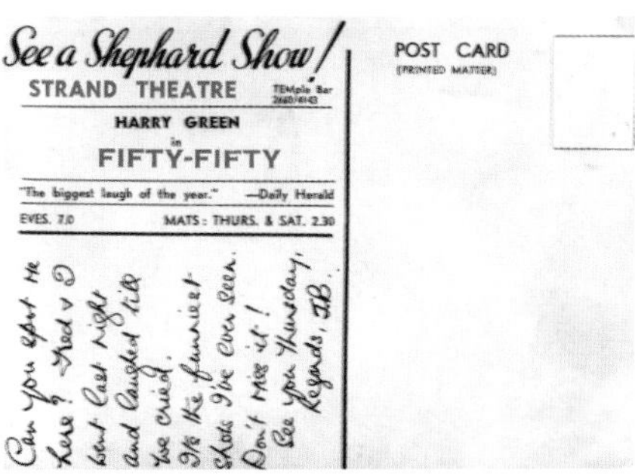

Theatre adverts often appeared on the back of a postcard as above, this unusual card is priced for the view on the front and could sell for £8

Miscellaneous

Comedians/Performers	£5
Playbill Reproductions	£10
Play Scenes/With Advert	£3

Where applicable, the value of Poster Type cards is determined by the name of the Artist. See main Artist Index.

BALLET

Artistes

Fonteyn, Margot	£10
Genee, Dame Adelina	£10
Markova, Alicia	£10
Nijinsky	£60
Nureyev, R	£35
Pavlova	£10
Other Artists	£8
Companies/Troupes	£6
Post-war	£3

THEATRES

Music Hall/Variety	£25
Opera Houses	£4
Piers/Winter Gardens	£3
Interiors	£4
London West End/Coloured	£4-£8

Prices for Theatres are for good, close-up mainly photographic studies and not for middle or far-distance views. Theatres forming part of a standard Street Scene are classed in that category.

LIFT-OFF, *Elephant a clown see- photograpł by Marsh of Bognor, Sussex £2*

CIRCUS

ADVERTISING

Barnum & Bailey

Poster Type	£30
Others	£25

Buffalo Bill's Wild West

Poster Type	£25
Others	£20

Miscellaneous

Poster Types	£30
Others	£15

MISCELLANEOUS

Acts/Performers	£8-20
Animals Caged	£8
Bands	£8
Circus Sites/Identified G.B.	£40+

Clowns

Early/Chromo Litho	£20
Photographic Performers	£15

Freaks

Animal	£10
Human	£6-£15
Giants	£6-£15
Midgets/Troupes	£6-£12

CHIEF BLACK BIRD.
WITH BUFFALO BILL'S WILD WEST.

Chief Back Beard appearing with the Buffalo Bill's Wild West, poster advert type £25

VARIETY ARTISTS

Bard, Wilkie	£6
Chevalier, Albert	£6
Chirgwin	£8
Elliott, G.H.	£8
Forde, Florrie	£6
Formby, George	£12
King, Hetty	£6
Lauder, Harry	£6
/Comic	£6
Leno Dan	£6
Lloyd Marie	£10
Miller, Max	£10
Robey, George	£4
Stratton, Eugene	£8
Tate, Harry	£6
Tich, Little	£8
Tilley. `Vesta	£5

A bit Tied up at the moment!
Escapologist Harry Kardoc, £15

RADIO/TELEVISION

Children's Programmes/Radio	£6
Radio Celebrities	£4
Studios	£6
Transmitting Stations	£5
Wireless Sets	£8
QSL Cards/Radio Amateurs	£1
Comic Sketches	£6
Children's TV/Sooty etc.	£3
Brooke Bond Chimps	£3
Radio Pictorial Series	£5

MISCELLANEOUS

Amateur Dramatics	£2
Escapologists/Stuntmen	£10-£20
Harry Houdini	£100+
Magicians/Conjurers	£25
Speciality Acts	£6
Ventriloquists	£20-£25
Drag Artists	£10

E. H. W. JENKINS "THE ENGLISH EARL"
VENTRILOQUIST AND MASTER OF CEREMONIES,
AS UNPREDICTABLE AS THE WEATHER.

GOTTLE 'O' GEER!
Ventriloquist E.W. JENKINS £20

Large letter card showing various pictures of actress Vesta Tilly, bargain at £2

Autographs

Known Stars	£3+
Unknown Artists	£1

*Prices quoted are for Autographs signed in ink. Printed Autographs have no value above that of the subject.**(See page 210 for more details on Autographs)*

Cabaret

French Skeletons	£1
Other Acts	£3

Concert Parties

Named Troupes	£6
Un-named	£2

Dancing

Ballroom/Stage etc.	£2
Greetings/Romance	£2

French Showgirls

`A Travers Les Coulisses'	£12
Moulin Rouge/Coloured	£12
Portraits/Miscellaneous	£3

TOPOGRAPHICAL

Stillman builders of North London. Top quality photographic, expect to pay up to £60

The most popular and eagerly sought after cards in the hobby, As has often been said before, the problem with Topographical cards is that there are a great many very common cards of any particular area. These include the standard High Street views, local buildings of interest, the church and the park etc.; originally produced in vast quantities by regional and national publishers. Once the collector has obtained these common views he does not buy them again. They remain in the box, as any postcard dealer will testify, for possibly years!

Being so common they keep turning up over and over again in the dealer's current buying. I would estimate that it would take an enthusiastic collector no more than six months to assemble a good collection of common cards such as these.

Then he joins the rest of us in seeking the more elusive, and far more interesting back streets and scenes of local social history interest e.g. the railway station, cinema, theatre, shop fronts, delivery vehicles, fairgrounds, trams, buses, fires, floods, disasters, post offices, public houses, windmills, local events etc. But these cards by their very nature were invariably produced in relatively small quantities by the local photographer, and today, some hundred years later, allowing for natural wastage, they are extremely thin on the ground. So as ever more collectors come to the hobby, all of them searching for these better cards, the prices go up and will continue to go up. Auction prices and internet auction prices can go to stratospheric heights when two eager collectors lock horns in a bidding war.

It is an oft-repeated maxim in the postcard trade that you can sell cards like these but you cannot buy them! Indeed many of the really superb street scenes are now so highly saleable that they often don't get as far as the dealer's box or album, but are offered privately to the collector of that particular town at a negotiated price!

So this is the Topographical market we are at present faced with. There is nothing we can do about it, save to re-double our efforts to find the cards which collectors want.

If I may now look briefly at the production of Topographical cards and at the methods involved, the following notes may be of interest to collectors. These are based on a paper written by JHD Smith in conjunction with Brian Lund, which was published in `*Picture Postcard Monthly*' in June 1982. They looked at the accepted definitions of `Real Photographic' and `Printed' cards, and suggested a more clearly defined structure, offering some thoughts toward a re-assessment of the Topographical nomenclature. To briefly summarise our conclusions, they were as follows:

Postcards were finished in two basically different methods:

1. By a photographic process.

2. By a Printing Machine process.

PHOTOGRAPHIC

Local Photographers

By small, local firms producing each photograph individually, or in very small batches onto an existing postcard back, and hand-cutting or guillotining the batches, possibly four at a time. The style of finish varies widely, from the superb clarity of the very best examples, to the image which has almost faded away, according to the skill of the photographer in the developing process. The caption was often hand-written, with the photographer's name or initials often appearing on the front of the card. These may be styled as the best examples of `Real Photographic' cards, and the work of photographers such as Bragg, Gibson, Garratt, Wellsted, Ross, Braddock, Perkins and Daniell, immediately spring to mind as pre-eminent in this field. There are of course many other local photographers who produced superb work, and here there is a great deal of research yet to be done. These men concentrated upon their own immediate locality, and as a result it is in this work that you will find the fascinating cards of local history interest referred to above, and thus it follows that in these cards we are now seeing the most significant advance in price.

Good quality, Sharp and bright images, produced by local firms using a photographic process

Regional Publishers

Postcards were produced in quantity by larger companies who covered a wide circulation area. They probably used a mass-production technique involving contact printing from a negative on to machines which could produce copies in large numbers. Many of these cards are designated `Real Photographic' on the back, and are often found with a white border framing the picture. They are characterised by a uniform, glossy finish, the machine controlled output being less susceptible to variations in tone. Leading firms who worked in this style include Sankey, Camburn and E.T. Bush, covering the areas of Cumbria, S.E. England and South Wales respectively. The subjects depicted tend to be high street and main street views, the railway station, cinema, theatre, post office, and other views of immediate local interest, although you will not find cards here showing a line of barefoot children queueing up at a soup kitchen, this being essentially the province of the local man. Cards in this section do not generally command such high prices, partly because they are more readily available, being produced in larger quantities, and also because the scenes they depict tend to be more `standard' than the off-beat work of the local photographer.

National Publishers

Also involved in postcard production, but this time on a national scale were big publishing houses such as Frith, Valentine, Davidson Bros, W.H.Smith (using various imprints including Kingsway Series and many others). Their work was machine produced and similar in all respects to that of the Regional Publishers both in style and content, but the difference lay in the fact that these were national publishing concerns who produced cards covering the length and breadth of the country. Prices here would fall into the same range as those for the Regional Publishers.

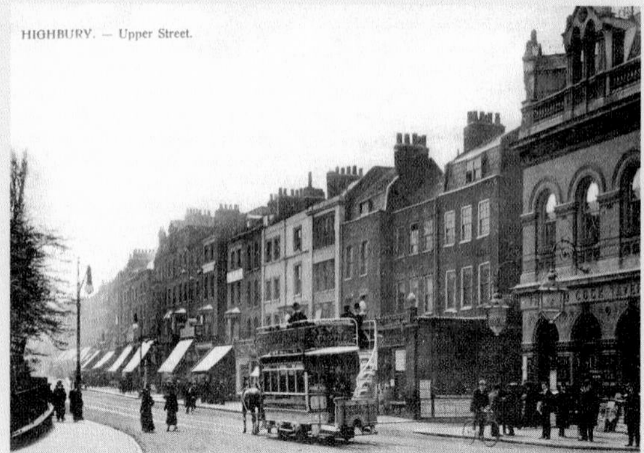

Printed postcard by London publisher £12

PRINTED CARDS

Without getting into a complex and perhaps misleading explanation of all the different printing techniques employed here, it is enough to state that if a card was not produced by one of the photographic methods given above, in other words if it does not have a glossy finish, then it must have been produced by one of the many printing processes available at the time. Basically the method employed involved splitting the original photographic image into dots, or what is known as the screen process, and then transferring this on to a printing plate. While this method enabled mass produced copies of quite appalling definition to flood the market, the finest printed cards are the equal of the finest photographics. Here again we have three main areas of commerce.

Local Publishers
Many local photographers produced cards in a variety of printed formats, and some may have combined these with their own original photographic work. Many local shops and stores had their names overprinted on to the backs of cards produced for them by the Regional Publishers. The content of these cards, while being essentially local in character, does fall into the same style as that of the Regional Publishers above, and prices would be at approximately the same levels.

Regional Publishers
The work of Charles Martin in London and the South East perhaps most clearly illustrates the very high standard to which many Regional Publishers aspired. If we may include Lucien Levy also in this classification, some of his work is certainly the equal of anything in the entire Topographical field. Subjects depicted were again similar to those of the Regional Publishers of Photographic cards, the `line of hungry children' being always the work of what has been termed `the back-street photographer'. Prices for these cards fall into line with the other regional photographic work above.

National Publishers
Here we come to those cards which today form the great bulk of stock to be found in any dealer's box. Endless mass-produced stereotyped views by Frith, Judges, Valentine, Tuck, Stengel and many other substantial publishing corporations. Printed in a wide variety of styles, with many cards coloured, and nearly all of them depicting the standard views and tourist areas of any town or city, as well as incalculable numbers of Churches, Cathedrals, Seasides, Scottish Lochs and Welsh Mountains! Some, of course, are more interesting than others, but overall, these are the cards which the collector soon obtains. Prices for the majority of them are at the lower end of the price scale.

MARKET REPORT

Prices are rising generally, partly fuelled by demand from Internet sellers and the realisation that collectors are prepared to pay a premium for the convenience of buying from their home computer.

However, the short sales window of internet auctions can be hit and miss for vendors and many dealers now find not everything on the net sells for full price. Indeed astute internet buyers can snap up real bargains and re-sell in the real world of fairs and markets at a good profit.

Taking a trip to one of the many fairs still running should still help you find bargains at every level of the topograhical field.

REMEMBER..
the higher prices in a range apply to the scarcest cards usually produced by local photographers. The lower prices in a range apply to printed cards by national publishers. Many common street scenes should be considered to fall into the category 'common views'

VILLAGES & COUNTRY TOWNS

Spectacular animated street scenes £30-£40
Animated street scenes £12-£25
Empty streets £4.50-£10
Common Views/Landscapes £2
Modern views/1945-1970 £2-£10

INDUSTRIALISED TOWNS AND CITIES

Spectacular animated street scenes £30+
Animated street scenes £20
Other street scenes £12
Empty streets £8
Common Views/City Centres etc. £2
Modern views/1945-1970 £2-£8

POST-WAR CARDS 1945-1980

Many of these cards have survived in small quantities. As they recede into history their relative scarcity is starting to be better understood and appreciated. Prices will continue to rise for post-war cards. The 1950s & 60s are doing well and even 1970s continental size cards are now being quietly collected

LONDON SUBURBAN

Spectacular animated street scenes £40+
Animated street scenes £25
Other street scenes £15
Empty streets £10
Common Views/Parks etc. £3
Modern views/1945-1980 £2-£10

City street scene photo type £8

London suburb, R/P £20

LONDON CENTRAL

Spectacular animated street scenes £25-£35
Animated street scenes £15-£25
Other street scenes R/Photo £10
Empty streets £6
Oxford St./Regent St. etc. £1.50
LL Published £5-£12
Common Views/Trafalgar Square etc. .50
Modern views/1945-1970 .50

Within these classifications many anomalies exist. For example, there are some superb animated LL cards of London Central, which at the same time are very common! With these, and similar examples, only knowledge and experience can be your guide. I have not tried to be too specific and break this down even further into considera-

London suburban, 1920s £15

tions of `RP, Printed, Coloured, Local and National Photographers etc., as this would only lead to confusion. I have not even tried to separate Real Photographic from Printed cards because, as we all know, there are some awful RPs, and some very fine Printed types. I have, however, given the main category to those superb Topographical views of both kinds which stand out in any collection.

*** Animated Street Scenes:** A card which is full of activity, life and movement, or which depicts a scene of particular relevance to that area, or is otherwise of unusual interest. These cards are very much the exception, often being produced by the local photographer. The majority of street scenes in any dealer's stock would be classified as `Other street scenes'.

MISCELLANEOUS

Abbeys/Convents/Priories	*25p-£3.50
Aerial Views	£4-£15
Archaeological sites, (Including standing stones, lost villages, digs etc.)	*25p-£5
Bridges/Viaducts	*£5-£10
Castles	*25p-£5
Cathedrals	*25p-50p
Chapels	*25p-£4
Churches (common)	25p-£1
Churches (better)	*£2-£8
Crystal Palace	£3
Follies/ estate statuary etc.	*£1-£5
Greetings (town names overprint)	£1-£2.50
Hotels	50p-£15
Lake District scenery	50p+
Landscapes	25p-£2
Manor Houses/County Houses	*50p-£8
Monuments/Memorials	*50p-£6
Multi-view	*50p-£4
Municipal Buildings	50p-£2
Parks	*25p-£5
Seaside	*25p-£5
Special Events	*£8-£35
Stately Homes (Chatsworth etc.)	25p-£1
Much photographed buildings	25p
War memorials	*50p-£6

Every dealer will have his own idea of the value of any card backed up by a specialised knowledge of his own area, so at best, the prices above should only be taken as a broad general average, capable of movement up or down as determined by the particular card.

** (a wide price range shown reflecting that some are very common and some extremely rare)*

Marching band *£15*

Perth street scene, photo type *£6*

A better church *£3*

Very nice Hotel, real photo *£15*

Gothard, in memorium £60

It is pointed out that for all relevant entries e.g. Fairs . Post Offices . Public Houses . Street Markets . Windmills etc. the stated price is a broad average figure for a card, either RP or Printed, fully identified and showing a 'Close-up at a named location', with Real Photographic cards being the most desirable. Unlocated cards and middle or far-distance views would be priced accordingly.

CANALS

Aqueducts/Bridges/Locks	£5-£12
Barges/Close-up	£40
Canal construction/Workers	£40
Disasters	£40
Events/Gatherings, etc.	£40
Military Canals	£3
Tunnels	£8

Narrow Canals

Spectacular Real Photographic	£50
Real Photographic £10/£15	
Coloured/Sepia/BW	£6
Common views/Hythe, Llangollen etc.	£2

Ship Canals

Caledonian/Crinan/Exeter etc.	£2
Manchester Ship Canal	£5

River Navigations

Traffic/Close-up	£15
General views	£6

As with other Subjects, a particularly good card or an unusual view on a seldom photographed Canal, would fetch a price well in excess of these general figures.

COAL MINING

Coal Miners

Groups/Portraits	£20/£30

Collieries

Surface/Close-up	£20/£40
/Middle Distance	£12
Somerset Coalfield	£25
Underground	£10
Models	£6
Pit Girls	£10
Open-cast Mining	£30
Gothard, In Memoriam	£20/£90

DISASTERS

Coast Erosion/Landslips	£15
/Black Rock/Brighton	£2
Explosions	£20
Floods	£20
Frozen Seas	£6
In Memoriam Cards	£20
Lightning Damage	£18
Snow Damage	£15
Storm Damage	£18
Subsidence	£20
Wrecked Buildings/Piers	£15
War Damage/WW1 Air Raids	
/Ramsgate	£12
/Scarborough	£8
Other locations	£15

Earthquakes

Essex 1884	£8
Other locations/GB	£20
Messina	£1.50
San Francisco	£3
Other locations/Foreign	£3

Events

Faversham 1916/Funeral scenes	£15
Lincoln Typhoid Outbreak 1905	£60+
Louth Floods 1920	£18
Lynmouth Floods 1952	£8
Newport Dock 1909	£50
Northwich Subsidence	£12
Norwich Floods	£12
Southend Pier	£10
Vanguard Motor Accident/ Handcross 1906	£10
Weston Super Mare Storm 1903	£12
Worthing Pier	£10

FAIRS

Amusement Parks	£5
Southend Kursaal	£5
Wall of Death/Action photos	£18
/Arenas	£8
Fetes	£12
Seaside Fairs/Water Chutes	£5

Markets

Animal Markets	£15
Street Markets	£15

See note on pricing at beginning of section.

London Markets

Club Row	£8

Real photo Hull Fair £25

Farringdon Road	£5
Petticoat Lane	£5
Billingsgate Market	£8
Smithfield Market	£8
Woolwich	£5

Travelling Fairs

Barnet Horse Fair	£22
Cosham Fair	£25
Hampstead Heath/A&G Taylor	£50
/Star Series	£5
Hull Fair	£20
Mitcham Fair	£25
Nottingham Goose Fair	£10
Oxford Fair	£15
Other named locations	£25

FIRE BRIGADE

Fire Stations	£20-£35

Fires

Bon Marche/Brixton	£5
Lewes	£6
Selby Abbey	£3
Other GB Fires	£12+

FISHING INDUSTRY

Deep Sea Fishing

Fish sales on quayside Real photo	£5-£40
Fish sales on quayside	£4-£15
Fish Markets	£3-£8
General quayside scenes	£3-£8

GIPSIES

Camps

GB locations	£25-£35
/Unlocated	£15
Alien Immigrants/Pub. Hartmann	£10
Macedonian Gipsies at Epping	£15

On the Road

GB locations	£35
/Unlocated	£12

HUNTING

Miscellaneous

Photographic groups/Named Hunts	£6
/Un-named Hunts	£3

INDUSTRIAL

Delabole Slate Quarry	£5
Gas Works	£15
Power Houses	£6
Saltworks	£25
Steelworks	£12

Cotton Mills

Interior/Machines	£8
Exterior views	£8
Lancashire Weaving scenes	£8

Factories

Interior/Machines	£8
Exterior views	£8
Machine Shops	£6
Cammell Laird/20 cards	
Industrial sketches	£6
Vickers of Barrow/Production scenes	
RP series/Valentine	£8
Woolwich Arsenal WHS Series	£6
Jute works	£10+
Shale mining	£20/£30

Pottery Industry

Factory Scenes	£6
Exteriors/Kilns etc.	£12

Fire engine, GB located, real photo £35

Gypsy children, printed card unlocated £15

Shop Front, great display of wares R/P located £35

Slate Quarries	£20/£30
Tin Mining/Cornish Mines	
RP/Close-up view	£25
/Middle distance	£15
Printed views	£10
Refining/Dressing processes/RP	£40

The great majority of Tin Mining cards were produced as Real Photographs by local photographers such as Bragg, Govier and Caddy etc.

Post Office R/P *£20*

Whaling stations	£20/£30
POST OFFICES	
Sorting Offices	£20
Villages	£20
Towns	
Main Office	£15
Sub Post Office	£25
Cities	
Main Offices	£8
Sub Post Office	£25

See note on pricing at beginning of section.

Delivery Vehicles/Staff Groups	
Posed outside building	£50
Breweries	
Guinness Brewery Scenes	£8
6x4 size	£6
Local Breweries	£10-£40

Real photo public house located *£50*

RETAIL TRADE (also see social history)

Shop Fronts	
Delivery Vehicles/Staff Groups posed outside building	£50
Special Displays/Meat Hanging etc.	£40
Grocer/Tobacconist/Newsagent etc.	
Spectacular Close-up RP/Located	£35
/Unlocated	£15
Other displays/Located	£20
/Unlocated	£5
Picture Postcard Displays	£50
Arcades	£10
Rationing queues	£40

Retail trade, Good quality shop front R/P unlocated sadly *£15*

Station Bookstalls/W.H.S. etc.	£20

See note on pricing at beginning of section. There are far more unlocated Shop Fronts than those which can clearly be assigned to a particular town or village.

Public Houses

Delivery Vehicles/Staff Groups posed outside building	£50
Close-up view	£25
Pub in street scene	£10

There are many very common pubs to be found on postcards. For example: The Star/Alfriston, Bull and Bush/Hampstead, Cat and Fiddle/New Forest, Jerusalem Inn/ Nottingham and many others too numerous to list. These are worth much less than the quoted prices and only through experience will you learn which ones they are.

WATERMILLS

Scarce types	£20
Middle range	£8
Common	£2
Fires/Disasters	£30
Art types	£1
Foreign	£1.50

WINDMILLS

Scarce types	£35
Middle range	£15
Common	£2
Fires/Disasters	£35
Art types	£1.50
Foreign	£3

See note on pricing at beginning of section. With both Watermills and Windmills it is difficult to be more specific, without listing and illustrating every card. In both cases there are some very common cards which are always turning up. With Watermills, those at Laxey, Groudle Glen and Guy's Cliff are familiar to all collectors,while in Windmills, Salvington, Rottingdean and Wimbledon are virtually unsaleable. Beyond these, there is a broad band of middle range cards, which although relatively common, are usually saleable if priced realistically. At the top of the range are cards which are seldom found, and where only a few copies may exist.

Also with Windmills there are many post-1945 cards which would carry half the prices. quoted above.

Only knowledge and experience can be your guide.

SCOTLAND TOPOGRAPHICAL

By Richard Stenlake

Market Report: The market in Scottish cards is very lively just now. Attendances at fairs are holding up well as although most Scottish dealers dabble with eBay few have embraced it completely. Scottish collectors still turn out to fairs in good numbers, but most are also supplementing their postcard 'diet' with internet buys. Internet sellers in need of stock are driving sales at fairs also. Simultaneous with all this a number of big collections have come up for sale recently ensuring a good flow of fresh material onto the market. Although it is a time of much change, with structural changes in the economy also at play as well as uncertainty about the independence referendum (don't get me started...), there is an air of dynamism in Scotland. As has been the case over the last 35 years good cards of Scottish islands always sell well and quickly. On the mainland certain towns and villages that used to sell well are now in the doldrums and neither sell at fairs nor on the internet, while others are 'hot'. There's little rhyme nor reason to this with the strange effect that neighbouring towns may be in opposite camps sales wise. Traditional 'Scottish' subjects like clan tartans and Scottish humour are only lukewarm as many of the collectors of these are now only looking for the rarest cards, but specialist Scottish themes like curling and whisky are riding high. Despite the hoo-hah about independence, Scottish political cards on the theme are still unpopular.

Please note: Where a price range is given the top end is for clear real photo cards or superb printed cards in good condition. Exceptional cards may be worth more. Conversely poorly printed, fuzzy, or damaged cards will be at the low end of the range and if especially unattractive lower than the bottom price given.

Beltane/Lanimer/ Common Riding etc.

Coronations	£8 - £10
Coronets/Queens	£2 - £4
Floats/Parades	£8 - £15
Proclamations etc.	£6 - £10
Riding of the Marches	£8 - £10

Clyde Steamers

Pre-war cards	£2 - £10
Post-war cards	50p - £2.50
At large piers	50p - £3.50
At small piers	£3 - £12

Coal Mining

Pitheads	£10 - £35
Lanarkshire Industry (Brandon Series)	£8 - £10
Mine Rescue Teams	£20+
Miners	£10+

Cotton Industry

Blantyre	£2 - £6
Catrine (mill)	£10+
Catrine (giant wheel)	£3 - £6
Johnstone	£4 - £6
New Lanark	£5 - £10
Paisley mills	£2 - £4
Paisley mill girls strike	£20
Spinningdale	£2
Stanley	£4 - £10

Curling

Printed	£5 - £10
Real Photo	£10 - £20
Curling stone quarries	£12 - £25

Granite Industry

Creetown/Dalbeattie	£10 - £20
Kemnay	£15+
Rubislaw	£8+

MISCELLANEOUS

Highland Cattle	25p - £3
Highland Washing	50p - £2
Jute Mills	£8 - £15
Loch Ness Monster	50p - £2
North Sea Oil (1970s)	50p - £2.50
Pipe Bands (Scottish)	£5 - £15

Political

Anarchists	£25+
Keir Hardie (portraits	£5 - £10
Keir Hardie (signed)	£15 - £20
Red Clydeside	£15+
Scottish Nationalism	£2 - £8
Porridge	£1+
Scottish Life & Character(Tuck)	£1

Shale Mining **£12 - £25**

NB shale was mined and roasted at the surface in retorts. Modern 'Fracking'extraction techniques are significantly different.

Shinty **£10 - £15**

Slate Quarries

Distant views	£4 - £5
Close-up	£20 - £40

Standing Stones etc.

Common	75p - £1.50
Middling	£2.50
Rare	£4 - £5

Tartan (see heraldic section)

Whaling

Harpooning etc.	£12+
Whaling Stations	£20 - £30

Whisky

Comic cards	£1 - £2
Distilleries	£8 - £15
Poster adverts	£10 - £25

WINDMILLS

Printed	£10 - £15
Real Photo	£15 - £25
Stumps	£10+

SCOTTISH ISLANDS

Scottish islands have always been popular. Islands have a mystique and are easily defined areas (unlike mainland counties whose boundaries shift with every whim of local government reorganisation). Collectors of postmarks like them too, as do transport enthusiasts who find plenty of material in the moving about of passengers and freight. Most of all islands are collected by their inhabitants who of course all love island life. Taken together these different interest groups combine to make a formidable market with constant demand for the better material.

Market report: Orkney and Shetland are currently red hot with a bull market very much being driven by a handful of 'moneybags' internet buyers. This bubble may well burst - be warned! The far-flung island group of St. Kilda, evacuated by the government in 1930 because the islanders were starving, despite a miserable history has the romance of a lost way of life that keeps it ever-popular and the highest-priced of all Scottish islands. The Outer Hebrides (Lewis, Harris, North & South Uist, Benbecula, Eriskay, Barra) sells strongly but post-1930 scenic cards of these islands are less in demand and very price-sensitive. Better cards of the Inner Hebrides (Coll, Tiree, Skye, Islay, Mull, Colonsay, Jura, Muick, Eigg, Rhum, Iona, Staffa etc) go quickly but commoner material lingers. The same applies for the Clyde Coast resort islands of Arran, Bute, and Cumbrae.

Postally used: No premium for postmarks at Tobermory, Stornoway, Kirkwall, Stromness, Rothesay, Millport, Brodick, Lerwick and other island towns unless unusual temporary rubber or skeleton types. Village postmarks are priced according to supply, demand and rarity. This is a very wide price range therefore as it covers many hundreds of different postmarks, Good legible strikes the right way up on clean cards are most desired. Prices range from £1 upwards to £25 and more (£70+ for St.

Kilda). Smaller remote settlements are higher priced (say £4 upwards) than larger accessible ones (£1 upwards). These prices are for good strikes (i.e. it's all there!). Poor strikes, smudged strikes, untidy, scruffy, damaged or dirty examples are worth only perhaps 10% or 20% of these prices - indeed should be priced solely on the basis of the picture side.

The Prime Minister at home: Fool's Gold. This card of Ramsay MacDonald is surprisingly common. Worth only £2 or £3 at best, maybe less!

The St. Kilda Parliament: The common St. Kilda type card, but still retails for £35 to £50 depending on publisher. £70+ if postally used from St. Kilda.

"Only a drachm": Gaelic card showing men taking a 'wee drap o' whisky probably on North or South Uist. This card was slightly remaindered at one time so current value about £8 to £10

A decidedly modern theme. Hard to find but undervalued as not much collected yet. Give it time though. This one about £4.

Interesting card in Scots language by publisher D & F Livingstone of Tayport. Charles Rennie Mackintosh type flower motifs seem at odds with the couthy saying which roughly translates as "May you always have food to go on your table".

Every face tells a story of a weary work-filled life in this study of real fisherfolk. There's no smiles for the camera. This is such a great card, social history at its

best. It's not that scarce, but it is superb in a voyeuristic capturing the harshness and misery sort of fashion. Price about £15 to £20.

Scottish coaching cards used to be well-collected and have gone out of fashion a bit. They are now looking reasonably priced and range from £2 to about £15 for the best examples. This is a scarce printed card for a commonish location so value about £10 to £12.

"Drunk again, Sandy?"
"I'm the same as yersel, Meenister-r-r."

Scottish humour at its best poking fun at two targets. Whisky interest helps but still only worth £1 to £1.50.

Desperately rare card published by the leftist International Pictorial Service of Glasgow about 1917/18. John MacLean was a 'Red Clydesider' who had links to the Bolsheviks. Easily worth £30, possibly more.

Real photo by national publisher William Ritchie & Sons showing holes being made for blasting at Ballachulish Slate Quarries. The slates themselves are much sought after for roof repairs in conservation areas as the quarry is closed. This 'boring' card is easily worth £40 to £50.

This 'Boring' card could be £50

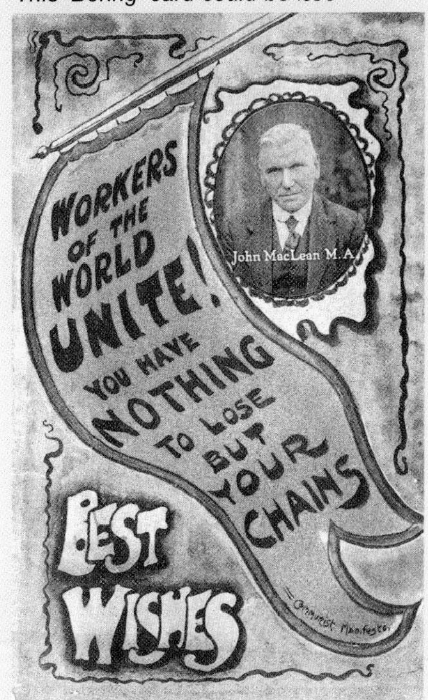

Up the workers! easily worth £30

SOCIAL HISTORY

This is Topographical by another name and the same comments apply. You can almost name your own price for the better RP studies and the scarce cards of local history interest. At the same time there are a great many interesting cards in this classification which are very reasonably priced.

AGRICULTURE

Agricultural Shows	£15
Carting	£12
Crofters	£6
Dalesmen	£5
Farm Machinery/Tractors etc	£12-£25
Farms	£8
Farmworkers	£6
Flower Picking	£6
Fruit Picking	£6
Herdsmen	£5
Trees	£1.50

Harvesting

Reaping	£5
Threshing machines/Located	£35
/Unlocated	£20
Hay Carts/RP studies	£8
General Harvesting scenes	£3

Hop Picking

Demonstrations in Kent	£75
Real Photographic scenes/Located	£20
/Unlocated	£10

There are many superb RP studies of Hop Picking. Everything depends upon location.

Cooper's Series/Maidstone/RP	£15
The "Kent" Series/Invicta	
Pub: G.A. Cooper/A.N. Hambrook	£8
Young & Cooper/Bw	£8
/Coloured	£4

There are certain Y&C coloured cards which are very common.

Filmer's Home Hop Picking Series	£8
T.A. Flemons/Tonbridge	£8

Farmers and farm machinery, R/P £20

"Solochrome" Series/E.A. Sweetman	£6
"Solograph" Series/E.A. Sweetman	£6

For Hampshire/Worcestershire etc. follow the price guide above.

Foreign Hop Picking	£5

Lavender Industry

Fields/Growing	£8
Picking	£10
Carting	£35

Ploughing

Oxen in Sussex/RP	£25
/Printed	£8
Plough Horses	£3
Ploughing/General scenes	£2

Sheep

Lambing	£6
Shearing	£12
Sheep Dips	£12
Sheepdog Trials	£12
Shepherds	£6
/South Downs/RP studies	£10

COAL MINING

Art Type	£2
Coal Picking	£60

Certain views of Collieries in South Wales, published by M.J.R.B. have been remaindered and are therefore worth considerably less than the prices given above.

Important Series

Kinsley Evictions 1905	£50

For full details on this series please refer to PPV 2003

M. Brookes/Pontypridd	£10
Cannock Chase	£10
Clay Cross Co./Set 25	£10
Timothy's Series/South Wales	£10
Other series	£10

A number of Collieries produced series of cards depicting work both at the surface and underground.

Disasters

Gothard, In Memoriam	£20/£90
Hamstead Colliery	£15
Senghenydd Colliery	£30
Other Named Events	£25

SOCIAL HISTORY

In Memoriam Cards	£25
Rescue Teams	£20

CRIME & PUNISHMENT

Judges/Barristers	£6
Prisons	£5
Prisoners at Work	£5
Warders at Dartmoor	£2
Prisoners at Portland	£2

CYCLING (also see Sport)

Close-up RP studies	£6
Cycle clubs Named location	£15-£20
Cycle shops	£25+
Tandems	£10
Tricycles	£15
Military	£10
Greetings/Romantic	£3
Comic Sketches	£3

Advert Cards

Poster Type	£40
Others	£15

See also SPORT

DOMESTIC LIFE

Corkscrews	£5
Knitting	£5
Weddings/Brides/Groups	£3
/Wedding Cakes	£2

Country Houses

Buildings	£5
Domestic Servants	£6
Gardens	£2
Kitchens	£5

Photography

Cameras/Equipment	£8
Greetings/Romantic	£4
Comic Sketches	£6
Stereoscopic cards	£4

These are cards with two adjacent pictures, best viewed through a Stereo viewer for full effect. There are many different series and subjects.

Telephones

Correspondence cards	£8
Telephone in photograph	£4
Telephone Exchanges/Operators	£20
Greetings/Romantic	£3
Comic Sketches	£2

FAIRS

Feats/Wagers

Walking Round the World	£12
/George M. Schilling	£7
/Man in the Iron Mask	£8
Niagara Falls Barrel	£8
Other Stunts	£10+
Fairground Equipment	£25+
RP studies/Published c.1950	£5

See note on pricing at beginning of section. There are in circulation many privately produced, postcard-size plain back photographs of Fairground equipment. Most of these have been printed in quantity from an existing negative and consequently have only a nominal value.

FIRE BRIGADE

Firemen	£15
Fire fighting/Identified	£15
/Unidentified	£6
Fire Stations	£20-£30
Tuck Oilettes	£8

Fire Engines

Hand Drawn	£45
Horse Drawn	£45
Motor	£40
Art Sketches	£3

FISHING INDUSTRY

Deep Sea Fishing

Fish sales on quayside Real photo	£5-£40
Fish sales on quayside	£4-£15
Fish Markets	£3-£8
General quayside scenes	£3-£8
Herring Girls	
/Gutting/Packing Herring	£6
/Spectacular RP studies	£15+
Fishermen	£3
Mending Nets	£3
Fishwives at Newhaven etc.	£2
French scenes/Concarneau etc.	£3
Other French scenes	£2

Cycle shop, R/P £25

(Please also check the topographical sections for more Social History)

Foreign scenes	£2

It is pointed out that in the 'Fish Markets' classification there are a number of very common cards, worth about £1.50 each, which are always turning up. Unfortunately it is not possible to list these individually without showing illustrations, but you have been warned.

Trawlers/Drifters

RP Trawler studies	£12
General studies	£6
/c.1960 RP studies	£1.50
On board Trawler	£12
Trawler fleet at sea	£3

Tuck Oilette Series

2317	Toilers of the Sea	£4
2761	Toilers of the Sea	£4
2817	Toilers of the Sea	£4
6690	Toilers of the Deep	£4

Local Industry

Keddle Net Fishing/Rye	£25
Prawn Fishermen/Bognor	£15
Coracle Fishermen	£5
Cockle Gatherers	£15
Cockle Vendors	£15

HUNTING

Tuck Oilette Series

2732	Fox and Stag Hunting	£4
2758	Hunting	£4
3596	Hunting in the Shires	£4
9801	In the Hunting Field	£4

Other photographic studies	£3
The Owl Series	£1.50
Comic Sketches	£2
Art Studies	£3

INDUSTRIAL

Gas Works	£15
Greenwich Telescope	£2
Printing Works	£6
/Evening News	£8
Royal Mint/Two sets of 12 cards	
Price per set	£1.50
Saltworks	£25
Science Museum Series	£3

Factories

Interior/Machines	£8
Machine Shops	£6
Men at work	£6

Pottery Industry

Factory Scenes	£6
Exteriors/Kilns etc.	£12

Industrial: Workers on site, £12

Craft Pottery/Throwing etc.	£10
Poole Pottery/14 cards	£4
Worcester Royal Porcelain Co. Ltd/ Set 6/Tuck Oilette	£1.50

Tin Mining (see topographical)

MEDICAL

Asylums	£5
Operations/Surgical	£8
Ward Scenes	£6
Cottage Hospitals	£5
Hospitals	£5
Nurses	£3
Red Cross	£5
St. John's Ambulance Brigade	£5+

Ambulances

Horse-Drawn	£35
Motor	£25

Dentistry

Surgeries	£15
Comic Sketches	£12

POLICE

Policemen/RP portraits	£6
Police Stations	£12
Special Constabulary/RP portraits	£5
Comic Sketches	£3
Art Studies	£4

POSTAL

Royal Mail Vans	£35
Hand Carts/Traps	£35
Pillar Boxes	£5
Romantic/Greetings	£3
Comic Telegrams	£3
Comic Sketches	£3

Mail Coaches

At named locations/G.B.	£25
Art Type	£5

POSTMEN

RP Studies	£12

Art Studies £5
Comic Sketches £4

Postmen of the World/Set 48
Kunzli Freres £10
Postmen of the British Empire/Set 14
Colman's Starch £10

POST OFFICES (see topographical)

RELIGION

ANGLICAN CHURCH

Bishops £1.50
Clergy named £1.50
Events/Processions £5

Evangelism
Caravans £25
Church Army £3
Conventions/Meetings £6
Gipsy Smith £3
Personalities £3
Wesleyan Churches £3

Oberammergau
Actors/Portraits £1
Production scenes/Views £1

ROMAN CATHOLICISM

Cardinals/Bishops £1.50
Priests named £1.50
Events/Processions etc. £2
Lourdes scenes £1

Popes
Coronation Souvenir Cards £5
Jubilee Cards £5
Mourning Cards/Leo XIII £5
Funeral Processions £3
Portraits £2

MISCELLANEOUS

Angels/Saints etc. £4
Lord's Prayer £1.50
Mission Societies £3
Missionaries £3

Ilfracombe farmers displaying their wares £35

/In the Pot £3
Monks/Local Industry £2
For Churches and Religious buildings see TOPOGRAPHICAL

RETAIL TRADE (also see topographical)

Delivery Vehicles
Hand Carts £35
Horse-drawn Carts £40
Milk Floats £50
Motor Vehicles £30
See also MOTOR TRANSPORT

RP Ox Roast Stratford-on-Avon £25

RURAL LIFE

Allendale Wolf £5
Barrel Organs/Men £60
Blacksmiths £18
Bootmakers £25
Brusher Mills £5
Children's Games £5
Chimney Sweeps £25
Cliff Climbers £8
Coopers £18
Cornish Pasties £2
Deer Stalking £3
Flower Shows £8
Hermits £12
Hunting/Shooting £3
Milkmaids £3
Odd Characters £12
Open Air Gatherings £5
Ox Roasts/Pig Roasts £25
Pea Picking £5
Peat Digging £6
Seaweed Gathering/Wracking £3
Spinning/Weaving £4
  Irish Spinning Wheels £1.50
Street Furniture/Troughs £6
Street Parades/Processions £15
Price is governed by the subject and location.
Tobacco Auctions/USA £6

Trug Making £40
Village Crafts £3
Village Folk £2
Village Life £3
There are a number of Tuck Oilette series on this theme, which would carry the price of the respective Artist.
Water Carts £30
Watercress Growing £20
Wheelwrights £30
Workers in the fields £5

Charcoal Burning
Actual work in progress/RP £25
Huts/Forest clearings etc. £5
Folklore
Banbury Cross £1.50
County Humour/Dialect £1.50
Customs & Traditions £1.50
Dunmow Flitch £8
Ducking Stools/Stocks £1.50
Epitaphs £1.50
Ghosts £2
Gretna Green £1
Lady Godiva £5
There are many cards of different personalities
playing this part.
Legends £1.50
Maypole Celebrations/Located £18
/Unlocated £5
Morris Dancers £15
Well Dressing £6
Witches £5
Funerals
Celebrities £18
Special Events/Processions £12
Other Funerals £6
Lacemaking
GB locations/Named Lacemakers £25
Industrial/Factory scenes £6
Belgium £4
France £8
Other Foreign £5
Performing Bears
GB locations £100
/Unlocated £30
Foreign £12

Refuse Collection
Dustcarts £40

SCHOOLS

Universities/Colleges £2
Public Schools/Eton etc. £2
Grammar/Secondary £6
Village Schools £5-10
Classroom groups/Identified £12

Milk delivery cart R/P £35

/Unidentified £3
School libraries £3

SEASIDE

Donkeys £3
Bathing Machines £5
Pierrot/Beach Shows £5
Piers £3+
Punch & Judy £12
Sand Models £3
Seaside Amusements £8

Beach Scenes
Animated RP £10
General scenes £1.50
HOLIDAY CAMPS
Butlins
Pre-1960 £4/£8
1961 onwards £3
Butlins produced cards with inset pix of their respective Holiday Camps.
Pontins/Warners etc.
Pre 1960 £3
1961 onwards £1.50
Local Camps/Holiday Villages
Pre 1960 £3-£8
1961 onwards £1.50
Caravan Parks £3
There exist many modern 6x4 size cards of Holiday Camps which would be worth less than the prices quoted above.

WELFARE ORGANISATIONS

Workhouses £12
N.S.P.C.C. £12
Y.M.C.A./Y.W.C.A. £3
John Grooms's Crippleage £2
Lord Mayor Treloar Home £2
Lord Mayor Treloar Hospital £3-£8
Newcastle-upon-Tyne Street Life/
Pub. Thompson & Lee £18

Youth Hostel R/P £3

Waifs and Strays	£3
Childrens' Homes	£6
Orphanages	£5

Charities/Fund Raising

Flag Days	£15
Fund Raising Animals	£12
T.B. Fund Raising	£8

See also MILITARY/WW1

Dr. Barnardo

Portraits	£3
Funeral Procession at Barkingside	£20
Homes	£3
Children at Work	£3
Children in group photos	£3
'Our Young Migrants in Canada'	£12

This was a scheme now discredited where Barnardos sent children to the Colonies. Believed to be two sets of 6 cards.

Salvation Army

Bands	£6
Gen. Booth/Visits G.B.	£20
Gen. Booth/Memorial Card	£8
Gen. Booth/Portraits	£3/£12
Miscellaneous interest	£3

YOUTH ORGANISATIONS

SCOUTING

Baden Powell

Tuck Empire Series	£25
Early Vignettes/Coloured	£25
/b.w.	£12
Relief of Mafeking	£30
Portraits	£15
Visits	£20

Portraits/Groups

Tuck R. & Sons/Payne H	£25
Other Series	£10
Camps/Located	£10
/Unlocated	£5
Scouts/Troops Identified	£10
/Unidentified	£2
Comic Sketches	£10-£15

National Series

Published by Millar & Lang in sets of 6 cards.

Prices are for individual cards.

Series 749	£10
Series 760	£10
Series 845	£10
Series 858	£10
Series 919	£10
Series 1000	£10
Series 1002	£10
Series 1044	£10
Series 1572	£10
Price per set of those listed above	£75
Other Millar & Lang issues	£8

Personalities

Jack Cornwell V.C.	£15

Miscellaneous

H.Q. Official Cards	£15
Jamborees	£15

A special postmark on these cards adds to their value.

Tuck R. & Sons/Our Boy Scouts/
Oilette Series 9950/Animal Heads

W.H. Ellam	£100
Price per set	£750

Scouts of the World/Set 111

USA 1968/Price for complete set	£75

GIRL GUIDES

Leaders

Lady Baden Powell	£10
Princess Mary	£5
Princess Elizabeth	£5
Other Leaders	£5

Portraits/Groups

Official Cards	£5
Identified	£5
Unidentified	£1.50

MISCELLANEOUS

Boys Brigade	£10
Church Lads Brigade	£6
Other Organisations	£3

"Up against it" Comic Scouting card £15

LONDON LIFE
and other Social History Series

Many Edwardian postcard firms published series of cards reflecting the Life and Labour of those times, while other companies produced long series covering Events and Disasters. These cards today are highly prized, and in many cases form a unique historical record of social conditions. With thanks to Alan Kelly for important updates listed in this section.

Market Report
Prices rise according to rarity, subject and quality of photo. Popular among collectors who are interested in London and Social History and keen to fill the gaps in a numbered series. The issues starting below are good quality series worth collecting.

ARISTOPHOT *No.400, 'Hyde Park Orator' £15*

ARISTOPHOT

383 Postman	£12
389 Horse Guards	£15
391 Flower Girls at Piccadilly	£10
392 Omnibus	£25
395 Policeman	£10
398 Omnibuses in a row	£15
399 Newspaper Boys	£15
400 Hyde Park Orator	£15
401 Feeding Pigeons	£15
404 District Messenger boy	£12
411 Dust Cart	£50
412 The Coal man	£20
413 Street Vendors	£15
414 Hansom Cab	£25
415 Sandwich Types	£10
417 Boot Cleaner	£12
418 Fine Ripe Cherries	£10
419 London Beer	£20

Beagles Smithfield meat market £25

BEAGLES J. & CO.

001 The Costermonger	£18
002 The Policeman	£18
003 The Shoe Black	£12
004 The German Band	£12
005 The Parcel Post	£20
006 The Flower Sellers	£10
006 The Horse Omnibus	£18
007 A Newsvendor	£15
008 The Flower Sellers	£10
009 The Street Organ	£15
010 The Knife Grinder	£15
011 Drinking Fountain & Cattle Trough	£10
012 The Motor Bus	£25
013 The Pavement Artist	£12
014 The Paper Boy	£12
015 The Telegraph Messenger	£12
016 The Electric Tram	£40
017 The District Messenger Boy	£12
018 The Milkman	£18
018 The Flower Sellers	£10
019 The Baker	£15
020 The Postman	£15
021 The Butcher Boy	£20
022 The Chelsea Pensioner	£10
411 Dust Cart	£25
646K A London Policeman	£12
646B Smithfield meat market	£25
647N Policeman holding up the traffic	£12
648E City of London Ambulance	£18
651H Billingsgate Fish Market	£20

W. HAGELBERG

Series 3490

Thames Embankment	£8
Coffee & Cocoa Stall	£8
Middlesex Street/Old Petticoat Lane	£8

JOHN WALKER

22607 Street Music	£25
22671 Petticoat Lane	£15
22672 Petticoat Lane	£15
22691 Bank Holiday	£30
22693 Bank Holiday Bioscope	£50

651.H. BILLINGSGATE FISH MARKET, LONDON.
BEAGLES' POSTCARDS
HUGE SUPPLIES OF FISH ARE DAILY SENT TO THIS OLD ESTABLISHED MARKET FOR DISTRIBUTION IN LONDON AND THROUGHOUT THE COUNTRY.
CLOSE AT HAND IS THE MONUMENT,
ERECTED TO COMMEMORATE THE GREAT FIRE OF LONDON 1666.

BEAGLES, *651H Billingsgate Fish Market £20*

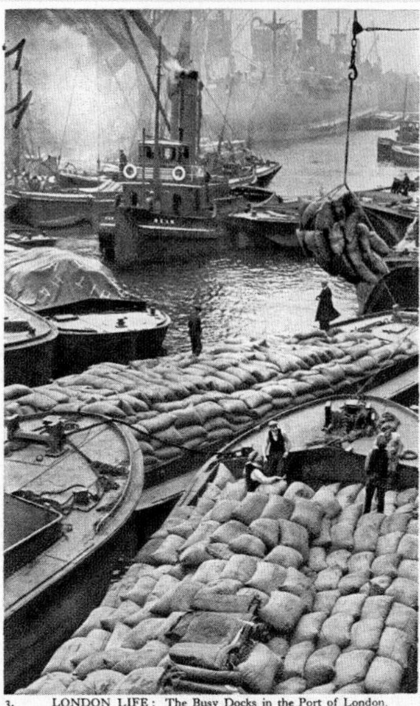

3. LONDON LIFE: The Busy Docks in the Port of London.

SKILTON, *London docks set of 12 £20*

302 Pavement Artist	£8
303 The Fireman	£12
325 Policeman	£8

G. SMITH

Types of London Life

01 Pavement Artist	£8
03 A Policeman	£12
04 Flower Seller at Piccadilly Circus	£12
05 Newsboy	£12
05a A Newsboy	£12
06 Shoe Black at Trafalgar Square	£12
08 The Fireman	£12
09 A Bus Driver	£15
10 Police Ambulance	£15
11 Policeman holding up Traffic at Bank	£12
12 Postman	£12
13 Messenger Boy	£12
14 Street Sweeper	£15
15 Fruit Seller	£15
16 Hot Chestnut Man	£15
17 The Lord Mayor's Coachman	£12
18 Punch & Judy Show at National Portrait Gallery	£15
19 A Horse Bus	£15
20 A Messenger Boy	£12
21 Hansom Cab driver	£20
22 Sentry at Buckingham Palace	£8
23 Sandwich Man	£15
T.24 A London Policeman	£12

Research by Philip Richards who informs me that although this is the main series of Gordon Smith "Types of London Life", there are certain titles known in another un-numbered series, as well as other cards in the style within the publisher's general range.

PHOTOCROM CO.

Celesque Series/Coloured London Types

The Bus Conductor	£10
The Smithfield Market Porter	£10
The Shoe Black	£10
The Flower Seller	£6
The Smithfield Market Porter	£6
The Pavement Artist	£6
The Recruiting Sergeant	£6
The Street Hawker	£10
The Newsboy	£6
The Life Guard	£6
The Orderly Boy	£10
The Postman	£10
The Chelsea Pensioner	£6
The Lighterman	£10

CHARLES SKILTON

Set of 12 cards c.1940	£20

TUCK R. & SONS

A10 A Policeman	£12
A11 The Recruiting Sergeant	£12
A12 A Fruit Hawker	£18
A13 Flower Vendors	£12
A14 A Messenger Boy	£12
A15 A Shoeblack	£18
A16 A Pavement Newsvendor	£12
A17 A Sandwichman & Newsvendor	£18

A18 A Cabman on the Rank £18
A19 A Policeman controlling Traffic £15
A20 A Pavement Hawker £18
A21 A Pavement Artist £12

WYNDHAM SERIES

6335 Hawking Butcher £30
7579 Fish Stall £30
7587 Mending Door Mats £30
7588 Penny Scales £30
7589 Salt & General Merchant £30
7590 Sweep snow away £30
7591 The Potman £30
7592 Shrimps £30
7593 Mixed Quartette £30
7594 Caravan Carpenter £30
7595 Hot Potatoes £30
7596 Fruit Merchant £30
7597 Pussy's Butcher £30
7598 Sweeps £30
7599 Muffins £30
7600 Toy Vendor £30
7601 Old Clo £30
7602 Dustman £30
7603 Shoeblack £30
7604 Shoeblack £30
7605 Street Musician £30
7606 Whelks £30
7607 Laces £30

STAR SERIES **Set of 36 cards**

01 Good Old Hampstead. The Cockney's Paradise
02 Milk Fresh from Tin Cow at St. James' Park.
03 The Nurse's Paradise, Hyde Park.
04 Feeding the Ducks in a London Park
05 Feeding the Pigeons in a London Park
06 The Fountains. Trafalgar Square.
07 Sweep O.
08 O.H.M.S.
09 The Little Bird will tell your Fortune for one Penny
10 Shoeblack and Cabby.
11 Fireman and Escape.
12 On Guard. Buckingham Palace.
13 Recruiting Sergeant and a Policeman. "On Point Duty".
14 Aliens.
15 Harmony.
16 A free Drink for Man's Best Friend.
17 Fine Fruit and Fresh Flowers. Farringdon Market, Farringdon Street.
18 Covent Garden.
19 All a Blowing and a Growing.
20 A Hot Day. Give us a Taster Jack.
21 Kerbstone Merchants. "Wonderful Pennorths". Ludgate Hill.

ARISTOPHOT 411 *Dust cart,* *£50*

22 Paper Kiosk outside the "Prudential" Holborn. A well-known Landmark.
23 Regent Circus. "Fresh from Market".
24 The Busy Bargees. River Thames.
25 Off to a Fire.
26 Changing the guard. Horseguards.
27 Fatigue Duty. Buckingham Palace Road.
28 Motor Bus.
29 Electric Tram and "2d" Tube Station.
30 A Free Drink in a London Park.
31 London Bridge
32 Piccadilly Circus
33 Rotten Row. Hyde Park.
34 Mansion House and Cheapside.
35 G.P.O. and St. Martin's le Grand.
36 Holborn Viaduct and City Temple.

Price Range: £3/£12. (The printing technique of this series leaves much to be desired).

A & G TAYLOR

Orthochrome Series/Coloured

243 Taking Lessons from the Artist	£6
245 Cat's Meat!	£10
246 The Ice Cream Merchant	£15
247 The Crossing Sweeper	£10
248 Brother Professionals	£6
250 On His Majesty's Service	£10
251 "Here you are, Sir! Shine Sir?"	£10
254 London Postman making collection	£10

ROTARY PHOTOGRAPHIC CO.

London Life/Series 10513

01 Fireman	£25
02 Postman	£25
03 Street Orderly Boy	£25
04 Taxi-Cab Driver	£25
05 Newspaper Boy	£25
06 Pavement Artist	£20
07 Hot Chestnut Seller	£35
08 Lifeguardsman Sentry	£20
09 Toy Seller	£25
10 "Votes for Women"	£75
11 District Messenger	£25
12 Flower Seller	£25
13 Omnibus Driver	£35
14 Hansom "Cabby"	£35
15 Bootblack	£30
16 Hawker	£25
17 City Police Constable	£25
18 Flower Sellers	£20
19 Fortune Teller	£25
20 The Brewers Man	£35

10513—50
LONDON LIFE. BOULTER'S LOCK ON ASCOT SUNDAY.
ROTARY PHOTO. E.C.

ROTARY, *No. 50 'Boulters lock on Ascot Sunday'* £35

21 District Messenger Boy £25
22 Big Bens Telescopeman £25
23 Post Office Telegraph Boy £30
24 LCC Tramcar Conductor £35
25 Reuter Telegraph Co.'s Messenger £20
26 The Milkman £35
27 The Baked Potato Man £35
28 A Woman Pavement Artist £25
29 City Police Motor Ambulance £30
30 "Votes for Women" £85
31 Billingsgate Porter £25
32 Smithfield Market Porter £35
33 Covent Garden Porters £35
34 Chelsea Pensioner £25
35 Firemen at Work £20
36 Street Fruit Hawker/ Coster Barrow £35
37 Street Orderly Man £35
38 Boy Scouts £35
39 Chimney Sweep £25
40 Sandwich Board Man £35
41 Automatic Road Sweeper £35
42 Royal Exchange Constable £25
43 Newspaper Boys with latest news £30
44 Ice Cream £45
45 An Apple Woman £25
46 Recruiting Sergeants £20
47 Coster in his Donkey Cart at Covent Garden Market £35
48 Flower Sellers at Oxford Circus £35
49 Underground Tube Train Conductor £45
50 Boulters Lock on Ascot Sunday £35
51 A Scene at Henley during Regatta Week £35
52 A Racecourse Scene at Epsom £35
53 The King is Coming £35
54 Opera enthusiasts. Queue outside Covent Garden Opera House £35
55 A Night Watchman £35
56 A Coffee Stall Supper, "Al Fresco" £45
57 A Whelk Stall £35
58 A Motor Bus. One of London's Red Generals £45
59 Postman collecting the Midnight Post £35
60 Fireman at work at a midnight Fire £30
61 An Underground Railway Lift Man £50
62 GPO Royal Mail Motor £35
63 Knives and Scissors Grinder £35
64 A Baker's Man £35
65 A Flower Seller £35
66 A Coal Man £40
67 A Butcher £35
68 A Hospital Nurse £45
69 Early Morning in Rotten Row, Hyde Park £25
70 Football. Chelsea V Aston Villa at Stamford Bridge £180
71 Arrest of a Militant Suffragette £95
72 Rushing to a Fire at Night £30
73 Steam Roller at work £55
74 The Dustman £45
75 A helpful member of our Dumb Friends League £35
76 A Boy Scout's Band £45
77 "Four Wheeler" Cab £45
78 A City Window Cleaner £35
79 Turkish Baths Advertiser £35
80 A Labour Demonstration £45
81 A Crossing Sweeper £35
82 In Smithfield Meat Market £35
83 Lifeguard at Whitehall £35
85 "The policeman's lot is not a happy one" £25
87 Feeding pigeons outside St. Paul's Cathedral £20
88 In Billingsgate Market £35
89 The Opening of the London Season £45
90 Queen Alexandra Buying Roses £25
91 A Coaching Meet in Hyde Park £20
95 Fire Brigade drilling before Chief Officers £45
96 Firemen wearing the smoke helmet £45
98 Motor Fire Engine and Escape £45
99 Fire Brigade drill at Headquarters £45
100 Fire Brigade Headquarters £75

There are also Tinted Cards known with a 10514 Series Number. More information is needed here. See right.

ROTARY (coloured series 10513)

C- An apple woman £25
D- Ice Cream £15

10513–52
LONDON LIFE. A RACECOURSE SCENE AT EPSOM.
ROTARY PHOTO. E.C.

ROTARY, *No 52 'A Racecourse Scene at Epsom' £35*

E- Fruit Hawker £25
L-The Baked Potato Man £20
P- Newspaper boys with latest news £20
R- Flower sellers at Oxford Circus £15
S- City Police Constable £25
T- Flower Sellers £15
W- Newspaper boy £25

LONDON LIFE/ART SERIES

Kyd £10
Rotophot
Cries of London £3
Sauber £5
Tuck R. & Sons
Oilette Series 9015 £6

TUCK'S SERIES 3762

Ice Cream Vendor £6
Safety first Policeman control traffic £5
Policeman control traffic £5

TUCK'S SERIES 3714

Postman £6
Fruit Stall £5
Muffin Man £5
Windmill Man £8
Knife Grinder £6
Series 10514
A-Children
E- Sandwich board man £5
J- Underground train conductor £12
Series 3762 set of 6 £6 per card

E.T.BOTTOM & CO, LONDON

Fish market £25
E.T. Bottom, Fruit Merchant £30

▶***JOHN WALKER SERIES:*** *Bank Holiday, Hampstead Heath, Cinematograph £50*

OVERSEAS TOPOGRAPHICAL

Please read the following explanation before consulting prices:

Every country listed in this section could support its own catalogue. Many of them produced literally millions of postcards, and although I have now begun to sub-classify many countries, a process which will be continued in future editions of this Catalogue, it must be clearly understood that at best, all one can really do in the pages which follow, is to put the reader in touch with the broad general price area for any particular card.

The degree of classification of any one country is a reflection of the demand for that country. France catalogues in much greater depth than Luxembourg for example, because the demand is there. Readers may like to think about this, when choosing a country to collect? With many countries there exist definite market indications which allow me to list Town and City Street Scenes, while other `non-collected' countries can at present only be covered either with a general `Street Scene' heading, or, in many cases, with just a single price for the whole country!

To achieve a logical presentation, I have in all cases used the term `Street Scenes', but where applicable, e.g in small islands, this is taken to mean all population centres, hut settlements, native villages, dirt-track roads etc. I don't need to be told that there are few `Streets' in Tibet or Nepal - I have deliberately chosen to use this term throughout the listings to achieve a correct balance.

Railway Stations are in all cases taken to be Town or Village stations. It is suggested that main City stations or termini be treated as `General Views', unless of course you are faced with a quite spectacular card. With all Foreign cards you will find a great many which are virtually worthless. These include Beach Scenes • Cathedrals • Churches • Countryside • Gardens • Historic Buildings • Lake Scenes • Landscapes • Mountains • Parks • Religious Buildings • River Scenes • Ruins • Stately Homes • Waterfalls • WW1 Shell Damage • Volcanoes etc.

As far as possible within the confines of a logical presentation, I have listed countries under the name by which they were known at the turn of the century. Where applicable, I have also given the modern name of the country in brackets, followed by the date this name was adopted. (This is not necessarily the date of independence).

Prices...

... are given for both Unused and Used cards. With Unused, prices may be taken as a broad, general average for the classification to which they refer. However, in all classifications there will be some very common cards which are worth much less than the stated figure, whilst on the other hand there will be cards which are worth more. With Used cards, prices are for Postcards which are of non philatelic origin, bearing the correct postal rate for the period and distance involved, and with a clear cancel on the address side only. The price given represents a basic value for any correctly used Postcard of that country.

It is pointed out that some postally used cards from certain countries or Islands are particularly rare, and may fetch a price considerably in excess of that quoted. In these cases, and where these conditions also apply to unused cards, a + sign has been entered.

The + sign has also been used where a realistic market value has not yet been established. This does not necessarily mean that the Postcard in used form is particularly rare, although certainly worth the price quoted. At best, all one can do within the limitations of a Catalogue of this kind, is to offer the reader a general indication of value for the cards in which he is interested.

Market Report

The economic woes of some of the southern European countries have had an impact on demand. Italy, Greece and Malta for example, have seen a decline in demand. Other countries with a strong exchange rate or emerging economies have seen prices hold firm – Australia, New Zealand, China, Turkey, Russia and Nigeria are setting the pace of life.

	Unused	Used
ADEN		
South Yemen 1967		£6
Street Scenes	£2	
General Views	£1.50	
AFGHANISTAN		£15+
Ethnic	£5	
Street Scenes	£12	
General Views	£5	
ALBANIA		£3+
Ethnic	£5	
Street Scenes	£6	
General Views	£3	
ALGERIA		£1
Street Scenes		£2
Ethnic	£2	
General Views	£1	
ANDAMAN ISLANDS		£15
General Views	£5	
ANDORRA		£5+
Street Scenes	£8	
General Views	£3	
ANGOLA		£5
Street Scenes	£6	
General Views	£2	
ANGUILLA		£20+
Street Scenes	£12	
General Views	£8	
ANTIGUA		£8+
Street Scenes	£10	
General Views	£2	
ARGENTINA		£2+
Ethnic	£5	
Railways	£8	
Street Scenes/Town	£3	

Finders Street Stn, Melbourne, Australia £8

	Unused	Used
/City	£1.50	
/Rural	£4	
General Views	£1.50	
ASCENSION		£25+
Royal Visit	£25	£100+
General Views	£15	
AUSTRALIA		£2
Aborigines	£15	
Bush Life	£6	
Dairy Industry	£3	
Farming	£3	
Industrial	£12	
Mining	£12	
Railway Stations	£15+	
Sheep Farming	£2	
Street Markets	£10	
Timber Industry	£6	
Trades/Workers	£6	
USA Fleet Visit	£18	
Street Scenes/Town	£10	
/City	£4	
/Rural	£10	
General Views	£2	
AUSTRIA		
Costume	£1.50	
Railway Stations	£8	
Street Markets	£5	
Gruss Aus	£8	
Street Scenes/Town	£3	
/City	£1	
/Rural	£5	
General Views	£1	
AZORES		£3
Street Scenes	£5	
General Views	£2	
BAHAMAS		£4
Hurricane 1933	£10	
Ethnic	£4	
Street Scenes/Town	£6	
/Rural	£8	
USA coloured views	£2	
General Views	£2	
BAHRAIN		£20+
Street Scenes	£12	
General Views	£8	
BARBADOS		£5
Railway	£12	

	Unused	Used
Ethnic	£3	
Street Scenes	£6	
General Views	£3	
BASUTOLAND		£5
Lesotho 1966	£15+	
Ethnic	£3	
Street Scenes/Town	£8	
/Rural	£12+	
General Views	£3	
BECHUANALAND		£5
Botswana 1966	£15+	
Ethnic	£5	
Street Scenes	£10+	
General Views	£3	
BELGIAN CONGO		
Zaire 1971		£4
Street Scenes	£6	
General Views	£1.50	
BELGIUM		.50
Costume	£1	
Dog Carts	£4	
Industrial	£6+	
Railway Stations	£8+	
Street Markets	£5	
Steam Trams	£15+	
Trades/Workers	£4	
WW1 Shell Damage	£1	
Street Scenes/Towns	£4	
/City	.50	
General Views	.50	
BERMUDA		£6+
Ethnic	£3	
Street Scenes/Town	£6	
General Views	£2	
BOLIVIA		£5+
Ethnic	£4	
Railways	£6	
Street Scenes/Town	£5	
/Rural	£6	
General Views	£2	
BORNEO		£25+
Street Scenes/Town	£20+	
/Rural	£20+	
Dutch	£6	
BOSNIA & HERZEGOVINA		
Yugoslavia 1929		£2
Street Scenes	£4	
General Views	£2	
BRAZIL		£3
Ethnic	£5	
Railways	£8	
Street Scenes/Town	£6	
Street Scenes/City	£2	

	Unused	Used
General Views	£1	
BRITISH GUIANA		
Guyana 1966		£8
Ethnic	£5	
Sugar Industry	£4	
Street Scenes/Town	£8	
/Rural	£10	
General Views	£3	
BRITISH HONDURAS		
Belize 1973		£15+
Street Scenes/Town	£10+	
/Rural	£15+	
General Views	£6	
BRITISH NEW GUINEA		
Papua New Guinea 1975		£15+
Ethnic	£10+	
Street Scenes	£20	
General Views	£8+	
BRITISH SOMALILAND		
Somalia 1960		£8
Street Scenes	£15	
General Views	£6	
BRITISH VIRGIN ISLANDS		£12
Street Scenes	£15	
General Views	£6	
BRUNEI		£25+
Street Scenes	£12	
General Views	£8	
BULGARIA		£1
Ethnic	£3	
Street Scenes	£4	
General Views	£1	
BURMA		£8
Ethnic	£3	
Street Scenes	£4	
General Views	£2	
CAICOS ISLANDS		£15
Street Scenes	£15+	
General Views	£12	

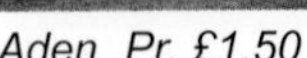

Aden Pr. £1.50

	Unused	Used
CAMBODIA		£8+
Kampuchea 1979		
Temples	£1	
Street Scenes	£8+	
General Views	£2	
CAMEROON		£10
Street Scenes	£10	
General Views	£3	
CANADA		£1
Farming	£1.50	
Indians	£6	
Industrial	£5	
Lake Steamers	£3	
Mining	£5	
Railway/CPR Views	£3	
Railway Stations	£8	
Street Markets	£3	
Trades/Workers	£3	
Street Scenes/Town	£4	
/City	£2	
/Rural	£8+	
General Views	£1	
CANAL ZONE		£3
Ethnic	£3	
Panama Canal	£3	
Street Scenes	£8	
General Views	£1.50	
CANARY ISLANDS		£3
Ethnic	£3	
Street Scenes	£5	
General Views	£1.50	
CAPE VERDE ISLANDS		£3
General Views	£3	
CAROLINE ISLANDS		£20
Pelew Islands, Ethnic	£6	
CAYMAN ISLANDS		£15+
General Views	£10	
CEYLON		
Sri Lanka 1972		£2
Ethnic	£3	
Tea Plantations	£3	
Street Scenes/Town	£4	
/City	£2	
Temples	£1.50	
General Views	£2	
CHAD		£6
Street Scenes	£8+	
General Views	£2	
CHATHAM ISLAND		£10+
General Views	£8	
CHILE		£3
Ethnic	£6	
Railways	£10+	
Street Scenes/Town	£5	
/City	£3	
General Views	£2	

China, Early, Pr. £10

	Unused	Used
CHINA		£10+
Ethnic	£6	
Street Scenes/City	£10	
/Towns	£12	
General Views	£6	
Temples/Pagodas	£6	
CHRISTMAS ISLAND		£25+
Atomic Tests	£15	
General Views	£18	
COCOS ISLANDS		£25+
General Views	£18	
COLOMBIA		£4
Ethnic	£4	
Railways	£10+	
Street Scenes	£5	
General Views	£2	
COMORO ISLANDS		£8+
General Views	£3	
COOK ISLANDS		£12+
Street Scenes	£10	
General Views	£8	
CORFU		£2
Street Scenes	£5	
General Views	£1	
COSTA RICA		£6+
Ethnic	£3	
Street Scenes	£8	
General Views	£3	
CRETE		£5
Ethnic	£10	
Street Scenes	£15	
General Views	£6	
CUBA		£3
Ethnic	£5	
Street Scenes	£4	
General Views	£2	
CURACAO		
Netherlands Antilles		£5+
Street Scenes	£6	
General Views	£2	

Cuba, Ethnic. £5

	Unused	Used
CYPRUS		£10
Ethnic	£10-£20	
Street Scenes	£15	
General Views	£6-£10	
CZECHOSLOVAKIA		£1
Street Scenes	£3	
General Views	£1	
DAHOMEY		
Benin 1975		£6
Street Scenes	£8	
General Views	£3	
DANISH WEST INDIES		
Virgin Islands/USA 1917		£15+
Ethnic	£5	
Street Scenes	£10	
General Views	£5	
DANZIG		
Poland 1945		£3
Street Scenes		£8
General Views	£3	
DENMARK		£1
Costume	£1	
Street Scenes/Town	£3	
/City	£1	
General Views	£1	
DOMINICA		£6
General Views	£3	
DOMINICAN REPUBLIC		£2
General Views	£3	
DUTCH GUIANA		
Suriname 1975		£5
General Views	£3	
DUTCH NEW GUINEA		

Early card of workers in Nicosia, Cyprus £20

	Unused	Used
Street Scenes	£6	
General Views	£3	
EASTER ISLAND		£25
General Views	£8	
ECUADOR		£4
Ethnic	£5	
Railways	£10+	
Street Scenes/Town	£6	
/City	£3	
General Views	£2	
EGYPT		£1
Ethnic	£2	
Street Scenes	£2	
General Views	£1	
ELLICE ISLANDS		
Tuvalu 1978		£10+
Street Scenes	£15	
General Views	£8	
EL SALVADOR		£4
Ethnic	£4	
Railway	£10+	
Street Scenes	£5	
General Views	£2	
ERITREA		
Ethiopia 1952		£3
Ethnic	£4	
Street Scenes	£8	
General Views	£1.50	
ESTONIA		
Russia 1940		£6
Ethnic	£3	
Street Scenes	£8	
General Views	£2	
ETHIOPIA		£5+
Ethnic	£3	
Street Scenes	£6	
General Views	£2	

Egypt, Heliopolis. £6

	Unused	Used
FALKLAND ISLANDS		£50+
Events	£50	
Penguins & Birds	£8	
Sheep Farming	£30	
Whaling	£50	
Street Scenes	£30	
General Views	£20	
FANNING ISLAND		£15+
General Views	£8+	
FAROE ISLANDS		£10+
General Views	£8	
FIJI		£6
Ethnic	£10	
StreetScenes	£15+	
General Views	£4-£8	
FINLAND		£3
Costume	£3	
Street Scenes/Town	£5	
/City	£2	
General Views	£1.50	
FIUME		
Yugoslavia 1947		£5
Street Scenes	£6	
General Views	£1.50	
FORMOSA		
Taiwan		£12+
Street Scenes	£10+	
General Views	£6	
FRENCH GUIANA		£4
General Views	£3	
FRENCH GUINEA		
Guinea 1958		£4
General Views	£4	
FRENCH OCEANIA		£10+
Street Scenes	£8	
General Views	£2	

Finland, Borga Market £5

	Unused	Used
FRENCH SOMALILAND		
Djibouti 1977		£5
Street Scenes	£8	
General Views	£2	
FRENCH SOUDAN		
Mali 1960		£3
Street Scenes	£5	
General Views	£2	
FRANCE		.50
Animal Markets	£6	
Costume	.50	
Dog Carts	£60+	
Farming	£4	
Fetes	£6	
Fishing Industry	£4	
Street/Fish Markets	£6	
Industrial	£5	
Mining	£5	
Railway Stations	£8	
Synagogues	£25	
Trades/Workers	£6	
Watermills	£3	
Windmills	£5	
Street Scenes/Villages	£8+	
/Town	£4+	
/City	£1	
GABON		£4
Street Scenes	£10	
General Views	£2	
GAMBIA		£8+
Street Scenes	£8	
General Views	£3	
GERMAN EAST AFRICA		£10+
Burundi 1962/Rwanda 1962/Tanzania 1961		
Ethnic	£5	
Occupation 1914/18	£6	
Street Scenes	£8	
General Views	£3	

	Unused	Used
GERMAN NEW GUINEA		
Papua New Guinea 1975		£20+
Ethnic	£8	
Street Scenes	£10	
General Views	£4	
GERMAN SOUTH WEST AFRICA		
Namibia		£8+
Ethnic	£8	
Street Scenes	£10	
General Views	£3	

Germany, Dusseldorf, early printed £4

	Unused	Used
GERMANY		£1
Animal Markets	£6	
Costume	£1.50	
Farming	£2	
Industrial	£5	
Mining	£5	
Railway Stations	£8	
Rhine Steamers	£3	
Street Markets	£6	
Synagogues	£25	
Trades/Workers	£6	
Street Scenes/Town	£4	
/City	£1	
General Views	.50	
GIBRALTAR		**£1**
Street Scenes	£2	
General Views	.50	
GILBERT ISLANDS		
Kiribati 1979		£20+
Street Scenes	£12	
General Views	£8	
GOLD COAST		
Ghana 1957		£6
Ethnic	£6	
Railway	£10	
Street Scenes	£8	
General Views	£3	

Greece, Turkish occupied Salonica, returned to Greek control a few years later, hence £20

	Unused	Used
GREECE		£3
Ethnic	£4	
Postal Stationery	£8	
Street Scenes	£8	
General Views	£2	
GREENLAND		£20+
Ethnic	£6	
General Views	£5	
GRENADA		£5+
Street Scenes	£6	
General Views	£2	
GUADELOUPE		£3
Street Scenes	£8	
General Views	£2	
GUAM		£10+
Street Scenes	£8	
General Views	£4	
GUATEMALA		£4
Street Scenes	£6	
General Views	£2	
HAITI		£3
Street Scenes	£6	
General Views	£3	
HAWAII		£5
Ethnic	£4	
Street Scenes colour	£3	
Street Scenes photo	£10	
General Views	£2	
HELIGOLAND		£2
Street scenes	£6	
General Views	£2	
HONDURAS		£4
Ethnic	£4	
Railway	£10	
Street Scenes	£8	
General Views	£3	

Hong Kong, Peak hotel and Railway *£5*

	Unused	Used
HONG KONG		£10
Ethnic	£6	
Peak Railway	£5	
Street Scenes Photo	£20	
Street Scenes colour	£10	
General Views	£6	
HUNGARY		£2
Ethnic	£3	
Street Scenes	£4	
General Views	£1	
ICELAND		£10+
Ethnic	£5	
Street Scenes	£8	
General Views	£3	
INDIA		£2
British Rule/Barracks etc.	£2	
Ethnic	£3	
Holy Sites	£1	
Court Size	£8	
Street Scenes	£3	
General Views	£1.50	
NWFP Photographic	£3	
IRAQ		£6
British Occupation	£4	
Street Scenes	£8	
General Views	£2	
ITALY		
Costume	£1	
Industrial	£10	
Railway Stations	£15	
River Steamers	£3	
Street Markets	£12	
Trades/Workers	£3	
Street Scenes/Town	£6+	
/City	.50	
Villages	£10	
IVORY COAST		£8
Street Scenes	£10	
General Views	£2	

	Unused	Used
JAMAICA		£3
Ethnic	£3	
Railway	£10	
Sugar Industry	£3	
Street Scenes	£6	
General Views	£2	
JAPAN		£2
Ethnic/Geishas	£3	
Shrines/Temples	£2	
Yokohama Earthquake	£3	
Street Scenes/City	£4	
/Towns	£5	
General Views	£1	

Java Pr. *£5*

	Unused	Used
JAVA-INDONESIA		£3
Street Scenes	£5	
General Views	£3	
KENYA		£4
Ethnic	£6	
Street Scenes	£6	
General Views	£3	
KOREA		£8+
Street Scenes	£8	
General Views	£3	
KUWAIT		£20+
Street Scenes	£15	
General Views	£8	
LABUAN		£20+
Street Scenes	£15+	
General Views	£10	
LAOS		£10
Street Scenes	£10	
General Views	£3	
LATVIA		
Russia 1940		£4
Ethnic	£5	
Street Scenes	£6	
General Views	£3	

Fiji, Pr. £8

Malta, coloured street scene Pr. £2

	Unused	Used
LEBANON		£5
Ethnic	£3	
Street Scenes	£4	
General Views	£1.50	
LIBERIA		£10+
Street Scenes	£8	
General Views	£2	
LIBYA		£2
General Views	£2	
LIECHTENSTEIN		£3
Street Scenes	£6	
General Views	£2	
LITHUANIA		
Russia 1940		£5
Ethnic	£6	
Street Scenes	£3	
General Views	£2	
LUXEMBOURG		.50
Street Scenes	£3	
General Views	.50	
MACAO		£25+
Street Scenes	£25	
General Views	£10	
MADAGASCAR		£3
Street Scenes	£6	
General Views	£1.50	
MADEIRA		£3
Street Scenes	£3	
General Views	£1.50	
MALAYA		
Malaysia 1963		£6
Ethnic	£4	
Railways	£12	
Rubber Industry	£3	
Street Scenes	£8	
General Views	£2	
MALDIVE ISLANDS		£10+
General Views	£8	

	Unused	Used
MALTA		£1
Ethnic	£3	
Street Scenes/RP	£6	
/Coloured	£2	
General Views	£2	
Early Undivided back	£4	
MARTINIQUE		£3
Volcano 1902	£3	
Street Scenes	£8	
General Views	£1.50	
MAURITANIA		£3
Street Scenes	£8	
General Views	£2	
MAURITIUS		£8
Railways	£15	
Street Scenes	£12	
General Views	£5	
MEXICO		£2
Ethnic	£3	
Railways	£10	
Street Scenes	£4	
General Views	£1.50	
MIDDLE CONGO		
Congo 1960		£6
Street Scenes	£8	
General Views	£2	
MOLUCCA ISLANDS		
General Views	£5	
MONACO		.50
Street Scenes	£1.50	
General Views	.50	
MONGOLIA		£20+
General Views	£6	
Ethnic	£6	
MONTENEGRO		
Yugoslavia 1929		£5
Street Scenes	£8	
General Views	£1.50	
MONTSERRAT		£12
General Views	£8	

Japan, Street with temples. £2

	Unused	Used
MOROCCO		£1
Street Scenes	£3	
General Views	£1	
Ethnic	£2	
MOZAMBIQUE		£4
Street Scenes	£5	
General Views	£1	
MUSCAT & OMAN		
Oman 1970		£30+
Street Scenes	£15	
General Views	£10	
NAURU		£25+
General Views	£10	
NEPAL		£20+
Ethnic	£6	
General Views	£5	
NETHERLANDS		.50
Canals	£1	
Costume	.50	
Customs & Traditions	£1	
Industrial	£3	
Railway Stations	£6	
Street Markets	£4	
Trades/Workers	£3	
Windmills	£1.50	
Street Scenes/Village	£6	
/Town	£2	
/City	.50	
General Views	.50	
NEVIS		£10+
General Views	£8	
NEW CALEDONIA		£10+
Street Scenes	£8	
General Views	£3	
NEWFOUNDLAND		£6
Fishing Industry	£6	
Railway Stations	£12	
Street Scenes	£10	
General Views	£5	

NZ, Palmerston North £6

	Unused	Used
NEW HEBRIDES		£15+
Vanuata 1980		
Street Scenes	£10+	
General Views	£5	
NEW ZEALAND		£1
Dairy Industry	£3	
Farming	£2	
Industrial	£6	
Maoris	£5	
Railway Stations	£12+	
Sheep Farming	£2	
Street Markets	£10	
Trades/Workers	£5	
Street Scenes/Town	£6	
/City	£4+	
General Views	£2+	
NICARAGUA		£6
Ethnic	£6	
Railways	£12+	
Street Scenes	£8+	
General Views	£3	
NIGER		£3
Ethnic	£8	
Street Scenes	£6	
General Views	£2	
NIGERIA		£4
Ethnic	£6	
Railways	£10	
Street Scenes	£6	
General Views	£4	
NIUE		£15+
General Views	£8	
NORFOLK ISLAND		£20+
General Views	£18	
Street Scenes	£20	
NORTH BORNEO		
Sabah 1964		£20+
Ethnic	£6	
Street Scenes	£15+	
General Views	£6	

Palestine, Tiberius R/P £6

Serbia, Hotel Paris, Pr. £4

	Unused	Used
NORTHERN RHODESIA		
Zambia 1964		£6
Ethnic	£4	
Railways	£15+	
Street Scenes	£8	
General Views	£2	
NORWAY		£1
Costume	£1	
Street Scenes/Town	£5	
/City	£3	
General Views	£1	
NYASALAND		
Malawi 1964		£4
Ethnic	£4	
Street Scenes	£6	
General Views	£3	
OUBANGUI-CHARI		
Central African Republic 1960		£5
General Views	£3	
PALESTINE		
Israel 1948		£1
British Occupation	£6	
Ethnic	£2	
Religious Sites	.50	
Street Scenes	£6	
General Views	£1	
PANAMA	£4	£4
Ethnic	£3	
Railways	£10+	
Street Scenes	£5	
General Views	£1.50	
PAPUA NEW GUINEA		£10
Street Scenes	£10	
General Views	£6	
PARAGUAY		£3
Ethnic	£6	
Railways	£12+	
Street Scenes	£8	
General Views	£2	

	Unused	Used
PEMBA ISLAND		£20+
Ethnic	£6	
General Views	£6	
PERIM ISLAND		
£15+		
General Views	£5	
PERSIA		
Iran 1935		£12
Street Scenes	£15	
General Views	£8	
PERU		£5
Ethnic	£5	
Railways	£10+	
Street Scenes	£6+	
General Views	£2	
PHILIPPINES		£3
Street Scenes	£8	
General Views	£2	
PITCAIRN ISLAND		£40+
Ethnic	£20	
General Views	£15	
POLAND		£3
Ethnic	£2	
Street Scenes	£5	
General Views	£3	
PORTUGAL		£1
Costume	£1.50	
Industrial	£4	
Railway Stations	£8	
Street Markets	£5	
Trades/Workers	£4	
Street Scenes/Town	£4	
/City	£1	
General Views	£1	
PORTUGUESE GUINEA		
Guinea-Bissau 1974		£5
Street Scenes	£8	
General Views	£1.50	

St Helena, The Wharf. £4

	Unused	Used
PORTUGUESE TIMOR		
East Timor		£5
Street Scenes		£8
General Views	£2	
PUERTO RICO		£4
Street Scenes	£10	
General Views	£4	
REUNION		£6
Ethnic	£6	
Street Scenes	£8	
General Views	£3	
ROMANIA		£1
Ethnic	£3	
Street Scenes	£6	
General Views	£2	
RUSSIA		£3
Costume	£3	
Ethnic	£8	
Industrial	£8	
Railway Stations	£15	
Street Markets	£15	
Trades/Workers	£15	
Street Scenes/Town	£8+	
/City	£3	
General Views	£4	
ST. HELENA		£12+
Boer War	£20	
Street Scenes	£5	
General Views	£4	
ST. KITTS		£8+
Street Scenes	£10	
General Views	£4	
ST. LUCIA		£8+
Street Scenes	£8	
General Views	£3	
ST. PIERRE & MIQUELON		£10+
Street Scenes	£10	
General Views	£4	
ST. THOMAS & PRINCE ISLAND		£6+
Street Scenes		£6
General Views	£2	

Yugoslavia R/P. £5

	Unused	Used
ST. VINCENT		£8+
Street Scenes	£8	
General Views	£3	
SAMOA		£12+
Ethnic	£6	
Street Scenes	£12	
General Views	£5	
SAN MARINO	£2	£2
Street Scenes	£4	
General Views	£2	
SARAWAK		£25+
Ethnic	£10	
Street Scenes	£20	
General Views	£10	
SARDINIA		£2
Street Scenes	£5	
General Views	£2	
SAUDI ARABIA		£15+
Street Scenes	£10	
General Views	£6	
SENEGAL		£3
Street Scenes	£5	
General Views	£2	
SERBIA		
Yugoslavia 1929		£3
Ethnic	£3	
Street Scenes	£3-£6	
General Views	£2	
SEYCHELLES		£25+
Street Scenes	£20+	
General Views	£10	
SIAM		
Thailand		£8+
Street Scenes	£10+	
General Views	£3	
SIERRA LEONE		£5
Ethnic	£4	
Railways	£10+	
Street Scenes	£6	
General Views	£3	

Switzerland, Lugano market Pr . £3

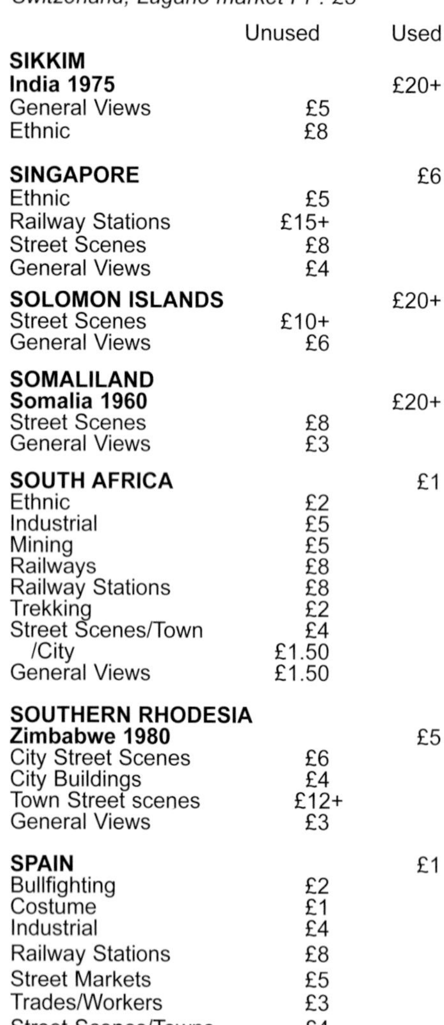

	Unused	Used
SIKKIM		
India 1975		£20+
General Views	£5	
Ethnic	£8	
SINGAPORE		£6
Ethnic	£5	
Railway Stations	£15+	
Street Scenes	£8	
General Views	£4	
SOLOMON ISLANDS		£20+
Street Scenes	£10+	
General Views	£6	
SOMALILAND		
Somalia 1960		£20+
Street Scenes	£8	
General Views	£3	
SOUTH AFRICA		£1
Ethnic	£2	
Industrial	£5	
Mining	£5	
Railways	£8	
Railway Stations	£8	
Trekking	£2	
Street Scenes/Town	£4	
/City	£1.50	
General Views	£1.50	
SOUTHERN RHODESIA		
Zimbabwe 1980		£5
City Street Scenes	£6	
City Buildings	£4	
Town Street scenes	£12+	
General Views	£3	
SPAIN		£1
Bullfighting	£2	
Costume	£1	
Industrial	£4	
Railway Stations	£8	
Street Markets	£5	
Trades/Workers	£3	
Street Scenes/Towns	£4	
/City	£2	
General Views	£1	

Sweden, Laxi, printed. £3

	Unused	Used
SPANISH GUINEA		
Equatorial Guinea 1968		£4
Street Scenes	£8	
General Views	£3	
SUDAN		£4
Ethnic	£4	
Street Scenes	£8	
General Views	£2	
SUMATRA		£3
Street Scenes	£6	
General Views	£1	
SWAZILAND		£10+
Ethnic	£4	
Street Scenes	£8	
General Views	£4	
SWEDEN		£1
Costume	.50	
Street Scenes/Town	£3	
/City	£1	
General Views	.50	
SWITZERLAND		
Costume	£1	
Customs & Traditions	£1	
Industrial	£3	
Lake Steamers	£2	
Mountain Railways	£2	
Railway Stations	£8	
Trades/Workers	£5	
Street Scenes/Town	£3	
/City	£1	
General Views	.50	
SYRIA		£3
Street Scenes	£4	
General Views	£1.50	
TANGANYIKA		
Tanzania 1961		£6
Ethnic	£5	
Street Scenes	£8	
General Views	£3	

Turkey, early printed Smyrne street scene £12

	Unused	Used
TASMANIA		£3
Street Scenes	£6	
General Views	£1.50	
THURSDAY ISLAND		£10+
General Views	£8	
TIBET		£40+
Ethnic	£12+	
General Views	£30+	
TIMOR		£15+
Street Scenes	£6	
General Views	£3	
TOBAGO		£5+
Street Scenes	£6	
General Views	£3	
TOGO		£6
Ethnic	£6	
Street Scenes	£5	
General Views	£4	
TONGA		£15+
Ethnic	£12	
General Views	£8	
TRANSJORDAN Jordan 1946		£4
Street Scenes	£6	
General Views	£1.50	
TRINIDAD		£3
Ethnic	£3	
Oil Industry	£5	
Street Scenes	£6	
General Views	£3	
TRISTAN DA CUNHA (PRE 1928)		£250+
Later issues	£25+	
TUNISIA		£2+
Street Scenes	£3	
General Views	£1	

	Unused	Used
TURKEY		£5+
Ethnic	£4	
Street Scenes/town	£6-£15	
Street Scenes/city	£3-£5	
General Views	£1.50	
TURKS ISLANDS		£20+
Street Scenes	£12	
General Views	£12	
UGANDA		£5+
Ethnic	£4	
Street Scenes	£6	
General Views	£3	
UPPER VOLTA Burkina 1984		£5+
Street Scenes	£8	
General Views	£1.50	
URUGUAY		£3
Ethnic	£4	
Railways	£10	
Street Scenes/Town	£5	
/City	£3	
General Views	£1.50	
U.S.A.		£1
Cattle	.50	
Indians	£6	
Industrial	£3	
Mining	£5	
Railway Stations	£6	
Steamboats	£3	
Street Scenes/Town	£4	
/City	£1	
General Views	.50	
VENEZUELA		£4
Ethnic	£5	
Railways	£10	
Street Scenes	£5	
General Views	£1.50	
VIETNAM		£3
Ethnic	£6	
Street Scenes	£8	
General Views	£3	
YEMEN		£5+
Street Scenes	£6	
General Views	£4	
YUGOSLAVIA		£2
Ethnic	£3	
Street Scenes	£5	
General Views	£1.50	
ZANZIBAR		£8
Ethnic	£8	
Street Scenes	£6	
General Views	£2	

IMPORTANT. Prices quoted are for complete, clear postmarks in every instance. Partial or indistinct strikes, generally have very little value.

CIRCULAR DATE STAMP

English type - £1
The most common of all postmarks

Scottish type - £1 upwards

SQUARED CIRCLES

Three different types
£2 each
For lesser used types
- £5 upwards to
£50

SINGLE RING

£1
upwards

Small 'thimble'
circular ring
£1.50
upwards

DUPLEX

£2 Minimum
Certain obscure or limited types
may be worth up to £10 each

MACHINE CANCELLATIONS £1-£3

Two different examples of the E (Crown) R Type.
Used in London (£7) Liverpool (£30)

STAMPS ON POSTCARDS

In response to many enquiries we receive about the value of Stamps found on Postcards, it must be pointed out that the picture postcard invariably carried the minimum postage rate, and these low-denomination Stamps are virtually worthless. Realistically, the only value in a used card would be if it has been stamped and posted from an 'unusual' country, or small island, or if it bears a cancellation of some interest.

INLAND POSTAGE RATES

1 October 1870 - 3 June 1918 - 1/2d
3 June 1918 - 13 June 1921 - 1d
13 June 1921 - 24 May 1922 - 1 1/2d
24 May 1922 - 1 May 1940 - 1d

FIRST DAY OF ISSUE

QUEEN VICTORIA		
1/2d Blue Green	17 April 1900	£500
KING EDWARD VII		
1/2d Blue Green	1 January 1902	£40
1d Red	1 January 1902	£40
1/2d Yellow Green	26 November 1904	£35
KING GEORGE V		
1/2d Green (three-quarter profile, hair dark)	22 June 1911	£30
1d Red (three-quarter profile, Lion unshaded)	22 June 1911	£40
1/2d Green (three-quarter profile, Hair light)	1 January 1912	£40
1d Red (three-quarter profile, Lion shaded)	1 January 1912	£45
*British Empire Exhibition 1924. (1d Red)	23 April 1924	£15
*British Empire Exhibition 1925. (1d Red)	9 May 1925	£30
U.P.U Congress 1929 (1/2d or 1d)	10 May 1929	£12
1/2d Green	19 November 1934	£5
1d Red	24 September 1934	£5
Silver Jubilee 1935. (1/2d or 1d)	7 May 1935	£6

* Postcards bearing Wembley Park 1924 or 1925 handstamp or slogan cancel on exhibition cards would justify a premium.

KING EDWARD VIII		
1/2d Green	1 September 1936	£6
1d Red	14 September 1936	£12
KING GEORGE VI		
1/2d Green	10 May 1937	£1
1d Red	10 May 1937	£1

POSTMARKS ON POSTCARDS

This is a vast and complex field, and part of the much wider area of Philately. There are thousands of different postal markings and stamps to be found on the backs of picture postcards, and indeed there is a similar number of specialised philatelic books devoted to all aspects of this subject.

In a postcard Catalogue of this kind, it is only possible to give a very rough indication of price for postmarks likely to be found on picture postcards. Readers requiring more specialised information or catalogues are referred to Stanley Gibbons new publication 'Collect Postmarks' as a useful guide to the broader issues of collecting postmarks. Available from Vera Trinder, see page 2 for details.

CACHETS

£1
Handstamps applied other than by the Official PO. Other common types are 'Summit of Snowdon', "Beachy Head'

METER MARKS

£1
Normally meant for business use

POSTAGE DUES

From £2 upwards
Surcharge marks for under-paid mail, many varieties

EXHIBITIONS

Edinburgh 1908
£8

Crystal Palace Code 3
(below date) £25

A complex field where price depends upon the particular exhibition and date
£1. - £50

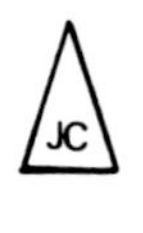

(i)

(ii)

(iii)

EXAMINATION MARKS

Post Office Examiner's marks applied to wrongly sorted mail. Usually stamped in black but type (iii) sometimes found in violet. £1 - £3 each
N.B. There is a larger type as (iii) which was used for checking the bulk posting of circulars, etc. Price 50p each

---

SKELETONS

A temporary hand-stamp used for a limited period. Of varying sizes usually 27 - 39 mm in diameter. Price subject to wide fluctuation
£4-£13 upwards

RUBBER DATE-STAMPS

often in blue or violet, used by smaller offices
£5 - £12 if superb coloured

ISLANDS

Circular Date Stamps Examples shown, Gorey £4, Sandwick Shetland £6. Others such as Lundy Island £50, St. Kilda £30. Chief offices of Jersey, Guernsey and I.O.M are common

RECEIVED FROM H.M.SHIP
NO CHARGE TO BE RAISED

RECEIVED FROM H M SHIP

£3
Naval security markings

DUMB CANCELS

£3
Naval security markings

SLOGANS

£1 upwards
Mostly common, but there are exceptions amongst many hundreds of different types

ARMY & FIELD POST OFFICES

A popular specialist field - with wide price fluctuations

Field Post Office G
France 1915
£1 upwards

P.B.2
1919 Archangel
£35

Autographs

WHAT IS AN AUTOGRAPH REALLY WORTH?

It is worth remembering a signature is always an autograph but an autograph is not always a signature.

What we are concerned with here is signatures, in autograph books, which is the most common and cheapest form, on photographs and postcards, and on letters which could be either typed, written by a secretary and then signed or completely hand written.

It must be remembered that the vast majority of autographs, especially on photographs and postcards will not be original, many will be machine, rubber stamped, signed by a third party, often a secretary or simply forged since the middle of the twentieth century the autopen machine has further complicated collecting as the signatures often can not be separated from genuine autograph unless you have two copies, the autopen signatures will be identical the handwritten ones will be slightly different as you can never sign two identical signatures.

S.F.Cody autograph on postcard £120

As with postcards, the value of an autograph is dependant on popularity and scarcity.

Here we have listed a cross section of Stars/Celebrities, some very old and some not so old, which we hope will help in explaining values of autographs.

GLOSSARY

Sig - Signature, in an autograph book or on a card, remember a signature alone on the back of a postcard is little better than an autograph in an autograph book.

Photo- Signature, on the front of a Postcard or Photo of the subject.

L.S. A letter written by a third party, usually a secretary and then signed by the subject.

T.L.S. A typed letter signed by the subject

A.L.S. A letter completely handwritten and signed by the subject. A Postcard hand written and signed would be priced about the same.

ARTISTS	Sig	Photo	T.L.S.	A.L.S.
Peter Blake	10	20	30	40
Salvador Dali	80	200	120	200
Tracy Emin	50	200	200	300
David Hockney	20	80	120	150
Damian Hirst	50	100	120	200
Edwin Landseer	20	-	40	100
Frederick Leighton	20	-	40	40
John Everett Millass	30	200	60	120
Henry Moore	40	100	80	140
Pablo Picasso	300	1000	800	1500
David Shepherd	10	20	30	40
Louis Wain	100	400	300	500
Frank Lloyd Wright	100	250	200	30

AUTHORS	Sig	Photo	T.L.S.	A.L.S.
J M Barrie	40	150	80	120
Enid Blyton	50	200	100	200
Michael Bond	5	20	20	30
Agatha Christie	100	350	250	350
Charles Dickens	150	-	500	800
Arthur Conan Doyle	80	250	150	250
Carol Ann Duffy	5	15	15	25
Ian Fleming	500	1500	1500	2000
Thomas Hardy	150	350	250	450
Rudyard Kirling	40	150	100	150
Alastair Maclean	40	120	80	100
J D Salinger	800	-	4000	4000
Leo Tolstoy	800	3000	1000	3000

AVIATION/SPACE	Sig	Photo	T.L.S.	A.L.S.
Samuel F Cody	40	120	120	180
Yuri Gagarin	80	200	160	300
Amy Johnson	50	120	150	300
Charles Lindbergh	250	1500	1000	2000
Patrick Moore	5	10	10	20
Helen Sharman	5	20	20	30
Igor Sikorsky	40	80	80	100
Claude Graham-White	25	70	90	100
Frank Whittle	50	120	100	150
Orville Wright	300	1200	800	1800
Wilbur Wright	1000	6000	3000	8000

ENTERTAINERS	Sig	Photo	T.L.S.	A.L.S.
Josephine Baker	80	150	150	250
Jeremy Brett	30	60	50	80
Clint Eastwood	20	40	50	100

ENTERTAINERS	Sig	Photo	T.L.S.	A.L.S.
Errol Flynn	100	200	250	350
William Hartnell	60	100	100	150
Audrey Hepburn	70	150	150	200
Katherine Hepburn	80	200	100	200
George Lazenby	20	40	50	80
David Niven	30	80	80	100
Flora Robson	5	20	20	30
Terry Thomas	50	80	80	120
Kenneth Williams	50	100	100	150
Orson Welles	80	150	120	200
Al Pacino	10	30	40	80
Brad Pitt	20	50	100	100
George Robey	2	15	20	30
Ginger Rogers	20	60	60	80
Elizabeth Taylor	100	500	300	600
Ellen Terry	5	30	30	40
Richard Todd	5	20	20	30
Patrick Troughton	60	120	120	170
John Wayne	500	1000	1000	1500

MILITARY	Sig	Photo	T.L.S.	A.L.S.
Douglas Bader	40	100	120	150
Albert Ball V.C.	300	600	600	800
John Churchill	300	-	600	1000
Alexander Haigh	30	80	100	150
Robert E Lee	1000	3500	3500	5000
Bernard Montgomery	50	150	150	200
William Reid V.C.	10	30	30	40
Irwin Rommel	200	400	400	600
Norman Schwarzkoff	10	50	50	70
Garnet Wolseley	15	80	100	150

POLITICS	Sig	Photo	T.L.S.	A.L.S.
Tony Blair	10	20	20	40
Gordon Brown	10	20	20	40
Arthur J Balfour	25	100	60	100
Winston Churchill	500	1500	1000	1500
Benjamin Disreali	80	80	150	300
Mohandas Gandhi	250	3000	1800	3000
William Gladstone	20	100	-	100
Edward Heath	10	20	20	30
John F Kennedy	700	1500	1500	2500
Adolf Hitler	700	1500	1000	3000
Robert Peel	10	-	100	150
Spencer Percival	80	-	150	300
Theodore Roosevelt	100	1000	1000	1500

Margaret Thatcher	20	60	80	150
Robert Walpole	40	-	200	400
SCIENCE	**Sig**	**Photo**	**T.L.S.**	**A.L.S.**
Francis Crick	30	100	100	150
Frederick Banting	200	600	600	900
Marie Curie	800	2500	3000	3500
Albert Einsteiin	700	3000	4000	5000
Michael Faraday	100	500	200	400
Sigmund Freud	800	4000	1500	3500
Joseph Lister	100	-	200	400
Guglielmo Marconi	100	300	300	400
Robert Oppenheimer	400	1000	1200	2000
Louis Pasteur	350	2000	700	1000
Frederick Treeves	40	250	200	250
James Watt	300	-	-	1200
MUSIC(CLASSICAL)	**Sig**	**Photo**	**T.L.S.**	**A.L.S.**
John Barbirolli	10	30	30	50
Adrian Boult	10	30	30	40
Benjamin Britten	80	200	200	300
Aaron Copland	40	100	150	200
W S Gilbert	120	400	250	400
Fritz Kreisler	40	80	80	100
Gustau Mahler	300	4000	1000	2000
Ignasi Paderewski	80	200	150	200
John Philip Souza	80	200	150	250
Arthus Sullivan	100	500	250	400
Michael Tippett	20	40	40	80
Michael Walton	40	100	100	200
MUSIC(OPERA)	**Sig**	**Photo**	**T.L.S.**	**A.L.S.**
Clara Butt	10	30	30	40
Maria Callas	300	800	500	700
Enrico Carusso	200	600	300	600
Kathleen Ferrier	100	200	200	250
Jenny Lind	50	-	-	150
Nellie Melba	40	100	100	150
Peter Pears	20	50	40	60
Lily Pons	40	120	80	100
Louisa Tetrazzi	20	70	90	120
Richard Tauber	20	50	50	80
MUSIC(POPULAR)	**Sig**	**Photo**	**T.L.S.**	**A.L.S.**
Beatles	2000	5000	-	-
Bob Dylan	80	150	200	400
Jimmy Hendrix	500	1500	1500	2000
Elton John	10	30	30	60
Oscar Peterson	10	20	20	40
Cole Porter	100	700	200	500
Elvis Presley	400	1000	1000	2000

Bruce Springsteen	50	100	100	150
Tina Turner	10	30	30	50
SPORT(CRICKET)	**Sig**	**Photo**	**T.L.S.**	**A.L.S.**
Ian Botham	5	10	20	30
Geoffrey Boycott	5	10	10	20
Donald Bradman	30	80	100	150
C B Fry	40	150	100	150
W G Grace	100	400	300	400
Walter Hammond	20	70	60	100
Tom Hayward	50	150	-	200
Douglas Jardine	40	150	100	150
Harold Larwood	30	150	100	150
Malcolm Marshall	20	50	60	80
Garfield Sobers	10	20	20	40
Pelham Warner	20	80	60	80
SPORT(FOOTBALL)	**Sig**	**Photo**	**T.L.S.**	**A.L.S.**
Alan Ball	25	60	60	80
Gordon Banks	10	20	20	30
David Beckham	10	30	40	60
Bobby Charlton	10	20	30	40
Dixie Dean	30	80	800	100
Roger Hunt	10	20	30	40
Stanley Matthews	30	60	60	80
Bobby Moore	200	350	400	500
Bob Paisley	30	60	50	80
Alf Ramsey	50	100	80	120
Wayne Rooney	20	40	40	60
Bill Shankly	30	60	50	80
SPORT(GOLF)	**Sig**	**Photo**	**T.L.S.**	**A.L.S.**
Seve Ballesteros	20	40	50	75
Nick Faldo	10	20	30	40
Walter Hagan	75	150	100	200
Tony Jacklin	10	20	20	30
Robert Jones(Jnr)	300	700	700	1000
Tom Morris(Snr)	400	800	800	1200
Jack Nicklaus	10	30	40	60
Greg Norman	10	20	20	30
Gary Player	10	30	40	60
Gene Sarazan	10	20	20	30
Tom Watson	10	20	20	30
Tiger Woods	80	150	150	200
SPORT(MOTOR)	**Sig**	**Photo**	**T.L.S.**	**A.L.S.**
Jenson Button	10	30	30	40
Bruce McLaren	100	150	200	300

Sport Motor Cont'd	Sig	Photo	T.L.S.	A.L.S.
Stirling Moss	10	20	20	40
Alain Prost	10	20	20	40
Lewis Hamilton	10	30	30	40
Barry Sheen	30	50	40	60
Michael Schumacher	20	50	70	100
Ayrton Senna	175	450	500	600
Jackie Stewart	10	20	20	40
John Surtees	10	20	20	30

SPORT(VARIOUS)	Sig	Photo	T.L.S.	A.L.S.
Lance Armstrong	20	50	50	70
Roger Bannnister	10	30	30	50
Bjorn Borg	10	20	20	40
Chris Hoy	5	10	10	20
Carl Lewis	10	20	20	30
Joe Louis	80	250	250	350
Jessie Owens	100	300	300	500
Babe Ruth	1500	5000	4000	5000
John L Sulivan	300	1000	1000	2000
Venus Williams	10	30	30	40

PEOPLE OF INTEREST	Sig	Photo	T.L.S.	A.L.S.
Hawley H Crippen	100	-	350	600
Joseph Fry	40	-	80	120
Edmund Hillery	20	50	50	80
Billy Graham	30	50	80	100
Reg Kray	30	60	80	100
Hiram Maxim	50	200	200	250
Fridjof Nansen	80	350	300	600
Lee Harvey Oswald	1500	-	5500	8000
Robert F Scott	200	-	300	800
Haile Selassie	150	900	400	600
Albert Schweitzer	100	400	300	400
John Stuart Mill	80	-	-	400
Victoria(Queen)	100	1000	200	400
Brigham Young	200	1500	800	1500

Sig - Signature, in an autograph book or on a card, remember a signature alone on the back of a postcard is little better than an autograph in an autograph book.

L.S. A letter written by a third party, usually a secretary and then signed by the subject.

T.L.S. A typed letter signed by the subject

A.L.S. A letter completely handwritten and signed by the subject. A Postcard hand-written and signed would be priced about the same.

PUBLISHER.. MEISSNER & BUCH

German company Meissner & Buch were pre-eminent in the field of picture postcards. Meissner and Buch produced postcards in Leipzig, Germany from 1876 to 1914

Series ..Title Subject
1000.... (12) Battleships and Cruisers Hans Bohrdt
1001.... Mothers and Children W.F.
1002.... Mothers and Children W.F.
1003.... Horse Racing..... C. Becker
1004..... Military Leaders. A. Beckort
1010.... (12) Military
1011.... (12) Venedig A. Prosdocimi
1012.... (12) Merchant Liners......
1013.....(12) Rothenburg...Otto Hummel
1015.... (12) Battleships and Cruisers
1016.... Aus 'Nansen, In Nacht Und Eis..... A. Goldfeld
1018.... (12) Roma............G. Gioja
1023.... (12) Hannover...Otto Hummel
1029.... (12) Von Der Alm
1032.... (12) Lago Di Como A. Prosdocimi
1033.... Blumenfee M.S.M.
1034.... (12) Aus Dem Thuringer Land (I)
1035.... Land Idyllen A. Mailick
1037.... Aus Dem Thuringer Land (II).. Otto Hummel
1039.... Lawn-Tennis...... B. Wennerberg
1040.... (12) Grusse Der Flora...... (?) M.B.
1041.... Weinnachtsgrusse
1047.... Unsere GartenfreundeC. Klein
1048.... (12) Kindlicher Frohsinn. M.S.M.
1049.... Chic
1052.... Aus Feld Und Garten...C. Klein
1053.... Die 4 Jahreszeiten
1055.... Wedgewood
1058.... Wir Gratulieren.. F.R.
1061.... Edlweiss
1062.... Firenze E. Bensa
1063.... (12) S. Marco.......A. Prosdocimi
1064.... (12) Lago Maggiore......... A. Prosdocimi
1065.... Aus Der Guten Alten Zeit
1066.... (12) Gluckliche Zeit......... M.S.M.
1067.... Wedgewood Gruppen M.S.M.
1068.... Aus Vergangenen Tagen
1069.... Wedgewood Figuren..M.S.M.
1070.... (24) Deutscher Sport
1076.... Flottengruss
1081.... Am Bluenhain
1082.... Frohe Tage M.S.M.
1084.... Graziose Gestalten
1085.... (12) Napoli. A. Prosdocimi
1087.... Schwesterliebe
1091.... (12) Viel Gluck
1092.... (12) Blumencorso
1093.... (12) Schone FrauenM.S.M.
1097.... (12) Strandleben... G. Grobe
1098.... (12) Uber Berg Und Thal
1112.... Beim Frohilchen Spiel H.P
.... = R.G. Hermann Paul

Series Title Subject
1124.... Auf Zum Tanz..... M.S.M.
1125.... Heitere Gemuter M.S.M.
1126.... Junge Frauen
1127.... Glucksterne
1128.... Geisha
1132.... Des Gartens Schmuck. C. Klein
1133.... Rosen C. Klein
1136.... Osterfreuden
1137.... Wilkommengrusse
1138.... Napoli
1139.... Nationaltrachten
1140.... Am Strand
1141.... Frohe Begegnung
1143.... Aus Der Biedermeierzeit......... M.S.M.
1147.... (12) Genova A. Prosdocimi
1149.... (12) Grusse Des Fruhlings
1151.... Jung Holland
1159.... Als Der Grossvater Die Grossmutter Nahm R.E.
1161.... Gluckslee
1162.... Fruhlings-Erwachen
1166.... Wedgewood Figuren
1170.... Gartenfreuden
1172.... Am Wasser
1179.... Zum Whol M.S.M.
1181.... Rosenpracht...... C. Klein
1182.... Zu Wasser Und Zu Lande
1184.... Im Versteck
1185.... Siesta
1186.... Frauen-Schonheiten
1189.... Am Weiher
1191.... Aus Der Rococozeit
1192.... Susse Madels
1193.... Altmeister Der Musik
1194.... Neuere Meister Der Musik
1195.... Aus Unserm Garten....C. Klein
1196.... Unter Bluhenden Blumen....... C. Klein
1197.... Erwachen Des Lenzes.. (?) M.B.
1199.... Zierden Der Fruhlings
1202.... Im Fruhlingskleid........C. Klein
1204.... Blumengeister
1207.... Blumen Am Zaun........ (?) M.B.
1210.... 12 Veitchen Duft. (?) M.B.
1212.... 12 Aus Dem Obstgarten...... C. Klein
1213.... 12 Aus Dem Baumblut. C. Klein
1215 ...12 Abseits Der Grossen Strasse..E.L.
1221.... 12 HerbstfreudenC. Klein
1224.... 12 Weidmannsheil
1225.... Spenden Des Sommers
1227.... Rheingold
1229.... Wald Idyll
1230.... Von Wald Und Wiese
1234.... Herzensfragen
1235.... In Den Augen Leigt Das Herz
1237.... Tage Des Friedens
1238.... Blumenpfade..... C. Klein

Series Title Subject
1239.... Blumen Auf Den Weg Gestreut
1241.... Von Blume Zu Blume .C. Klein
1242.... Was Sich Leibt Das Neckt Such
1244.... Junder OsterzeitM.S.M.
1246.... Von Blute Zur Frucht ..C. Klein
1249.... Von Herz Zu Herzen....M.S.M.
1251.... Dein Heim Dein Gluck
1259.... Venezia A. Prosdocimi
1263.... Frohen Herzen Frohe Stunden.F.W. Hayes
1264.... Von BergeshohnF.W. Hayes
1265.... Auf Lichten Pfaden
1269.... Japanische Schonheiten
1272.... Worpswede E. Koster
1274.... Gluck Auf Den Wag
1275.... Gute Kameraden
1277.... 12 Keine Srog' Um Den Weg
1285.... Auf Blumen Durchs Leben C. Klein
1288.... Augenweide....... C. Klein
1296.... Ostergluck A.W.
1298.... Aus Grossmutters Jugend M.S.M.
1299.... Pfingstfreunden
1305.... Gaben Zum Laben ......C. Klein
1308.... O Sonneschein
1311.... Blumenkinder
1313.... Regen Und Sonnenschein
1323.... Der Maler Auf Dem Lande
1328.... Mother and child.........EW
1334.... Winterfreuden-Kinderfreuden
1337.... Auf Dem Wege Zum Gluck
1338.... Wenn Ich Ein Voglein War
1339.... Wer Nicht Leibt Wein, Weib U. Gesang
1350.... Heimatsklange
1355.... Frohes Schaffen In Freier Natur!
1357.... Wir Bringen Gluck
1359.... Bluhende Weit
1360.... Mit Veilchen Umrahmt
1368.... Gluhende Farben Auf Wald End Flur
1370.... Im Sturm Der Zeit
1375.... Von Haus Und Herd
1378.... Kinderhumor
1379.... Frohsinn Und Herd
1386.... Ein Mauschen Im Hauschen
1390.... Fruhlingskinder
1391.... Roslein Auf Der Heiden C. Klein
1392.... Ein Blumengrub
1394.... Kleine Leckermaulchen
1398.... Von Baum Und Strauch ?M.B.
1400.... Gratulanten Aus Fernen Landen
1402.... Feldblumen C. Klein
1410.... Gutefreunde
1417.... Gluckliche Reise
1424.... Daheim Und Draussen
1429.... Abendfrieden
1431.... Weihnachtsboten
1433.... Weihnachts-Stimmung Paul Hey

INDEX

A

B

C

D

E

F

G

M

N

O

P

Q

R

S

T

U, V

W, Y, Z